"This book provides a powerful and nec⟨ American church addicted to cheap grace. With pastoral insight and care, the authors expose the destructive half-truths and clichés that mislead so many well-meaning Christians. They replace these distortions with the richest insights and practices of the Protestant tradition and the Scriptures that directed it. This is Protestant theology at its very best, because this is theology from and for the church. Every pastor and teacher should read this book."

—**Keith L. Johnson**, Wheaton College

"Good works are an often neglected or misunderstood scriptural theme. McCall, Friedeman, and Friedeman correct many misconceptions and set forth their own understanding in this important work. They examine the role of good works historically, biblically, theologically, and practically. I am grateful for this contribution and hope it precipitates further conversation and study."

—**Thomas Schreiner**, The Southern Baptist Theological Seminary

"Unfortunately, in some Protestant circles since the Reformation, good works have undeservedly gotten a bad name. In fact, precisely for saying 'Faith without works is dead,' James's letter was called by Luther 'a right strawy epistle,' and he questioned its inclusion in the New Testament. This book takes on numerous caricatures such as 'Good works have nothing to do with salvation' in a refreshing and detailed way, and the result is the best single study I know of on this subject. Salvation involves far more than initial justification, and there is a reason why Paul said, 'Work out your salvation with fear and trembling,' and yes it involves *doing*, not just believing or having saving faith. This book itself is a 'good work.' And after all, Titus 2:14 reminded us to be 'zealous for good works.' I highly recommend this study."

—**Ben Witherington III**, Asbury Theological Seminary

"McCall, Friedeman, and Friedeman offer a gift to the church in this challenge to reclaim good works in the Protestant tradition. With clarity and conviction, they argue that true faith in Christ will necessarily result in good works. Such a conclusion need not lead to legalism but can encourage an empowered and motivated body equipped by the

Spirit to love God and love others. Ultimately, this book is a needed corrective to cognition-centered faith that may not actually be faith at all."

—**Christa L. McKirland**, Carey Baptist College; executive director
of Logia International

"Saved by good works? Yes! Not only Catholics but also Protestants have traditionally taught this. *The Doctrine of Good Works* shows how diverse Protestant traditions and thinkers have articulated a positive doctrine of saving good works while prioritizing grace and faith. Far from simply correcting caricatures, McCall, Friedeman, and Friedeman contribute positively to the current theological conversation about how to best systematize what Scripture teaches about salvation. Their results are made practical by inspiring case studies. Highly recommended."

—**Matthew W. Bates**, Quincy University; author
of *Salvation by Allegiance Alone*

THE
DOCTRINE
of
GOOD
WORKS

THE
DOCTRINE
of
GOOD
WORKS

*Reclaiming a Neglected
Protestant Teaching*

Thomas H. McCall, Caleb T. Friedeman,
and Matt T. Friedeman

Baker Academic
a division of Baker Publishing Group
Grand Rapids, Michigan

© 2023 by Thomas H. McCall, Caleb T. Friedeman, and Matt T. Friedeman

Published by Baker Academic
a division of Baker Publishing Group
Grand Rapids, Michigan
www.bakeracademic.com

Printed in the United States of America

Library of Congress Cataloging-in-Publication Data
Names: McCall, Thomas H., author. | Friedeman, Caleb T., author. | Friedeman, Matt, author.
Title: The doctrine of good works : reclaiming a neglected Protestant teaching / Thomas H. McCall,
    Caleb T. Friedeman, and Matt T. Friedeman.
Description: Grand Rapids, Michigan : Baker Academic, a division of Baker Publishing Group, [2023] |
    Includes bibliographical references and index.
Identifiers: LCCN 2022053301 | ISBN 9781540965202 (paperback) | ISBN 9781540966582 (casebound) |
    ISBN 9781493442003 (ebook) | ISBN 9781493442010 (pdf)
Subjects: LCSH: Good works (Theology) | Protestant churches—Doctrines.
Classification: LCC BT773 .M395 2023 | DDC 269/.2—dc23/eng/20230224
LC record available at https://lccn.loc.gov/2022053301

Baker Publishing Group publications use paper produced from sustainable forestry practices and postconsumer waste whenever possible.

24   25   26   27   28   29   7   6   5   4   3

To John M. Perkins,
an extraordinary model of good works
and abundant living

Contents

Introduction: Recovering an Essential Doctrine   xi

1. Truly Good and Actually Necessary: *Good Works in Protestant Theology*   1
2. The Greatest Commandments Announced: *Good Works in the Old Testament*   25
3. The Greatest Commandments Fulfilled: *Good Works in the New Testament*   61
4. Holiness as Love of God and Love of Neighbor: *Toward a Theology of Good Works*   99
5. The Working Church: *Case Studies in Living Faith*   127
6. Strategic Pastoral Leadership: *Toward Valuing Works in the Local Church*   161

Conclusion: *United with Christ, Filled with the Spirit, Zealous for Good Works*   187

Scripture Index   193
Subject Index   201

Introduction

Recovering an Essential Doctrine

To say that Christianity has a crisis of credibility is an understatement. Some skeptics raise criticisms of the truth or rationality of Christian belief; in cultures that are impacted or even dominated by secularism and metaphysical naturalism, theistic belief in general and Christian faith in particular look increasingly strange and even unfathomable. Christians are stepping up to meet such challenges to the rationality and truth claims of their faith, and their engagement in apologetics is important work. But there is another crisis of credibility, and it deserves attention. This crisis is focused not so much on the rational defense of Christianity as on "real life" issues of justice and mercy. The crisis is not primarily epistemological but is instead moral in nature; the deep concerns and pressing criticisms are not about the rationality of the Christian faith so much as they are concerned with the plausibility of the gospel. Or to put the matter somewhat differently, people are hardly interested in the truth claims of Christianity unless and until they see that it matters. They are not likely even to take the rational defense of the faith seriously until they see it lived out. They will not be inclined to give serious consideration to the truth claims of Christianity until there is something about it that makes them hope that it might be true, and they will not be committed to it until they are attracted to it.

James tells us, "Religion that is pure and undefiled before God, the Father, is this: to care for orphans and widows in their distress, and to keep oneself unstained by the world" (James 1:27 NRSV). But there is a current generation that does not see it. They do not see behavior that suggests that care for others is essential to evangelical Protestant Christian faith. Instead, they see people who are fearful and committed to protecting themselves and their "rights." They do not see people who are "unspotted from the world." Instead, they see leaders of denominations and parachurch organizations who appear obsessed with status and hungry for political power. They see a message of salvation that is strictly about what happens after they are dead—or depending on which version of the "prosperity gospel" might be in view, perhaps one that offers health and wealth or better access to the "American dream" for those who are already highly privileged. They look at evangelical Protestant Christianity, and they do not see "religion that is pure and undefiled." And in many cases, they simply do not want what they see. For many seekers and searchers who observe the practice of Christianity, Christianity is at best irrelevant and at worst a sinister threat.

Perhaps we could simply chalk this rejection of vibrant evangelical faith up to a misunderstanding of it. Or maybe we can blame it on hypocrisy. There is some truth in that, and placing blame on misunderstanding and hypocrisy might be convenient. Sometimes the problems of credibility are engendered or exaggerated by hypocrisy. Fair enough. But to dismiss this crisis as mere misunderstanding or even as hypocrisy would be to miss a very important point. For in other cases, the problem is not that Christians are misunderstanding or failing to live out their faith with consistency; in some instances, it appears that people indeed *are* living out the faith that they have been taught. Consider the following statements:

- Christians aren't perfect, just forgiven.
- We are saved by faith alone, and good works have nothing to do with it.
- If you've said the "Sinner's Prayer," your salvation is eternally guaranteed.
- Rejoice in the fact that there is nothing that you or anyone else could ever do to undo what Christ has done for you.

- Your good works don't get you saved, and they cannot keep you saved either.
- Good works cannot earn salvation, for it is by grace alone.
- To be concerned about good works is to reject the gospel—it's either your works or Christ's work for you. Which are you going to trust for your salvation?

Such statements abound within popular evangelical preaching and teaching. Indeed, in some circles it seems that good works are seen not only as unnecessary but even as dangerous: if we are saved by faith rather than good works, then good works might be the one thing that threatens one's salvation.

There are elements of truth, of course, to be found in the popular clichés. But in many cases, they obscure and mislead, and at any rate, we should not be surprised when Christians and non-Christians alike conclude that the essentials of Christianity have little or nothing to do with how people live their lives in relation to God and their fellow humans. When earnest Christians are repeatedly told that their *good works have nothing to do with salvation*, why should we be surprised when they believe what they hear? Why would we be puzzled when they live accordingly? And why should we be surprised when non-Christians think that Christianity does not fundamentally change anything that matters in this life?

It might be tempting to say that the problem is due only to popular-level oversimplifications and misunderstandings of complex theological truths. And, again, surely there is some merit to this consideration. But it seems to us that the situation is not so simple and that we cannot simply dismiss the problem as one of popular-level misunderstanding. In many evangelical theology textbooks of recent vintage, there is little or no sustained treatment of the doctrine of good works.[1] In addition, a great deal of contemporary evangelical theology simply equates salvation with justification. As an example, consider the claims of Millard

---

1. Textbooks commonly used in evangelical theological education do not contain a *locus* (or similar sustained treatment) on the doctrine of good works. See, e.g., Millard Erickson, *Christian Theology*, 3rd ed. (Grand Rapids: Baker Academic, 2013); Michael F. Bird, *Evangelical Theology: A Biblical and Systematic Introduction* (Grand Rapids: Zondervan, 2013); Wayne A. Grudem, *Systematic Theology: An Introduction to Biblical Doctrine*, 2nd ed. (Grand Rapids: Zondervan Academic, 2020).

Erickson when he says that "salvation is not by works. A person is declared righteous in the sight of God, not because of having done good
works, but because of having believed."[2] Erickson insists that good
works are only the evidence of genuine faith. What about those biblical passages that might seem to teach the necessity of good works?
Erickson says that when such passages are "seen in their contexts and
in relation to the texts that speak of justification by faith," they "do not
teach that works are a means of receiving salvation."[3] As we will see in
the following chapters, Erickson's statement tracks well with historic
Protestant teaching on justification in one respect: he is insisting that
justification is by grace through faith rather than by works. But as we
also will see, Erickson's account departs from classic Protestant doctrine in some important ways. Notice how he equates justification with
salvation *simpliciter*: "salvation" is simply being "declared righteous."
This equation is resisted by the historic Protestant traditions. And when
Erickson denies that good works are a "means of receiving salvation,"
he is diametrically opposed to important elements of confessional and
scholastic Reformed theology.

Even a more historically grounded Protestant work of theology such
as *Christian Dogmatics: Reformed Theology for the Church Catholic* fails
to include any focused attention on the doctrine of good works.[4] More
broadly, confessional Reformed theology of recent vintage largely
downplays or ignores the doctrine.[5] And when concern for good works
and the "obedience of faith" is taken seriously, contemporary Reformed
and evangelical theologians sometimes react by charging those who
express such concern with rejecting the heritage of the Reformation
and even the gospel.

In his foreword to a recent book on the doctrine of justification, John
Piper refers to an arresting question raised by the author, Tom Schreiner:
"How can a person be right with God?" The answer is both clear and
unsurprising: "The stunning Christian answer is: *sola fide*—faith alone."

2. Erickson, *Christian Theology*, 938.
3. Erickson, *Christian Theology*, 940. Cf. Bird, *Evangelical Theology*, 569–70.
4. Michael Allen and Scott R. Swain, eds., *Christian Dogmatics: Reformed Theology for the Church Catholic* (Grand Rapids: Baker Academic, 2016).
5. E.g., the series New Studies in Dogmatics, edited by Michael Allen and Scott Swain, contains no volume on the doctrine of good works. By contrast, it includes two volumes on the doctrine of justification.

But as soon as he gives this answer, Piper goes on to say something that is equally clear but also more surprising and disturbing: "But be sure you hear this carefully and precisely: [Schreiner] says *right with God* by faith alone, not *attain heaven* by faith alone." He explains further, "There are other conditions for attaining heaven, but no others for entering a right relationship to God." For while we are justified by faith alone, any faith that is alone "is not faith in union with Christ." To the contrary, faith that is in union with Christ is faith that "is living and active with Christ's power," and the "obedience of faith" is not required for entering a right relationship with God but *is* "required for heaven."[6] The response from some theologians who are well known as Reformed has been very negative: Piper is said to be not only theologically deficient from a Reformed perspective but also offering a dangerous alternative to the true gospel that rejects the most fundamental insights of the Reformation. Critics charge Piper with not understanding "what the Reformation was really trying to do." His views are said to be "highly problematic," and he is judged to have "fundamentally turned his back on the Reformation" as well as to be making claims that are "contradictory to the gospel and contradictory to the Word of God."[7] Piper holds that good works are not necessary for justification, but he also insists that good works are necessary for final salvation. For this, he is charged with rejecting the true gospel.

So when Christians and non-Christians alike conclude that a life of loving obedience and good works has nothing to do with the essentials of Christianity, it may be that they are only believing what they have been told. But what if what they have been told is not correct? And what if, instead of seeing a special-interest group or political bloc interested in self-defense and self-promotion, they understood Christianity to be good for the world and Christians to be people who are "zealous for good works" (Titus 2:14 ESV)? What if the good news of Christianity

6. John Piper, foreword to *Faith Alone—The Doctrine of Justification: What the Reformers Taught . . . and Why It Still Matters*, by Thomas R. Schreiner, Five Solas Series (Grand Rapids: Zondervan, 2015), 11.

7. R. Scott Clark, "Heidelcast 149: Q & A on How [to] Pray, When to Drop the H Bomb, What Did OT Believers Know, and Why Final Justification through Good Works Is Bad News," April 24, 2020, in *The Heidelcast*, podcast, MP3 audio, 1:19:22, https://heidelblog.net/2020/04/heidelcast-149-q-a-on-how-pray-when-to-drop-the-h-bomb-what-did-ot-believers-know-and-why-final-justification-through-good-works-is-bad-news/.

really includes good works within it? What if loving God with all one's heart, mind, and strength—and the "works of piety" that flow from that love—really were understood to be integral to the gospel? What if loving one's neighbor as oneself—and the "works of mercy" that flow from that love—really was seen as essential to the good news that God saves sinners from their sin and for himself?

Hence, this volume. From the very beginning of Scripture, we find that God is a working God and that his image-bearers best represent him as we work meaningfully, doing the things he wants us to do.[8] In the New Testament, the Son of God appears as a rabbi who performs works of both piety and mercy and calls and expects his followers to do the same. A vision of God's people as a people who do good works—good works of love of God and good works of love of neighbor—is at the very core of a biblical message. It is a vision that was understood by the Reformers and their confessional and scholastic heirs. And it is a vision that is desperately needed today.

In this book, we argue from Scripture and the resources of the Protestant confessional traditions for a recovery of a positive doctrine of good works. We begin with a historical survey of the doctrine of good works in the major Protestant traditions. What emerges from this history is a set of conclusions that invite us to revisit the biblical teachings about good works. Following this, we offer a theological summary, and then we turn toward a pastoral, theological application of the doctrine of good works. Throughout, we make a case for a positive Protestant doctrine of good works. It is positive in the sense that good works are actually integral to the good news, and it is Protestant with respect to basic and fundamental theological commitments. The view that emerges is one that is both deeply theological and imminently practical, one that celebrates God's gracious work on our behalf while also taking seriously the importance of genuine, faithful obedience and love.

---

8. In using masculine personal pronouns for God, we do not mean to imply that God is male. We recognize, with Beth Felker Jones, that the use of "masculine personal pronouns for God is not unproblematic" but that the use of them seems to be "the least problematic route" (Beth Felker Jones, *Practicing Christian Doctrine* [Grand Rapids: Baker Academic, 2014], 174). See further the discussion of Amy Peeler, *Women and the Gender of God* (Grand Rapids: Eerdmans, 2022).

CHAPTER 1

Truly Good and Actually Necessary

Good Works in Protestant Theology

I t is no secret that good works are important in the early church and throughout the Middle Ages; patristic and medieval theologians are concerned to encourage good works,[1] and they routinely insist upon the importance and necessity of these works. Good works of "piety" (those related directly to love of God, most commonly expressed in personal and corporate worship) are vitally important for the Christian life, and good works of "mercy" (those related directly to love of neighbor, most commonly expressed in the commitment to care and the pursuit of justice) are as well. In many cases, these are closely linked, for Christians should not claim to love God if they do not love and serve their neighbors.

Theologians of the early church are prone to encourage Christians to be active in seeking ways to serve their neighbors. For instance, John Chrysostom says, "Paul urges that they not wait for those who are needy to come to them but that they seek out those who need their assistance. Thus the considerate man shows his concern, and with great zeal will perform his duty. For in acts of mercy it is not those who receive the kindness who are benefited, so much as those who do the kindness.

---

1. Portions of this chapter were first published as Thomas H. McCall, "On 'Doing What You Can': Toward Recovery of a Protestant Doctrine of Good Works," *Trinity Journal* 41 (2020): 165–83. Used with permission.

They make the greater gain. For it gives them confidence toward God."[2] Notice what Chrysostom says here: followers of Christ are not to wait until someone asks; instead, they are to take the first step. To do so is the "duty" of the Christian. It is not an option. It is not something to be done only when convenient or only when one happens to be feeling generous or grateful. No, it is the *duty* of the one who follows Jesus. And it actually benefits not only the one in need but also the one meeting the need, for it increases their filial confidence in God.

Chrysostom's position is anything but unique in early Christianity. But how does it relate to distinctly *Protestant* theology? Are good works really important in the Christian life? Surely they are—but *how* are they important? Are they necessary for salvation? Not merely important, but actually necessary? Not merely necessary for Christian witness, not just important for *showing* that one has genuine faith, but truly *necessary for salvation*? Many contemporary evangelical Christians might respond with an unhesitating and emphatic no. Many might insist that such a denial was central to the Reformation and indeed essential to any truly Protestant theology. After all, what was the Reformation about if it was not about salvation by grace rather than through works?

But for much classical Protestant theology, the answers to such questions are a resounding yes. It is, of course, true that justification is by grace alone and received through faith alone. It is true that sinners are justified and accepted as righteous because of the righteousness of Christ given (or "imputed") to them. At the same time, however, it is also true that good works are nothing less than necessary: to be a Christian is to be someone who is transformed so that they can and will do good works. For many classical Protestant theologians, good works are necessary for salvation—and not merely as the "result" or "fruit" or evidence of salvation.

Good Works in Lutheran Theology

Lutheran theology is sometimes understood to downplay, denigrate, ignore, or even deny the place and importance of good works in the process of salvation and the Christian life. As Benjamin T. G. Mayes

2. John Chrysostom, *Homilies on Titus* 6, in Thomas C. Oden, *The Good Works Reader*, Classic Christian Readers (Grand Rapids: Eerdmans, 2007), 57.

observes, there is "a popular Lutheran phrase that goes something like 'God does not need your good works, but your neighbor does,' and thus it is claimed that good works are not necessary for salvation but only for the good of one's neighbor."[3] But such an account of Lutheran soteriology is an unfortunate misunderstanding, at least with respect to historic Lutheran confessional and scholastic theology.

The Nature and Importance of Good Works

Lutheran confessional theology is justly famous for its resolute insistence on the doctrine of justification by grace alone received through faith alone. The Augsburg Confession (1530) maintains that no one is justified by works; instead, all those who are justified are received into God's favor "for Christ's sake."[4] It is *sinners* who are justified, and they are justified as the righteousness of Christ is imputed to them. But as they are justified, they are also regenerated, and as those who are born again begin new life, they are enabled and expected to live lives of "New Obedience." They are justified by grace alone through faith alone, but this faith "should bring forth good fruits" that are "good works commanded of God, because it is God's will."[5] No one earns merit toward salvation; it is not as if doing good works helps the sinner gain favor. Nonetheless, the new life of those who are freely justified is a life characterized by good works.

The Augsburg Confession juxtaposes its position against two alternatives. The first such alternative is the teaching that salvation is strictly by good works. On this view, sinners earn salvation through "childish and needless works" such as keeping holidays and fasts, making pilgrimages, and reciting rosaries.[6] The second alternative teaches that "we are not justified by works alone" but instead are justified by "faith and works."[7] Interestingly, Augsburg judges this error to be "more tolerable"

---

3. Benjamin T. G. Mayes, general editor's introduction to *On Good Works*, by Johann Gerhard, trans. Richard J. Dinda, ed. Benjamin T. G. Mayes, Joshua J. Hayes, and Aaron Jensen, Theological Commonplaces 20 (St. Louis: Concordia, 2019), xiii.

4. The Augsburg Confession, art. 4, in *The Evangelical Protestant Creeds, with Translations*, vol. 3 of *The Creeds of Christendom: With a History and Critical Notes*, ed. Philip Schaff, 6th ed. (Grand Rapids: Baker Academic, 2007), 10.

5. Augsburg Confession, art. 6 (p. 11).

6. Augsburg Confession, art. 20 (p. 20).

7. Augsburg Confession, art. 20 (p. 21).

than the first, but it still weighs it in the balances and finds it wanting.[8] Against such teaching, the Lutheran doctrine insists that "our works cannot reconcile God, or deserve remission of sins, grace, and justification."[9] No, these are obtained by "faith only," and anyone who trusts in their own works to "merit grace" actually "despises the merit and grace of Christ."[10]

What are good works? David Hollaz (1648–1713) defines them as "free acts of justified persons, performed through the renewing grace of the Holy Spirit, according to the prescription of divine Law, true faith in Christ preceding, to the honor of God and the edification of men."[11] Johannes Quenstedt (1617–88) says that a good work is an action that "God commands, and which is done with the disposition, manner, and purpose for which it has been commanded."[12] The Lutheran scholastics offer extended and rigorous discussion, and they provide important distinctions. Thus Johann Gerhard (1582–1637), through hundreds of pages of detailed biblical exegesis, careful historical theology, and conceptual analysis and logical argumentation, distinguishes between various types of good works and then defends a properly Lutheran account of the doctrine. He points out that some good works are internal and thus seen only by God, while others are external and thus obvious to others. Some are aimed directly toward God; others are performed for the benefit of oneself or one's neighbor. Some are good morally, and others are good spiritually.[13] Hollaz notes that when one puts the "internal" with the "external," what we have is nothing less than "the entire obedience and inherent righteousness of the regenerate" person.[14]

Good works are truly *good*, even though they may fall short of perfection in various ways. Hollaz states, "The works of the regenerate and justified men are called good, not absolutely, as if they were perfectly good, but in their kind, because (*a*) they derive their origin from the

8. Augsburg Confession, art. 20 (p. 21).
9. Augsburg Confession, art. 20 (p. 21).
10. Augsburg Confession, art. 20 (p. 21).
11. David Hollaz, *Examen Theologicum Acroamaticum* (1707), quoted in *The Doctrinal Theology of the Evangelical Lutheran Church*, ed. Heinrich Schmid, 4th ed. (Philadelphia: Lutheran Publication Society, 1898), 493.
12. Johannes Quenstedt, *Theologia Didactico-Polemica* (1685), quoted in Schmid, *Doctrinal Theology*, 493.
13. Gerhard, *On Good Works*, 7–14.
14. Hollaz, *Examen Theologicum Acroamaticum*, quoted in Schmid, *Doctrinal Theology*, 493.

good Spirit of God; (b) they proceed from a good heart; (c) they are in some degree conformed to the good will of God, expressed in the Law; and (d) they design a good end, the glory of God."[15] Hollaz is explicit and clear: the good works of regenerated and justified persons "do not reach that degree of perfection that they cannot increase, nor do they perfectly correspond to the divine Law."[16] They are, nonetheless, rightly called "good" if they meet the requisite conditions.

Gerhard is careful to spell out the causes of good works. He is clear that the "principal efficient cause" is the Holy Spirit.[17] No one does, and no one can do, good works by their own strength. The "instrumental cause" is the Word of God.[18] But Gerhard also accounts for the reality of genuine human agency and responsibility. Notably, the "cooperating cause" is "the mind and will of man that has been renewed by the Holy Spirit."[19] The human agency to which Gerhard refers is an agency that is and must be empowered by divine grace, for the human will alone can neither effect nor even attempt to do good apart from grace. For the "cooperation of the reborn in good works by no means excludes but requires the constant aid of the Holy Spirit."[20] The "Holy Spirit gives new powers to those who are in Christ through faith, regenerates them, gives them life, and efficaciously changes their mind and will so that as new and spiritual people they are eager for a new life and produce the acts of the life of the Spirit."[21] But as it is true that nothing good can be done without the gracious empowerment of the Holy Spirit, so also it is true that human agency is free and genuine. Good works simply are a vital part of the Christian life, and Christians are not only called but also commanded to perform them.

The Necessity of Good Works

But are good works actually in some sense *necessary*? Clearly, they are important, but are they necessary? What happens if they are absent

---

15. Hollaz, *Examen Theologicum Acroamaticum*, quoted in Schmid, *Doctrinal Theology*, 493 (in this quotation and the next one we have omitted biblical citations).

16. Hollaz, *Examen Theologicum Acroamaticum*, quoted in Schmid, *Doctrinal Theology*, 494.

17. Gerhard, *Good Works*, 15.

18. Gerhard, *Good Works*, 15–16.

19. Gerhard, *Good Works*, 16.

20. Gerhard, *Good Works*, 16.

21. Gerhard, *Good Works*, 16.

or impotent? The Lutheran confessional tradition denies that their theology forbids good works, and the tradition likewise denies that their theology undercuts the proper motivation for such works. Thus the Augsburg Confession says that when Lutherans are accused of forbidding good works, such accusations are false.[22] The Formula of Concord (1577) echoes many of these points, and it provides further clarification on several. Justification is by grace through faith alone, and neither "antecedent contrition" nor "subsequent new obedience" are operative in justification.[23] At the same time, however, we are told in no uncertain terms that any faith that is "true and living" is faith that "works by love," and "good works always follow justifying faith."[24] For while we are justified by faith alone, genuine faith "is never alone, but always has charity and hope in its train."[25]

The Formula of Concord deals with two controversies in this area. The first concerns the debate between those who teach that good works are necessary for salvation and those who teach that good works are detrimental to salvation. The second concerns the proper understanding of the terms "necessity" and "freedom" in relation to good works. So should we affirm that good works are necessary? If so, should we say that they are necessary *for salvation*—or should we search for another sense in which they are properly said to be necessary? In dealing with these controversies, the Concordists issue a set of affirmations and a set of corresponding denials. Concord affirms that "good works must certainly and without all doubt follow a true faith . . . , as fruits of a good tree."[26] Good works are not meritorious for justification, but nonetheless all who have been regenerated by the Holy Spirit "are debtors to do good works."[27] Moreover, Concord affirms that the terms "necessary" and "necessity" are appropriate as long as it is understood that these refer not to constraint but instead to the obligation to be obedient to God. So on one hand, good works are excluded not only from justification but also from any discussion of eternal salvation, and Concord flatly denies that the phrase "good works are necessary to salvation" should

---

22. Augsburg Confession, art. 20 (p. 20).
23. The Formula of Concord, art. 3, in Schaff, *Evangelical Protestant Creeds*, 118.
24. Formula of Concord, art. 3 (p. 118).
25. Formula of Concord, art. 3 (p. 118).
26. Formula of Concord, art. 4 (p. 122).
27. Formula of Concord, art. 4 (p. 123).

be used.[28] On the other hand, Concord also "repudiates and condemns" the notion that good works are somehow detrimental to salvation, and it also insists that those who commit grave sins forfeit salvation. For "we repudiate and condemn that dogma that faith in Christ is not lost, and that the Holy Spirit, even though a man sin wittingly and willingly, nevertheless dwells in him; and that the holy and elect retain the Holy Spirit, even though they fall into adultery and other crimes, and persevere in the same."[29]

The Lutheran scholastic theologians follow the confessions but add more nuance and depth. Quenstedt denies that good works are necessary in any sense of constraint, but he avers that such actions indeed are necessary in the sense of duty. Moreover, good works are necessary in the sense of debt; redeemed and reborn persons have a debt of gratitude. Good works are also necessary in the sense of "presence," for if they are not there, then there is no salvation. More precisely, such works are furthermore necessary as the consequence of justification.[30] Quenstedt rejects outright any notion that good works are "indifferent or arbitrary."[31] To the contrary, he says that they are necessary. Indeed, they are necessary for all who are truly justified and regenerate. And how are they necessary? In what sense(s) can good works be said to be necessary? Not, he says, in any sense of constraint or compulsion. Nor, he denies, can good works be said to be necessary as a means to gain or merit salvation. Good works are not necessary as a means to an end, as a source of merit, as an indispensable condition, or as a "conserving cause."[32] So how are good works necessary? His answer extends to four reasons: "We hold good works to be necessary, by the necessity, (1) of the divine command; (2) of our duty, or of gratitude due for the benefits of creation, redemption, etc.; (3) of presence (that believers may not lose the grace of God and faith, and fall from the hope of inheritance . . .); (4) of a divinely appointed order and sequence to justification and faith, because as effects they necessarily follow their cause."[33]

---

28. Formula of Concord, art. 4 (pp. 122, 125).
29. Formula of Concord, art. 4 (p. 126).
30. Quenstedt, *Theologia Didactico-Polemica*, quoted in Schmid, *Doctrinal Theology*, 497.
31. Quenstedt, *Theologia Didactico-Polemica*, quoted in Schmid, *Doctrinal Theology*, 497.
32. Quenstedt, *Theologica Didactico-Polemica*, quoted in Schmid, *Doctrinal Theology*, 497.
33. Quenstedt, *Theologica Didactico-Polemica*, quoted in Schmid, *Doctrinal Theology*, 497 (in this quotation we have omitted biblical citations).

Similarly, Gerhard directly addresses the question, Are good works necessary? His answer is clear: yes, without any shadow of doubt, good works are necessary. But while clear and direct, his answer is also nuanced and careful. He first notes that there are different kinds of necessity. Drawing from patristic theologians such as Augustine and John of Damascus and medieval theologians such as Albert Magnus, Thomas Aquinas, and Gabriel Biel, as well as insights from Aristotle, he distinguishes between various relevant senses of necessity. Building from these insights and arguing directly from biblical exegesis, he denies that good works are of necessity for salvific merit, and he likewise rejects any notion of necessity as compulsion or involuntariness. He affirms that good works are necessary because they are commanded by God and "in a general sense of the necessity of the consequent."[34]

Gerhard spells out several senses in which it is rightly said that good works are necessary. For the *analogia fidei* (analogy of faith) teaches that it is not left up to the whims or judgments of the regenerate "whether or not they want to serve God with good works"; to the contrary, it is God's will that rational creatures generally obey him, and in no way is this duty abrogated for the regenerate.[35] More directly, good works are commanded in Scripture. Beyond this, to do less would be to encourage the antinomians and "works-haters."[36]

Good works are necessary because they are commanded by God. But they are also necessary because they naturally follow and bear witness to the genuine faith of justification. As "new creatures," by good works repentant believers demonstrate their salvation.[37] Beyond this, however, good works are necessary according to the "necessity of hypothesis."[38] As Gerhard explains this concept, "Unless we wish to cast away our faith, lose God's grace and eternal life, and summon punishments of every kind, it is incumbent on us to pursue good works."[39] By good works, believers not only "produce true fruits of faith" but also make their "calling firm."[40] Note the strength of Gerhard's claims: failure to

34. Gerhard, *Good Works*, 26.
35. Gerhard, *Good Works*, 26.
36. Gerhard, *Good Works*, 26.
37. Gerhard, *Good Works*, 30–31.
38. Gerhard, *Good Works*, 31.
39. Gerhard, *Good Works*, 31.
40. Gerhard, *Good Works*, 31.

do good works will "summon punishments of every kind." He spells this out more explicitly; punishments of every kind include not only "temporal" punishments but also "eternal punishments established for wicked work and idleness."[41] Make no mistake: those who neglect good works risk losing "eternal life."

Are good works necessary *for* salvation? Gerhard stops just short of saying that good works are necessary in this sense. He is clearly concerned about the possibility that such a statement is susceptible to misunderstanding; at best, it is ambiguous and fraught with the potential for dangerous misinterpretation. He is, however, aware that Christian theologians of other major Christian traditions do not hesitate to make such an affirmation. It is not only Roman Catholic theology that does so, for both the Remonstrants, or Arminians, and the Reformed do so as well. But he looks for better ways to state the important truth that good works are necessary. And when specifying what they are necessary for, he is clear: good works are necessary to avoid eternal separation from God. He resists the language used by both the Remonstrants and the Reformed, but he joins them in warning about the eternal punishments that come with the loss or rejection of faith and good works. Arguing from a catena of biblical passages (e.g., Ps. 5:4; Ezek. 17:15; Zech. 8:17; Rom. 1:32; 1 Thess. 4:6; Heb. 10:38), Gerhard mounts the following argument:

1. All who pollute themselves with ruling sins (*peccatis regnantibus*) are considered hateful by God and judged by him to be worthy of death;
2. Some of the reborn pollute themselves with such sins;
3. Therefore, some of those who are regenerate are judged by God to be worthy of death.[42]

Gerhard understands the explicit warnings against apostasy to be exactly that—warnings to be heeded by regenerate believers in order to avoid forfeiting grace and going to eternal damnation. Moreover, he sees indirect but nonetheless powerful evidence in Scripture that

41. Gerhard, *Good Works*, 31.
42. Gerhard, *Good Works*, 238.

supplements these explicit warnings. Key here are the analogies of
athletic competition, warfare, and marriage. By such metaphors and
analogies, believers are warned not to stop before receiving the prize
and to battle valiantly against the forces of darkness and the enemies
of our souls. He says that "some of the reborn can come to a stop before the finish line and fall down before victory," and "just as the most
intimate bond in marriage is dissolved by the committing of adultery,
so also the covenant of this spiritual marriage is only on the condition
of keeping the marriage promise."[43] Thus he concludes by agreeing
with the Augsburg Confession: it is possible "that through sins against
conscience the righteous or reborn lose God's grace not only totally but
also finally, unless they are converted again."[44] Faith, he says, "can be
considered apart from works but cannot exist apart from works"; while
faith and works can be distinguished, "they are and remain always connected in reality."[45] For "by faith Christ dwells in our hearts. How can
good works be banished where Christ is?"[46]

In summary, we can see the following points with clarity. Are good
works necessary for the Christian? If so, in what sense or senses are
they necessary? The confessional and scholastic theologians are insistent that good works are not necessary in the sense of constraint.
They are adamant that good works do not achieve merit or in any way
help a sinner to earn salvation; properly speaking, good works are not
necessary to attain salvation or maintain salvation. But good works are
necessary in other ways. First, good works are necessary because they
are commanded by God. Second, good works are necessary because
those who are justified and regenerate owe a debt of gratitude to their
Creator and Redeemer. Third, good works are necessary in the sense
that they are the result or "fruit" of justifying faith. It is vitally important
to understand the relation between faith and works and to keep the
"direction" in proper focus: good works play no causal role in justification, but the faith by which sinners are justified is the same faith that
actively produces the "fruit" of good works. And fourth, good works are
necessary in the sense of what Quenstedt calls "presence" and Gerhard

43. Gerhard, *Good Works*, 239.
44. Gerhard, *Good Works*, 247.
45. Gerhard, *Good Works*, 73.
46. Gerhard, *Good Works*, 73.

refers to as the "necessity of hypothesis." This is the affirmation that the pursuit of good works is necessary to avoid the loss of "God's grace and eternal life." For failure to perform such good works will "summon punishments of every kind," and this includes not only those that are temporal, but also eternal life.

Good Works in Reformed Theology

The Reformed theological tradition holds commitments that are similar in many respects to fundamental Lutheran convictions. But Reformed theologians will go beyond their Lutheran counterparts in several ways.

The Nature and Importance of Good Works

The major Reformed confessional statements teach that good works are a vital and important part of the Christian life. For example, the Gallic Confession (1559), also known as the French Confession of Faith, insists that the same God who justifies freely also regenerates sinners; just as we receive by faith the grace that justifies, so also we receive by faith the grace that is necessary and sufficient to lead holy lives. Against the charges that belief in justification *sola fide* (by faith alone) will result in lawlessness and carelessness, the Gallic Confession says that genuine faith will of necessity produce good works.[47] Such good works are never meritorious and cannot secure either justification or adoption by God, but they really do proceed from the Holy Spirit and are realities in the lives of people of genuine faith.[48]

Similarly, the Belgic Confession (1561), while admitting that any good works performed by humans will be polluted and imperfect, defends the reality and importance of good works. For while the hope of salvation cannot be grounded upon them and they cannot be meritorious, nonetheless they are real and vital. The same Holy Spirit who regenerates sinners also enables and expects the redeemed to do good works that are truly acceptable and pleasing to God.[49] In accord with such

47. The French Confession of Faith, art. 22, in Schaff, *Evangelical Protestant Creeds*, 372.
48. French Confession of Faith, art. 22 (p. 372).
49. The Belgic Confession, art. 24, in Schaff, *Evangelical Protestant Creeds*, 411–12.

statements, the Scots Confession (1560) says that the cause of good works is the Spirit of Jesus Christ.[50]

According to the Canons of Dordt (1619), good works strengthen the assurance of salvation in the believer; along with the Word of God written and the internal testimony of the Holy Spirit, "a serious and holy desire to preserve a good conscience, and to perform good works" is a sign that one is truly regenerate.[51] The Westminster Confession of Faith (1646) warns against associating just any sort of activity with good works, for only the actions performed in obedience to divine commands count as good works. Moreover, believers are warned: "We can not, by our best works, merit pardon of sin, or eternal life at the hand of God."[52] But even as it warns against abuses and misunderstandings, Westminster also enjoins good works as vitally important in the life of the Christian. Several benefits are highlighted. First, good works are the evidence of genuine faith; just as a good tree produces good fruit, so also a Christian life will show evidence of Christian virtue even as it produces good works. Second, good works are an obvious and powerful testimony to the gratitude of the believer for the divine gift of grace. Third, through good works the assurance of the believer is confirmed and strengthened. Fourth, good works help to edify others in the life of grace; not only do good works help the one doing the work, but also they serve as a poignant witness to fellow Christians. Fifth, just as good works are a powerful witness to fellow believers and unbelieving neighbors alike, so also it is a striking testimony to the adversaries of genuine Christianity. Sixth, good works bring glory to God.[53]

The Necessity of Good Works

The Belgic Confession insists that good works are necessary in the life of the truly justified and regenerate person: "It is impossible that this holy faith can be unfruitful."[54] For the faith that is revealed in the Bible is a faith that works in love, and this love "excites man to the prac-

50. The Scots Confession of Faith, art. 13, in Schaff, *Evangelical Protestant Creeds*, 452.
51. The Canons of the Synod of Dordt, part 5, art. 10, in Schaff, *Evangelical Protestant Creeds*, 594.
52. The Westminster Confession of Faith, chap. 16, art. 5, in Schaff, *Evangelical Protestant Creeds*, 634.
53. Westminster Confession of Faith, chap. 16, art. 2 (p. 633).
54. Belgic Confession, art. 24 (p. 411).

tice of those works which God has commanded in his Word."[55] Going further, the Westminster Confession says that those who have done the good works that are the "fruit unto holiness" will finally "have the end, eternal life."[56]

It should be obvious that the Reformed, as well as the Lutherans, insist that good works are necessary. Indeed, they say that such works are necessary *for salvation*. Good works are not necessary for justification per se, for human sinners cannot justify themselves by their own efforts. Nonetheless, good works are vitally important in Reformed theology and, in point of fact, are nothing short of necessary for salvation. For there is more to salvation than justification, and the order or process of salvation cannot be whittled down to the doctrine of justification. While important, justification is not the sum total of salvation for the Reformed, and being saved is not reducible to being pronounced righteous or acquitted of guilt. Francis Turretin (1623–87) speaks for early modern Reformed scholasticism more broadly when he faces the question "Are good works necessary for salvation?" His answer leaves no room for doubt: "We affirm."[57]

Turretin affirms the necessity of good works for salvation; so, too, does Lucas Trelcatius Jr. (1573–1607). Trelcatius is notable for our discussion because he was a colleague and sometime opponent of Jacob Arminius at Leiden. Trelcatius has a thoroughly developed doctrine of good works. He holds (much like we have seen in the thought of Gerhard on the Lutheran side) that good works are properly distinguished as those that are internal and invisible and those that are external and visible.[58] He distinguishes further between the efficient, material, formal, and final causes of good works. The efficient cause is split further between primary and secondary efficient causes; the primary efficient cause is, of course, the triune God, who is Father, Son, and Holy Spirit.[59] Secondary efficient causality is further understood with yet another distinction between those that are external and those that are internal.

55. Belgic Confession, art. 24 (p. 411).
56. Westminster Confession of Faith, chap. 16, art. 2 (p. 633).
57. Francis Turretin, *Institutes of Elenctic Theology*, trans. George Musgrave Giger, ed. James T. Dennison Jr., 3 vols. (Phillipsburg, NJ: P&R, 1994), 2:702. Turretin's Latin original, *Institutio Theologiae Elencticae*, was published in three parts in Geneva, between 1679 and 1685.
58. Lucas Trelcatius Jr., *Opuscula Theologica Omnia* (Amsterdam, 1614), 5:266.
59. Trelcatius, *Opuscula Theologica*, 5:267.

Notably, both internal and external secondary causes are rightly understood, he insists, to be instrumental.[60] The material cause is the law of God that has been prescribed for us (further distinguished into two tables). The formal cause is conformity to this law; and while it is always imperfect and never meritorious (*meritum ergo bonorum nullem est*), nonetheless such conformity is necessary.[61] The impulsive and final cause is threefold: it is properly understood with respect to God, to others, and to ourselves. With respect to God, the glory of God is ultimate.[62] With respect to others, it is important to understand that good works provide examples of genuine faith and piety to those who do not believe and remain alien to the faith. And note carefully Trelcatius's understanding of good works with respect to the believers who are enjoined to do them: it is by good works that one has an external testimony of faith *and* confirms one's own election to salvation.[63]

As we have seen, a commonplace with respect to the doctrine of good works in Reformed theology is the affirmation that good works are necessary as the evidence of salvation.[64] Theodore Beza (1519–1605) says that good works are necessary for salvation because they have a necessary connection to true faith; without good works there is no true faith, but with true faith there will always be good works.[65] Just as a healthy tree will produce good fruit that is evidence of both the kind of tree it is and the tree's health, so also will the life of the person who is truly justified and regenerate be productive of the "fruit" of good works. As Amandus Polanus (1561–1610) states the point, good works are the necessary demonstration of living and vital faith.[66]

So far, there is widespread agreement: good works are necessary for salvation because good works are the necessary consequence of true saving faith. However, many major Reformed theologians go further in their articulation of the necessity of good works. Some Reformed theo-

60. Trelcatius, *Opuscula Theologica*, 5:267–68.

61. Trelcatius, *Opuscula Theologica*, 5:269.

62. Trelcatius, *Opuscula Theologica*, 5:270–71.

63. Trelcatius, *Opuscula Theologica*, 5:270.

64. E.g., the Anglican Thirty-Nine Articles, art. 12, in Schaff, *Evangelical Protestant Creeds*, 494; the Scots Confession, art. 13; the Belgic Confession, art. 24; the Westminster Confession of Faith, chap. 16.

65. Theodore Beza, *Opera*, vol. 1, *Tractationum Theologicarum*, 2nd ed. (Anchora Evstathi Vignon, 1576), 675.

66. Amandus Polanus, *Collegium Anti-Bellarminianum* (Basel, 1613), 101.

logians understand good works to be a *medium* or *means* of salvation. Others make a case that good works are nothing less than a *condition* of salvation. Still others argue that good works are actually a *cause* of salvation, and then they differ among themselves on the kind of cause in view. Let us consider these in order.

Among Anglican theologians who identify as (or who are commonly considered) Reformed, it is not uncommon to find an insistence that good works are necessary as a God-appointed *means* for receiving the gift of salvation. It is in this sense that John Edwards (1637–1716) maintains that good works are necessary, and Henry Compton (1632–1713) says, "It is agreed by all sober men, that a virtuous and holy life is necessary to salvation; not as giving a right, but as the necessary means to obtain that right, which is purchased by Christ's blood."[67] Prominent Reformed theologians on the Continent concur. Johannes Wollebius (1589–1629) also insists that the principal efficient cause of good works is the Holy Spirit and that their instrumental cause is faith.[68] Thus he denies that good works are necessary to obtain soteriological merit, but he stoutly maintains that good works are, strictly speaking, necessary with respect to both *precept* and *means*.[69] Such works are necessary by precept, of course, because they are commanded by God. We have already seen this notion in Lutheran theology, and this is quite straightforward. But Wollebius goes further. He says that good works are necessary as a medium or means as well. He offers this illustration: Consider someone who comes into an inheritance in another city. It is an inheritance; it is not something that has been earned. Instead, it is a gift. There is nothing that the inheritor has done or might do in the future to merit the gift. There is nothing that they have done or can do to make themselves worthy of the inheritance or that would in any sense earn it. The inheritance comes from another, and the wealth of it was secured by another and then given to them. Nonetheless, the person inheriting the gift must travel to the city in order to receive it. If they fail to travel to the city, the inheritance that has been provided

---

67. Quoted in Stephen Hampton, *Anti-Arminians: The Anglican Reformed Tradition from Charles II to George I* (Oxford: Oxford University Press, 2008), 124.

68. Johannes Wollebius, *Christianae Theologiae Compendium* (Basel, 1634), 2.1.3, p. 291.

69. Wollebius, *Compendium* 2.1.15, p. 295 (*Necessaria sunt bona opera, necessitate praecepti et medii, non autem necessitate causae et meritii*).

for them and offered to them does them no good. The parallel that Wollebius is drawing is quite direct: as the person who is receiving the inheritance does nothing to earn or merit the gift, neither does the sinner do anything to earn or merit salvation; but as the person receiving the inheritance must go somewhere to get it, so also the repentant and believing sinner must perform good works to actually obtain or receive the salvation merited by Christ and freely offered to the desperate sinner.[70] Wollebius is not alone in his use of this analogy, for it is employed by English-speaking divines as well.[71]

Many Reformed theologians overtly make good works a *condition* of salvation.[72] Indeed, as Johann Heinrich Alsted (1588–1638) observes, the performance of good works is necessary according to "presence" as the "sign and effect of true faith," as a "medium" of salvation, and as the "*conditio et causa sine qua non*" (condition and cause, without which not).[73] Stephen Hampton notes that Edwards goes so far as to say that Paul "separates works from justification, yet he doth not separate them from justifying faith."[74] Petrus van Mastricht (1630–1706) insists that good works are necessary not only by divine command but also as a condition.[75] Hampton compares the thought of Thomas Barlow (1608/9–91) to George Bull (1634–1710). Bull was known for his departure from standard Reformed teaching on justification; notoriously, he was understood to hold that good works are necessary for justification. Hampton notes that in rejecting Bull's doctrine, the Reformed divine Barlow denied that good works are a condition of justification, but then he insisted that good works indeed are a condition of salvation understood more broadly. As Hampton puts it, "Barlow requires from the believer exactly what Bull required, but he requires it for salvation, not for justification."[76]

Some Reformed theologians go even further. Some do not hesitate to refer to good works as a *cause* of salvation. Indeed, Alsted says that

---

70. Wollebius, *Compendium* 2.1.15, p. 295.

71. See the discussion in Hampton, *Anti-Arminians*, 124–25.

72. See the discussion in Ryan M. Hurd, "*Dei Viā Regiā*: The Westminster Divine Anthony Tucker on the Necessity of Good Works for Salvation," *Westminster Theological Journal* 81, no. 1 (2019): 1–17.

73. Heinrich Alsted, *Theologica Polemica* (Hanover, 1620), 496.

74. Hampton, *Anti-Arminians*, 123.

75. Petrus van Mastricht, *Theoretico-Practica Theologia*, 2nd ed. (Utrecht, 1698), 6.8.27, pp. 744–45.

76. Hampton, *Anti-Arminians*, 99.

good works are not only a condition *sine qua non* but also a *causa sine qua non*.[77] But what does it mean to say that good works are the cause of salvation? The Reformed theologians who champion this position have inherited a nuanced and sophisticated account of causality, and it is important in these discussions.[78] What "causes" something else? What causes some event to happen or some entity to exist? The standard scholastic account employed by the Reformed maintains that any acceptable answers to such questions will be complex: any adequate account of causation will distinguish between primary and secondary causality, and any such account will distinguish between material, formal, efficient, final, and instrumental causes. Let us consider a mundane illustration: What causes, say, a house to exist? To get a handle on how Reformed scholastics thought about the metaphysics of causation, consider the following types of causes. The *material cause* of the house is the raw materials that are used in the construction of the house. In other words, the house would not exist without the bricks, concrete, and lumber of which the house is composed. Thus the bricks, concrete, and lumber are necessary for the existence of the house. If the bricks, concrete, and lumber did not exist, the house would not exist; they are the material cause of the house. But if all we have is a stack of bricks and a pile of logs, we still do not have a house. More is needed. The *formal cause* of the house is necessary too; this is the idea of the house that can be sketched as a blueprint of the house. But if we have only a stash of bricks and lumber and an architectural design, we still do not have a house. For the actual house to exist, someone must build it. Thus an *efficient cause* is needed as well. Efficient causes can then be divided into *primary* and *secondary* causes; the primary efficient cause of all that happens in the world is none other than God, and secondary causes are agents who operate in the world as they are empowered by primary causality. *Instrumental causes* are akin to the tools that are used to build the house. Finally, for the house to exist, there must be a *final cause*. This is the reason for which the house is built; this is the motivation or purpose that guides the efficient cause in acting.

77. Alsted, *Theologica Polemica*, 496.

78. For further explanation, see Richard A. Muller, *Dictionary of Latin and Greek Theological Terms: Drawn Principally from Protestant Scholastic Theology* (Grand Rapids: Baker Academic, 1985), 61–62; Edward Feser, *Scholastic Metaphysics: A Contemporary Introduction* (Heusenstamm: Editiones Scholasticae, 2014), 88–159.

With these clarifications in mind, we are now in a position to ask this question: What kind of cause are good works? Here intuitions differ, and various proposals are made. Jerome Zanchi (1516–90) holds that good works are an instrumental cause.[79] Samuel Rutherford (1600?–1661) and Gisbertus Voetius (1589–1676) agree: good works have causal powers, but such powers are instrumental (rather than material, formal, primarily efficient, or final).[80]

Johannes Piscator (1546–1625) takes a rather different and somewhat more radical line.[81] For he also believes that good works play a causal role in salvation, and he goes so far as to say that the causation in question is nothing short of efficient causation.[82] He makes it clear that he is talking about an inferior and secondary efficient cause. Divine grace is always the ultimate efficient cause, but it is properly understood as a primary efficient cause that empowers and also demands the performance of good works as a secondary efficient cause. His analogy is arresting: someone who is given a treasure buried on a mountain not only must climb the mountain but also must dig the treasure from the summit of the peak.[83] The treasure, of course, is analogous to salvation. The climb up the mountain illustrates the necessity of means; here Piscator is in line with theologians such as Wollebius. But the effort to dig out the treasure illustrates something further. This is akin to the performance of good works, and here it is nothing short of an efficient cause. Digging it out of the ground secures the treasure, and the treasure is not obtained without the effort of digging. This is an efficient cause. It is an efficient cause that is secondary and inferior, for the secondary causal agent is always dependent on the primary cause for the agency itself. But it is an efficient cause nonetheless.

The position taken by John Davenant (1572–1641) appears to go even further in some ways, for he maintains that there is a sense in which

79. Jerome Zanchi, *De Natura Dei, Seu de Divinis Attributus* (Nuestadt, 1593), 5.2.3, p. 670.

80. Samuel Rutherford, *Examen Arminianismi* (Utrecht, 1668); Gisbertus Voetius, *Thersites Heautontimorenos hoc est Remonstrantium Hyperaspistes* (Utrecht, 1635), 168.

81. Due to his views on the imputation of Christ's active righteousness, Piscator might be considered a dubious exemplar of Reformed theology. But Heber Carlos de Campos has argued (persuasively, in our view) that Piscator was, in general, thoroughly Reformed on the doctrine of justification. See Heber Carlos de Campos, *Doctrine in Development: Johannes Piscator and the Debates over Christ's Active Obedience* (Grand Rapids: Reformation Heritage Books, 2017).

82. Johannes Piscator, *Analysis Logica Sex Epistolarum Pauli*, 2nd ed. (Herborn, 1593), 88.

83. Johannes Piscator, cited in William Forbes, *Considerationes Modestae et Pacificae Controversiarum de Justificatione* (Oxford: J. H. Parker, 1850), 312–13.

good works are necessary for justification too (rather than salvation understood more broadly). He directly tackles the question of "whether good works can be said to be necessary to our justification or salvation."[84] He notes that there is some disagreement among the Reformed on how to handle this question, for some deny it, while others "have no hesitation in declaring that good works are necessary to salvation."[85] In his judgment, most of the disagreement is merely verbal or semantic rather than substantive, and he seeks to bring clarity to the matter.

Davenant does so by issuing a series of cautions and caveats. He insists that contextual sensitivity is critical. When dialoguing with Roman Catholic theologians or instructing unlearned people, "it is not safe or wise to use or admit" that good works are necessary for justification (or salvation more broadly).[86] For although it is true that these propositions "may by means of explanation be reduced to a sound sense," nonetheless it is common and all too easy for one to hear this and conclude that good works are somehow meritorious or that they earn salvation.[87] Davenant also denies that good works are necessary if by "good works" is meant performances that are perfect.[88] And he is insistent that good works are not necessary for justification (or salvation more broadly) if we "understand necessary in the sense of a meritorious cause."[89] For good works are not meritorious in any sense; they do not bring the sinner into a state of justification, and they "are not necessary in the way of merit, even for preserving a state of justification and salvation."[90]

With such caveats and cautions in place, however, note that Davenant affirms that there indeed is a proper sense in which it is true that good works are necessary for justification. For while good works are not in any way a merit-earning or efficient cause of justification, nonetheless it is true that some good works are necessary for justification as

84. John Davenant, *A Treatise on Justification; or, The Disputatio de Justitia Habituali et Actuali; Together with Translations of the "Determinationes" of the Same Prelate, by the Rev. Josiah Allport*, vol. 1 (London: Hamilton, Adams, 1844), 295.

85. Davenant, *Justification*, 295.

86. Davenant, *Justification*, 295.

87. Davenant, *Justification*, 295.

88. Davenant, *Justification*, 297–98.

89. Davenant, *Justification*, 298.

90. Davenant, *Justification*, 299.

"concurrent or preliminary conditions."[91] His point is that God justifies those who are "full of compunction and contrition" as they are "following the leading of the Word and the Divine Spirit," not those who are "doing nothing" or those who are "rebellious and intractable."[92] He appeals to illustrations to illuminate his point: as those who are sick must approach the physician and receive the proper medication and treatment, and as those who are destitute must entreat the almsgiver and "stretch out his hand" to receive the alms, so also must one perform good works toward God.[93] To be clear, the good works do not *cause* justification or acquire merit. But they are necessary not only to receive but also to retain and preserve the state of justification. Although there is no merit in good works, nonetheless they are necessary "as means or conditions, without which God will not preserve in men the grace of justification."[94]

Davenant insists that good works are necessary for justification and salvation, and the warnings that accompany this insistence are stark and dire. He draws a direct comparison between natural, bodily life and spiritual life:

> As therefore it is necessarily required, for the preservation of natural life, that everyone should studiously avoid falling into fire, water, precipices, poisons, and all other things which endanger the health of the body; so it is necessarily required for the preservation of spiritual life, that a man should avoid unbelief, impenitence, and all other things dangerous and hurtful to the health of the soul; which cannot be avoided unless the opposite and contrary actions are exercised.[95]

Davenant argues that because good works do not earn merit or cause justification, they need not be performed perfectly. At the same time, however, it is also true that "it is impossible to reach the goal of salvation, when the pursuit of good works is altogether evaded and rejected, and a loose rein is given to the lust after evil works."[96] What happens

---

91. Davenant, *Justification*, 299.
92. Davenant, *Justification*, 299–300.
93. Davenant, *Justification*, 300.
94. Davenant, *Justification*, 301.
95. Davenant, *Justification*, 301–2.
96. Davenant, *Justification*, 302.

if a believer should "wander from this path of good works" and onto a "bye-path"? Davenant's answer is clear and bracing:

> I say, that whilst traveling this bye-path, he is proceeding straight to hell; and that he will never arrive at the heavenly city, unless he recover himself and return into the true way. So says the Apostle, 1 Cor. vi. 9, 10; *Be not deceived: Neither fornicators, nor idolaters—nor covetous, nor drunkards, &c., shall inherit the kingdom of God.* And Gal. v. 19–21: *The works of the flesh are manifest, which are these; adultery, fornication, idolatry—drunkenness, &c. Of which I tell you before, that they which do such things shall not inherit the kingdom of God.*[97]

Of course, not all Protestants agree fully with Davenant. John Wesley (1703–91), for example, insists, "Faith, therefore, is the *necessary* condition of justification. Yea, and the *only necessary* condition thereof."[98] But if Davenant goes beyond many of his fellow Protestants in saying that good works are necessary for justification, he is fully in line with them in many respects.

Turretin's summary of the necessity of good works in salvation is instructive. He resolutely and emphatically denies that good works merit eternal life.[99] But he also insists that good works are truly called "good" when done by those who are regenerate and righteous.[100] Are such good works necessary for salvation? Turretin notes that there are three camps. There are the "Libertines," who deny that good works are necessary and who "make good works arbitrary and indifferent [*arbitraria et adiaphora*], that we may perform or omit at pleasure."[101] There is a second group that is in opposition to the Libertines, and Turretin describes them as those who "affirm and press the necessity of merit and causality"; these people make good works necessary with respect to acquiring a right to salvation.[102] Turretin rejects both views; against them, he insists that good works are necessary but denies that they have any powers of efficient causality, and he rejects any notion that they

---

97. Davenant, *Justification*, 303 (italics original).

98. John Wesley, "Justification by Faith," in *Wesley's 52 Standard Sermons*, ed. N. Burwash (Salem, OH: Schmul, 1988), 49.

99. Turretin, *Institutes*, 2:710–24.

100. Turretin, *Institutes*, 2:706–10.

101. Turretin, *Institutes*, 2:702.

102. Turretin, *Institutes*, 2:702.

merit or earn salvation. Instead, he says, such good works are necessary as the means and way of possessing salvation. He argues,

> Works can be understood in three ways: either with reference to justification or sanctification or glorification. They are related to justification not antecedently, efficiently, and meritoriously, but consequently and declaratively. They are related to sanctification constitutively because they constitute and promote it. They are related to glorification antecedently and ordinatively.[103]

In this dense passage, Turretin relates good works to various aspects of the *ordo salutis* (order of salvation). With respect to justification, good works do not come before the divine pronouncement and acceptance of sinners as righteous. Such acceptance is done on the basis of the righteousness of Christ imputed to believing and repentant sinners. Good works follow the divine acquittal; they do not precede it. Nor are good works efficacious in the procurement of the divine verdict. And in no sense do they earn merit before God. To the contrary, good works follow justification. They do not establish the grounds for it, but they bear witness to the reality of it.

In regard to glorification, good works are indeed necessary for this moment of the *ordo salutis*. Good works come before the event of glorification, and they are ordained by God as the *way* or *means* of glorification. Good works are thus related to glorification as the means to the end, because "grace is glory begun, as glory is grace consummated."[104]

Sanctification comes between justification and glorification, and it is, for Turretin (and for the Reformed orthodox more generally), an essential component of salvation. Good works actually *constitute* sanctification, for it is by the doing of good works that repentant and believing sinners grow in grace and holiness. The practice of good works contributes to three things that are of paramount importance: the glory of God, the edification of our neighbors, and our own salvation. Thus good works are "necessary above all things" (*necessarium eam esse supra omnia facile consat*).[105]

---

103. Turretin, *Institutes*, 2:705.
104. Turretin, *Institutes*, 2:705.
105. Turretin, *Institutes*, 2:705.

Yesterday and Today: Moving Forward in Retrieval

In summary, we can see that the doctrine of good works is an important, if often overlooked, element of historic Protestant theology. It is not a uniquely or even distinctly Roman Catholic doctrinal locus. To the contrary, discussion of it is common within Reformed and Lutheran confessional theologies. Nor is it the case that the Protestant discussions are uniformly negative. Yes, the Lutheran and Reformed divines alike are concerned to avoid any notion of works righteousness. They are exercised to reject any temptations to think that our good works somehow earn or merit salvation. But much of their discussions are positive; they teach that good works are truly good and should be pursued as part of the normal Christian life. For by our good works we bring glory to God, testify to God's goodness and saving power, assist and edify our neighbors, and indeed "work out [our] own salvation with fear and trembling" (Phil. 2:12 ESV).

Martin Luther (1483–1546) insists that salvation is more than justification. Those who are truly saved by grace "get a new and clean heart," and from this new and clean heart flow "good works which follow such faith, renewal, and forgiveness."[106] Although such good works will be less than perfect, "whatever is still sinful or imperfect in these works will not be reckoned as sin or defect for the sake of the same Christ," who justifies us by his righteousness.[107] What happens if good works do not accompany justification? Luther's response is unmistakably clear: "If good works do not follow, then faith is false and not true."[108] Confessional and scholastic Lutheran theology follows and echoes these themes.

Clearly, there is some variegation within early modern Reformed theology with respect to the exact relation of good works to salvation. Virtually everyone thinks that good works are necessary as evidence of justifying faith. Many Reformed scholastics also think of good works as a means of receiving salvation. Others go further and maintain that good works are a condition of salvation. Some of the Reformed orthodox argue that good works are actually a cause of salvation. Despite such

---

106. Martin Luther, Smalcald Articles 3.13, in *Martin Luther's Basic Theological Writings*, ed. Timothy Lull (Minneapolis: Fortress, 1989), 534.

107. Luther, Smalcald Articles 3.13, p. 534.

108. Luther, Smalcald Articles 3.13, p. 534.

intramural disagreements, however, there is much common ground. What is common to these explanations is an affirmation that stands out with sparkling clarity: good works are nothing less than necessary for salvation.

Confessional and scholastic Protestant theologians understood Scripture to teach that good works are important. Indeed, good works are nothing less than *necessary*. They understood this biblical teaching to be forceful and convicting, and they insisted that it could be ignored only at great peril. In the twenty-first century, there are prominent strands of evangelical theology that deny that good works have anything to do with salvation. Some theologians even warn that concern for good works signals a departure from Protestant teaching, and some even indicate that such a concern threatens a proper understanding of the gospel. There are other strands of evangelical theology that do not go quite so far but nonetheless tend to downplay or ignore the importance and necessity of good works. Many of these evangelical Protestant theologies claim to be the true heirs of the Reformation and the defenders of historic Protestantism. If the major theologians of Protestant confessionalism and scholasticism were here today, they might want to know why.

CHAPTER 2

The Greatest Commandments Announced

Good Works in the Old Testament

A s we saw in chapter 1, Protestant theologians historically have devoted significant attention to the doctrine of good works, even to the point of viewing good works as necessary in some sense for salvation. But is this position warranted? The doctrine of *sola scriptura* lies close to the heart of Protestant theology, so any attempt to recover a *Protestant* doctrine of good works must ultimately appeal to Scripture. The present chapter and the one that follows develop a biblical theology of good works, focusing on the Old and New Testaments, respectively. To discuss the significance of good works in even a single corpus of Scripture (e.g., the Pentateuch or Paul's Letters) could easily occupy a whole book, so here we will simply attempt to capture the major emphases that emerge within each Testament and to synthesize Scripture's overarching teaching regarding good works.

Created for Good Works, Corrupted by Sin (Gen. 1–3)

Humans in a fallen world might be forgiven for viewing work(s) as a necessary evil; we know all too well the dehumanizing effects of meaningless, unproductive, and oppressive work. The biblical account of creation and fall in Genesis 1–3, however, tells a different story. Genesis

1–2 presents work not as burdensome toil but as something good that God both does and creates humans to do, and Genesis 3 describes how this original intent was marred by the fall.

In the Image of a Working God

One of the first things that we discover about God on the opening pages of the Bible is that he is a worker. In the panoramic creation account of Genesis 1:1–2:3, the first six days are replete with divine activity: God speaks, and things come into existence.[1] But does such activity constitute work? The author removes any doubt on this point in Genesis 2:2–3: "By the seventh day God had finished the *work* he had been *doing*; so on the seventh day he rested from all his *work*. Then God blessed the seventh day and made it holy, because on it he rested from all the *work* of creating that he had *done*."[2] Three times here the author sums up God's creative activity as "work" (*mela'kah*), something that one "does" (*'asah*). God himself characterizes his work as "good" (1:4, 10, 12, 18, 21, 25) and, at its completion, "very good" (1:31).

All of this provides important context for understanding the creation of humans in 1:26–27:

> [26] Then God said, "Let us make [humankind] in our image, in our likeness, so that they may rule over the fish in the sea and the birds in the sky, over the livestock and all the wild animals, and over all the creatures that move along the ground."
>
>> [27] So God created [humankind] in his own image,
>>   in the image of God he created them;
>>   male and female he created them.

Much ink has been spilled over what it means for humans to be made in God's image and likeness.[3] Two relatively uncontroversial points are suf-

---

1. Victor P. Hamilton rightly notes, "The only item in Gen. 1 that is created by *fiat*, strictly speaking, is light. . . . Everything else is created, or emerges, in Gen. 1 by *fiat* plus some subsequent activity that is divinely instigated" (*The Book of Genesis: Chapters 1–17*, New International Commentary on the Old Testament [Grand Rapids: Eerdmans, 1990], 119). God's creative activity in Gen. 1 therefore includes both speech and other divine actions that enact that speech.

2. Italics in biblical quotations have been added for emphasis.

3. For a recent discussion citing extensive bibliography, see Peter J. Gentry and Stephen J. Wellum, *Kingdom through Covenant: A Biblical-Theological Understanding of the Covenants*, 2nd ed. (Wheaton: Crossway, 2018), 216–44.

ficient for our purposes. First, being made in the image and likeness of God means that humans resemble and represent God in a way that other creatures do not. Whereas God makes all other creatures "according to their kinds" (1:21, 24–25), he makes humans alone in his own image and likeness. This suggests that being made in the image and likeness of God is constitutive of human identity; it is what makes us human.[4] And while humans might resemble God in numerous ways, the God we find revealed in Genesis 1:1–25 is above all a Creator and Ruler, one who makes things and orders them.[5] It therefore seems likely that to be human involves reflecting the creative and ruling activity of God himself. Second, this initial impression is confirmed by the following context, where we find that being made in the image and likeness of God entails a vocation. God initially states that he is creating humans in his image and likeness "so that they may rule" over all other creatures (1:26). And after he creates humans, he commissions them: "Be fruitful and increase in number; fill the earth and subdue it. Rule over the fish in the sea and the birds in the sky and over every living creature that moves on the ground" (1:28).

It is important to note that only at this point—with humans created and commissioned to act as vice-regents over creation—does God call his creation "very good" (1:31). Genesis 1:1–2:3 therefore presents doing God-ordained work as a good and even necessary part of what it means to be human.[6] In God's original intent, good works do not conflict with one's relationship with God; on the contrary, they are its logical outflow.

Good Works in the Garden

Genesis 2:4–25 also presents human work as part of God's original intent, albeit from a different angle. Whereas Genesis 1:1–2:3 provides

4. While Gen. 1:26–27 explicitly describes only the first humans as being made in God's image and likeness, Scripture is clear elsewhere that this status extends to all humans (Gen. 9:6; James 3:9; cf. Ps. 8; 1 Cor. 11:7).

5. Andy Crouch, *Culture Making: Recovering Our Creative Calling* (Downers Grove, IL: IVP Books, 2008), 21.

6. Contra Scott Hafemann, "Work as the Divine Curse: Toil and Grace East of Eden," *Bulletin of Ecclesial Theology* 2, no. 1 (2015): 1–4. Hafemann contends that "men and women were created to eat and drink, but not to work" (1). However, he defines the verb "work" idiosyncratically as action "whose goal it is to obtain what is needed to sustain one's life" (1n3). Hafemann argues that the first humans had no such external necessity. The problem, of course, is that external necessity is not essential to the concept of work. As noted above, Gen. 2 describes God's creative activity as "work," and God certainly does not create out of any external necessity.

a sweeping view of creation, Genesis 2:4–25 zooms in to focus on the origin of the first humans. In this way, it functions as a commentary of sorts on 1:26–27. After a brief introduction (2:4), the account seems to be organized around a twofold problem-solution structure:

Problem: no man to work the ground (2:5–6)
   Solution: God forms man and places him in the garden (2:7–17)
Problem: no suitable helper for the man (2:18–20)
   Solution: God makes woman and presents her to the man
      (2:21–25)

In the first problem-solution, the author explains that there were no plants on the earth, "for the LORD God had not sent rain on the earth and there was no one [*'adam*] to work [*la'abod*, from *'abad*] the ground [*'adamah*]" (2:5). God then creates man (*'adam*) from the dust of the ground (*'adamah*) as a solution to this problem and places him in the garden of Eden (2:7–8). Genesis 2:15 seems to confirm that God creates man for the purpose of working the garden: "The LORD God took the man and put him in the Garden of Eden to work it [*le'obdah*, from *'abad*] and take care of it [*leshomrah*, from *shamar*]." Note that here the author uses the same verb for "work" (*'abad*) as in 2:5. Man thus seems to address the need articulated in 2:5. In the second problem-solution, God creates woman to fill man's need for a suitable helper in this vocation. Such an interpretation suggests that work is an integral part of God's original intent for humanity.

Some interpreters, however, have challenged this reading. Umberto Cassuto, John Sailhamer, and Scott Hafemann, for example, all argue that the clause "there was no man to work the ground" (Gen. 2:5) simply anticipates humanity's fallen state (3:23), as opposed to presenting the problem to which man constitutes the solution.[7] They also contend that the two infinitives in Genesis 2:15 that describe God's purpose for placing man in the garden should be translated not as "to work it and take care of it" (NIV) but as "to serve and to guard" (Cassuto) or "to worship and to

---

7. Umberto Cassuto, *A Commentary on the Book of Genesis, Part 1: From Adam to Noah*, trans. Israel Abrahams (Jerusalem: Magnes, 1961), 102–3; John H. Sailhamer, "Genesis," in *The Expositor's Bible Commentary*, vol. 2 (Grand Rapids: Zondervan, 1990), 40; Hafemann, "Work," 8.

obey" (Sailhamer).[8] On this basis, all three scholars contend that God creates man not for *work* but for *worship* (i.e., priestly or sacrificial service).

In our view, there are two significant problems with this reading.
First, as noted above, Genesis 1:26–27 presents humans as being made
in the image of a working God, and Genesis 2:4–25 develops this concept. Given this context, it would be odd for the author to present work
as a purely postfall phenomenon. Second, even if Cassuto and company
are correct about the translation of Genesis 2:15 (and this is by no means
certain),[9] they have not eliminated work from the garden. Whether we
wish to describe the man's intended activity as agricultural service,
priestly service, or some other sort of service, the fact remains that God
places the man in the garden to *do* something that is productive and not
merely for leisure. It is therefore not surprising that the worship-not-
work view of human activity in the garden of Eden remains a minority
perspective. Victor Hamilton sums up the consensus view well:

> Manual labor is a God-given privilege, not a sentence or a penalty.[10]

The point is made clear here that physical labor is not a consequence of
sin. Work enters the picture before sin does, and if man had never sinned
he still would be working. Eden certainly is not a paradise in which man

---

8. Cassuto, *Genesis*, 121–23; Sailhamer, "Genesis," 45; Hafemann, "Work," 5–7. Cassuto cites Genesis Rabbah 16.5 as precedent for this interpretation.

9. The final *he* on the two infinitives (*le'obdah, leshomrah*) typically is understood as a feminine
suffix and thus is written with a *mappiq* (so the NIV: "to work and take care of *it*"). However, there is
no obvious feminine antecedent for the suffix to refer to. "Garden" (*gan*) usually is masculine, "Eden"
is neither masculine nor feminine, and while "ground" (*'adamah*) is feminine, it last occurred in
2:9. Cassuto (followed by Sailhamer and Hafemann) notes this issue and argues that the *he* should
be understood as part of the infinitives, functionally making both infinitives intransitive. However,
there are at least two solutions that would preserve the feminine suffix: (1) "garden" (*gan*) might
have variable gender and be feminine here (see Wilhelm Gesenius, *Gesenius' Hebrew and Chaldee
Lexicon to the Old Testament Scriptures*, trans. Samuel P. Tregelles [Grand Rapids: Eerdmans, 1971],
175; Ludwig Koehler, Walter Baumgartner, and Johann J. Stamm, *The Hebrew and Aramaic Lexicon
of the Old Testament*, trans. and ed. Mervyn E. J. Richardson, 5 vols. [Leiden: Brill, 1994–99], 1:198);
(2) "ground" (*'adamah*) might be the antecedent despite its absence from the immediately preceding
verses. Indeed, since 2:5 notes that "there was no man to *work* the *ground*," it is not unreasonable
to think that when God creates man "to *work* and take care of *it*," the "it" is the ground mentioned
earlier. But even if the infinitives are intransitive, this would not require the alternative meaning
that Cassuto suggests; *'abad* can mean "work" whether transitive or intransitive. Indeed, Helmer
Ringgren contends that "without an object, [*'abad*] usually means 'to work'" (G. Johannes Botterweck
and Helmer Ringgren, eds., *Theological Dictionary of the Old Testament*, trans. John T. Willis et al.,
17 vols. [Grand Rapids: Eerdmans, 1974–2021], s.v. "עָבַד," 10:381).

10. Victor P. Hamilton, *Handbook on the Pentateuch* (Grand Rapids: Baker, 1982), 27.

passes his time in idyllic and uninterrupted bliss with absolutely no demands on his daily schedule.[11]

The interpretation of Genesis 1–2 developed above has significant implications for a biblical theology of good works. In these opening chapters of Scripture, we find that human work (i.e., productive activity) is not a result of the fall but is an integral part of God's original intent for humanity. God creates humans to do good works, and doing good works is therefore part of what it means to be a human in right relationship with God. Work, in other words, is originally a form of worship. Of course, as we will see below, Adam and Eve's rebellion results in the corruption of humans and human work, but Genesis 1–2 reminds us that from the beginning it was not so. God's original intent was that Adam and Eve do good works, multiplying the people of God and expanding the place of God to fill the whole earth with the presence of God, all to the glory of God.

The Corruption of Work

Genesis 3 narrates humans' tragic rebellion against God and the resulting corruption of God's original intent. Earlier, God had given Adam a single, simple command: "You are free to eat from any tree in the garden; but you must not eat from the tree of the knowledge of good and evil, for when you eat from it you will certainly die" (2:16–17). The serpent, however, approaches Eve and argues that eating the forbidden fruit will result not in death but in God-like powers (3:4–5). Thus, when Adam and Eve eat the fruit, they are committing an act of rebellion against God, declaring their autonomy from him and attempting to displace him as God.

God's judgment on Adam and Eve constitutes "not just the removal of blessings, but the *reversal* of blessings. What had been a blessing now becomes a curse, a benefit becomes a burden, paradise is exchanged

11. Hamilton, *Book of Genesis*, 171. For interpreters who take a similar view, see Gerhard von Rad, *Genesis: A Commentary*, rev. ed., Old Testament Library (Philadelphia: Westminster, 1972), 80; Walter Brueggemann, *Genesis*, Interpretation (Atlanta: John Knox, 1982), 46; Nahum M. Sarna, *Genesis*, JPS Torah Commentary (Philadelphia: Jewish Publication Society, 1989), 20; Claus Westermann, *Genesis 1–11*, trans. John J. Scullion, Continental Commentary (Minneapolis: Fortress, 1994), 222; Bruce K. Waltke with Cathi J. Fredricks, *Genesis: A Commentary* (Grand Rapids: Zondervan, 2001), 87; Bill T. Arnold, *Genesis*, New Cambridge Bible Commentary (Cambridge: Cambridge University Press, 2009), 59.

for prison."[12] Whereas Eve had been given the privilege of partnering with Adam in multiplying humanity and ruling over creation (1:28), God now declares that she will experience severe pain in childbearing and alienation from Adam, her would-be partner (3:16). Similarly, whereas Adam had been given the blessing of fruitful labor in the garden, God now proclaims,

> [17] Cursed is the ground ['adamah] because of you;
>   through painful toil you will eat food from it
>   all the days of your life.
> [18] It will produce thorns and thistles for you,
>   and you will eat the plants of the field.
> [19] By the sweat of your brow
>   you will eat your food
>   until you return to the ground. (3:17–19)

The 'adamah will now rebel against Adam, transforming his previously productive labor into grueling toil. The statement "By the sweat of your brow you will eat your food until you return to the ground" (3:19) is particularly interesting. While the "sweat" may simply refer to difficult physical labor, it is doubtful that Adam's prior activity in the garden had involved no sweat-inducing work. Daniel Fleming has shown that in several ancient Near Eastern texts, sweat is associated with and caused by anxious fear.[13] In light of this background, it seems likely that Adam's punishment is not only that he will work harder but also that he will experience "a deeper anguish, the fear that for all the effort and pain, death will await [him] when the soil does not produce its life-giving grain."[14] The rebellion of humans thus corrupts not only us but also our relationship to work. We must note, however, that the fundamental problem is not work itself but humans.

Genesis 1–3 therefore presents a nuanced view of humans' relationship to work(s). On the one hand, God creates humans to do good works.

---

12. Sandra L. Richter, *The Epic of Eden: A Christian Entry into the Old Testament* (Downers Grove, IL: IVP Academic, 2008), 106 (italics original).

13. Daniel E. Fleming, "By the Sweat of Your Brow: Adam, Anat, Athirat and Ashurbanipal," in *Ugarit and the Bible: Proceedings of the International Symposium on Ugarit and the Bible, Manchester, September 1992*, ed. George J. Brooke, Adrian H. W. Curtis, and John F. Healey, Ugaritisch-biblische Literatur 11 (Münster: Ugarit-Verlag, 1994), 93–100. We owe this reference to Richter, *Epic of Eden*, 111.

14. Fleming, "Sweat," 100.

On the other hand, Adam and Eve's rebellion against God results in the corruption of humans and, by extension, of how we interact with one another and the world around us. Work is thus not caused by the fall but corrupted by it. Such a beginning to the biblical metanarrative suggests that while the relationship between humans and works is sure to be a complex one, God's goal is not to rid humans of work but rather to redeem us so we can do the good for which we were created.

Faith That Works (Abraham)

The story of Abraham is a significant one for the doctrine of good works, not least because Paul and James cite it as an example of justification by faith and of justification by works, respectively (Rom. 4:1–25; Gal. 3:1–9; James 2:18–24). We will discuss the relationship between Paul and James in the next chapter, but here we will see that in the story of Abraham, at least, faith and works do not stand in tension but complement each other.

Call and Response

Within the plotline of Genesis, Abraham and his descendants constitute a solution to the Adam problem. The sin of Adam and Eve has caused a vicious cycle of human wickedness and death, and even the fresh start with righteous Noah (Gen. 6:9) and his family has led to the debacle of Babel, a city built for human self-glorification and in rebellion against God (11:4; cf. 1:28). God's solution to this problem is to call one man and to bless him so that he (and his descendants) can be a blessing to the nations:

> ¹ The LORD had said to Abram, "Go from your country, your people and your father's household to the land I will show you.
> ² "I will make you into a great nation,
>   and I will bless you;
> I will make your name great,
>   and you will be a blessing.
> ³ I will bless those who bless you,
>   and whoever curses you I will curse;
> and all peoples on earth
>   will be blessed through you." (Gen. 12:1–3)

Several points about this call are key with respect to good works. First, God's promise to bless Abram and to make him into a great nation is the first of many passages in Genesis about Abram/Abraham and his descendants that recall God's commission to Adam and Eve.[15]

God *blessed* them and said to them, "*Be fruitful* and *increase in number*; fill the earth and subdue it. Rule over the fish in the sea and the birds in the sky and over every living creature that moves on the ground." (1:28)

I will *make you into a great nation*, and I will *bless* you; I will make your name great, and you will be a *blessing*. I will *bless* those who bless you. . . . (12:2–3)

I will make my covenant between me and you and will greatly *increase your numbers*. . . . I will make you very *fruitful*. . . . The whole land of Canaan . . . I will give as an everlasting possession to you and your descendants after you. (17:2, 6, 8)

Because you have done this . . . , I will surely *bless* you and *make* your descendants as *numerous* as the stars in the sky and as the sand on the seashore. . . . And through your offspring all nations on earth will be *blessed*, because you have obeyed me. (22:16–18)

This pattern extends through the rest of Genesis (26:3–4, 24; 28:3; 35:11–12; 47:27; 48:3–4) and further in the Pentateuch (Exod. 1:7; 23:30; 32:13; Lev. 26:9; Deut. 1:10–11; 7:13–14; 8:1; 28:63; 30:5, 16). As N. T. Wright notes, "At major turning-points in the story . . . the narrative quietly insists that Abraham and his progeny inherit the role of Adam and Eve."[16] This point is significant, for it suggests that just as God originally created Adam and Eve for good works, he now calls Abram and his descendants for good works.[17]

15. N. T. Wright, *The Climax of the Covenant: Christ and the Law in Pauline Theology* (Minneapolis: Fortress, 1991), 21–23. Cf. Wright, *The New Testament and the People of God*, Christian Origins and the Question of God 1 (Minneapolis: Fortress, 1992), 263; Gentry and Wellum, *Kingdom through Covenant*, 262–63. The language is used also of Noah and his descendants in Gen. 9:1, 7.

16. Wright, *New Testament*, 263. Cf. Wright, *Climax of the Covenant*, 22.

17. It is true that God's command to Adam and Eve becomes a promise to Abraham and his descendants (Wright, *Climax of the Covenant*, 22; Wright, *New Testament*, 263). However, this change seems intended not to eliminate human action or responsibility but rather to emphasize God's provision for Abraham and his descendants in a fallen world.

Second, while Abram's call is unconditioned, it is not unconditional.[18] Genesis does not tell us why God calls Abram as opposed to someone else, but it does not seem to be because Abram is inherently worthy or has "earned it." In this sense, the call is unconditioned. Yet there do seem to be conditions to this call. The most immediate is "Go from your country, your people and your father's household to the land I will show you" (Gen. 12:1). We do not know what would have happened if Abram had refused and stayed in Haran, but we may assume that he would not have become the "father of many nations" (17:5) or "the man of faith" (Gal. 3:9). We know Abram because of his obedient response: "So Abram went, as the LORD had told him" (Gen. 12:4). The gracious yet conditional nature of Abram's relationship with God, both here and elsewhere, should caution us against creating a dichotomy between grace/faith and good works. On the contrary, as the author of Hebrews would later point out, "*By faith* Abraham, when called to go . . . , obeyed and went" (Heb. 11:8).

Third, Abram's call is missional. God blesses Abram *to be a blessing* to all the peoples of the earth (Gen. 12:2–3). The divine blessings that Abram and his descendants will receive are not only for them. Rather, Israel is meant to be a channel through which God's blessings flow to the world. But while the channel metaphor is helpful, we must also remember that Israel is meant to be not merely a passive conduit but an active witness to the nations, as will become clear as the biblical story progresses. A rabbinic commentary on Genesis captures this well when it portrays God as saying, "I will create Adam first, so that if he sins, Abraham may come and set things right" (Genesis Rabbah 14.6).[19] The great privilege of Abram and his children is to participate in God's work of saving the world.

Covenant

The language of "covenant" enters the Abram story in Genesis 15. Genesis tells us that Abram was seventy-five when he left Haran. However, a few chapters (and perhaps some years) later, God's promise of

18. We owe this distinction to John M. G. Barclay, *Paul and the Gift* (Grand Rapids: Eerdmans, 2015), 500.

19. Harry Freedman and Maurice Simon, eds., *Midrash Rabbah*, 3rd ed., 10 vols. (London: Soncino, 1983), 1:114. We owe this reference to Wright, *New Testament*, 251.

offspring remains unfulfilled. It is therefore not surprising that when God says to Abram in a vision, "Fear not, Abram, I am your shield; your reward shall be very great" (15:1 ESV), Abram responds, "Sovereign LORD, what can you give me since I remain childless and the one who will inherit my estate is Eliezer of Damascus?" (15:2). It seems that in the absence of a biological son, Abram has decided to adopt one of his servants as his heir. The Lord, however, assures Abram that the promised child will be a biological son and promises him that his offspring will be as numerous as the stars (15:4–5). The author then notes, "Abram believed the LORD, and he credited it to him as righteousness" (15:6). As Paul would later note, Abram here simply has faith in what God has spoken, and it is on this basis (rather than on preexisting qualifications or worth that Abram has amassed) that God credits righteousness to him (Rom. 4:1–25).

God speaks again in Genesis 15:7: "I am the LORD, who brought you out of Ur of the Chaldeans to give you this land to take possession of it." Abram, who has been a sojourner in "this land" for some time now, understandably replies, "Sovereign LORD, how can I know that I will gain possession of it?" (15:8). God responds by commanding Abram to bring him various animals: "a heifer, a goat and a ram, each three years old, along with a dove and a young pigeon" (15:9). To the modern mind, this seems like an odd way of answering Abram's question, but it seems to make sense to Abram, for without further instruction he cuts the larger animals in two and arranges the halves opposite each other (15:10), effectively creating a blood path between them. God makes promises to Abram about how his descendants will inherit the land, and then "a smoking firepot with a blazing torch"—a symbol of God's presence—passes between the animal pieces (15:17).[20] The author sums up the whole affair by saying, "On that day the LORD made a covenant [berith] with Abram . . ." (15:18).

The concept of covenant was common in the ancient Near East and involved two or more parties (individuals, tribes, nations, etc.) binding themselves together through oaths.[21] A covenant was, in essence, a

---

20. For fire and smoke as symbols of God's presence, see Gentry and Wellum, *Kingdom through Covenant*, 287, citing Exod. 3:2; 13:21; 19:18; 20:18.

21. George E. Mendenhall, "Covenant Forms in Israelite Traditions," *Biblical Archaeologist* 17, no. 3 (1954): 50–76; Botterweck and Ringgren, *Theological Dictionary*, s.v. "בְּרִית," 2:253–79; Bill T. Arnold

relationship-creating and relationship-defining agreement. Covenants "were always ratified by the sacrifice of . . . animals," and "this practice was so consistent that the act of making a covenant was idiomatically expressed by the phrase 'to cut a covenant.'"[22] We find this idiom in Genesis 15:18: "The LORD made [*karath*, literally "cut"] a covenant with Abram." The covenant partners would sometimes pass between the pieces of the slaughtered animals as a way of saying, "May the same happen to me if I break my word."[23] In Genesis 15, however, it is only God who passes down the blood path and pledges his own life to keep this covenant.

Two major types of covenants in the ancient Near East were the suzerain-vassal treaty and the royal grant. Peter Gentry and Stephen Wellum describe these well: "The first type is a diplomatic treaty between a great king, or suzerain, and client kings, or vassals. The focus of these treaties was to reinforce the interest of the suzerain by arguments from history and oathbound affirmations of loyalty on the part of the vassal-states, backed up by divine sanctions. The second type of treaty involved a grant of property or even a privileged position of a priestly or royal office given as a favor by a god or king."[24] Scholars generally agree that the covenant of Moses is similar in form to the suzerain-vassal treaty and that the covenants of Abram and David more resemble the royal grant. On this basis, some portray the Mosaic covenant as conditional (requiring Israel's obedience) and the Abrahamic and Davidic covenants as unconditional.[25] Yet precisely because a covenant is a *mutual* agreement, we should be wary of such stark dichotomies.[26] As Moshe Weinfeld states, "While the grant is mainly a promise by the donor to the recipient, it presupposes the loyalty of the latter. By the

and Bryan E. Beyer, eds., *Readings from the Ancient Near East: Primary Sources for Old Testament Study*, Encountering Biblical Studies (Grand Rapids: Baker Academic, 2002), 96–103; Richter, *Epic of Eden*, 69–91, esp. 72–79.

  22. Richter, *Epic of Eden*, 77.
  23. Richter, *Epic of Eden*, 77; Gentry and Wellum, *Kingdom through Covenant*, 287–94. Cf. Jer. 34:18–22.
  24. Gentry and Wellum, *Kingdom through Covenant*, 166.
  25. E.g., "Major Covenants in the Old Testament," in *NIV Zondervan Study Bible*, ed. D. A. Carson (Grand Rapids: Zondervan, 2015), 41. The associate editors for the Old Testament content are Richard S. Hess and T. Desmond Alexander, and they are also listed as primary authors of the Genesis material.
  26. Frank M. Cross, "Kinship and Covenant in Ancient Israel," in *From Epic to Canon: History and Literature in Ancient Israel* (Baltimore: Johns Hopkins University Press, 1998), 15–16.

same token the treaty, whose principal concern is with the obligation of the vassal, presupposes the sovereign's promise to protect his vassal's country and dynasty."[27] It seems best to conclude with John A. Davies that these two covenant types express "differing emphases of the same relationship, on a continuum rather than being polar opposites."[28] Thus, while Abram's covenant does stress God's benevolence, we need not assume that it expects no good works.

Indeed, God explicitly commands good works of Abram when he affirms this covenant in Genesis 17.[29] The Lord appears to Abram, saying, "I am God Almighty; walk before me faithfully and be blameless" (17:1). After giving Abram a new name (Abraham, "father of many") and reminding him of his promises, God delivers a covenantal command: "Every male among you shall be circumcised" (17:10). This circumcision will be "the sign of the covenant" (17:11), applies to every male who is eight days old (17:12), and is a serious enough matter that any uncircumcised male "will be cut off from his people" because he has broken the covenant (17:14). Abraham's covenant, it seems, is *both* gracious *and* requires a certain response from Abraham and his descendants.

The Obedience of Faith

Our final episode from Abraham's life comes from Genesis 22. Abraham has finally received the promised child, Isaac (21:1–3), and the baby has grown into a boy. Abraham's trial of faith is over, we might think. Not so. God now tests Abraham, saying, "Take your son, your only son, whom you love—Isaac—and go to the region of Moriah. Sacrifice him there as a burnt offering on a mountain I will show you" (22:2). One can only imagine the angst and confusion that these words must have caused Abraham. The child for whom Abraham has waited for twenty-five years (cf. 21:5) has now arrived, and God is asking him to sacrifice his son, the one on whom all the promises hinge? Yet Abraham obeys, and as he raises the knife to slay Isaac, God stays his hand, saying, "Do

---

27. Moshe Weinfeld, *Deuteronomy and the Deuteronomic School* (Oxford: Clarendon, 1972), 74. We owe this reference to Gentry and Wellum, *Kingdom through Covenant*, 166.

28. John A. Davies, *A Royal Priesthood: Literary and Intertextual Perspectives on an Image of Israel in Exodus 19:6*, Journal for the Study of the Old Testament Supplement Series 395 (London: T&T Clark, 2004), 183. Cf. Gentry and Wellum, *Kingdom through Covenant*, 167.

29. For Gen. 17 as an affirmation of the covenant in Gen. 15, as opposed to being a separate covenant, see Gentry and Wellum, *Kingdom through Covenant*, 294–318, esp. 312–18.

not lay a hand on the boy. . . . Do not do anything to him. Now I know that you fear God, because you have not withheld from me your son, your only son" (22:12).

James later cites this story, saying,

> [20] Do you want evidence that faith without deeds is useless? [21] Was not our father Abraham considered righteous for what he did when he offered his son Isaac on the altar? [22] You see that his faith and his actions were working together, and his faith was made complete by what he did. [23] And the scripture was fulfilled that says, "Abraham believed God, and it was credited to him as righteousness." (James 2:20–23, quoting Gen. 15:6)

We will explore the relationship between faith and works in both James and Paul more fully in the following chapter, but here we simply wish to point out that James interprets Abraham's response to God's testing as deeds/actions/works that are a necessary complement to his initial faith in Genesis 15:6. Abraham is "the man of faith" (Gal. 3:9), to be sure, but his is a faith that works.

Good Works as Covenant Faithfulness (Moses and the Law)

We now come to Moses and the law. In the preceding material, we have attempted to show that good works are an integral part of God's intent for his people. Here, however, our focus must be somewhat different. Few of us need to be convinced that works figure prominently in the law of Moses; the question is whether this is a good thing. For many modern Christians, the copious pages of legal code in Exodus through Deuteronomy seem daunting, if not burdensome. Our squeamishness about works and the law more broadly is due in large measure to a certain interpretation of Paul's teaching on these topics in the New Testament. Yet we do well to remember that the same Paul declared that "the law is good" (Rom. 7:16; cf. 1 Tim. 1:8). The problem is not the law itself or the works that it requires, but rather sin and how it uses the law against fallen humans (Rom. 7:7–11). Here we will argue that the law is indeed good, meant to guide Israel into right relationship with God and neighbor so that God's blessings can flow through them to the nations.[30]

---

30. See Gentry and Wellum, *Kingdom through Covenant*, 342.

Works and the Covenant

Context, they say, is king. If someone asks you to give them twenty dollars, for example, it makes a significant difference whether the person in question is a stranger holding you at gunpoint or your spouse requesting lunch money for your children. One request is a crime to make, the other a crime to refuse. In the case of the Mosaic law, the crucial context is covenant. This is true on two levels. First, in our study of Abraham above we observed how God calls Abraham and makes a covenant with him so that he and his family can be a blessing to the nations. As Abraham's descendants, the Israelites are heirs to that covenant. Indeed, it is *because* they are Abraham's offspring that God has delivered them from Egypt (Gen. 15:13–14; Exod. 2:24). Second, God makes a further covenant with Israel at Mount Sinai, and all of the "works of the law" are given against the backdrop of this covenant relationship.

Exodus 19:3–6, which recounts Moses's first encounter with God at Sinai, summarizes the purpose of the covenant:

> [3] Then Moses went up to God, and the LORD called to him from the mountain and said, "This is what you are to say to the descendants of Jacob and what you are to tell the people of Israel: [4] 'You yourselves have seen what I did to Egypt, and how I carried you on eagles' wings and brought you to myself. [5] Now if you obey me fully and keep my covenant, then out of all nations you will be my treasured possession. Although the whole earth is mine, [6] you will be for me a kingdom of priests and a holy nation.' These are the words you are to speak to the Israelites."

YHWH begins by summing up what he has done for the Israelites in bringing them out of Egypt ("You yourselves have seen . . ."). Notice that the last action that God mentions is "I . . . brought you to myself" (19:4). This suggests that God's ultimate goal in the exodus is not merely to bring Israel out of Egypt but to bring them into relationship with himself. Only in the context of this story and intent does God declare, "Now if you obey me fully and keep my covenant . . ." (19:5). Three titles follow that develop the covenantal relationship that Israel will have with YHWH and the nations. The first, "treasured possession" (*segulah*), can refer to a king's treasure (1 Chron. 29:3; Eccles. 2:8), but in Malachi 3:17 it is also linked with filial service: "'On the day when I act,' says the LORD Almighty, 'they [those who fear the LORD] will be my treasured possession [*segulah*]. I will spare them, just as a father has compassion and spares his son who serves him.'" As Gentry and Wellum note, "When Yahweh calls Israel to be his personal treasure, he is speaking of the kind of devoted service given by a son."[31] The second and third titles, "kingdom of priests" (*mamleketh kohanim*) and "holy nation" (*goy qadosh*), are closely linked. Priests, of course, had special access to God's presence and mediated between God and the rest of Israel. As "a kingdom of priests," Israel will mediate God's grace to the rest of the peoples. Similarly, as "a holy nation," Israel will be consecrated and set apart for YHWH, the Holy One, and their YHWH-shaped life will bear witness to the nations. Indeed, it is precisely by living as a "holy nation" (reflecting God's character) that Israel will be a "kingdom of priests." In short, the Mosaic covenant is meant to cultivate right relationship between Israel and YHWH so that Israel can fulfill the Abrahamic promise to be a blessing to the nations. The people of Israel willingly accept this covenant and the responsibilities it entails, saying, "We will do everything the LORD has said" (Exod. 19:8).

The fact that this covenant required specific works would not have been a surprise to Moses or his contemporaries. In our discussion of Abraham, we introduced the concept of covenant and noted two major types of covenants: the suzerain-vassal treaty and the royal grant. In its most widely attested form, the suzerain-vassal treaty consisted of six parts:[32]

1. Preamble
2. Historical prologue
3. Stipulations
4. Deposition and provision for periodic reading
5. List of witnesses
6. Curses and blessings

31. Gentry and Wellum, *Kingdom through Covenant*, 356. Drawing on the analysis by Davies (*Royal Priesthood*, 53), the authors note that Akkadian and Ugaritic parallels corroborate this usage.
32. Adapted from Richter, *Epic of Eden*, 84. The form is specifically that of the Hittite suzerain-vassal treaties of the second millennium BC.

Scholars have observed that the Mosaic covenant recalls this form at numerous points.[33] Here we simply wish to make two observations regarding the treaty form and its use in the Mosaic covenant. First, the historical prologue, which rehearses the suzerain's acts of benevolence toward the vassal, *precedes* the stipulations that communicate the suzerain's expectations for his vassal. As Jon Levenson states, "The function of the prologue is to ground the obligations of Israel to YHWH in the history of his gracious acts on her behalf."[34] Second, the stipulations are not only a standard part of the form; they are an element that God chooses to preserve when he defines his relationship with Israel. Together, the prologue and the stipulations emphasize both that the Mosaic covenant is gracious and that it expects a response.

The Center: Love of God and Neighbor

When asked, "Which is the greatest commandment in the Law?" Jesus replies, "'Love the Lord your God with all your heart and with all your soul and with all your mind.' This is the first and greatest commandment. And the second is like it: 'Love your neighbor as yourself.' All the Law and the Prophets hang on these two commandments" (Matt. 22:37–40; cf. Mark 12:29–31; Luke 10:27–28). As the last phrase implies, Jesus is identifying not only the two most important commandments in the law but also the ones that sum up all the others. On Jesus's reading, then, the law of Moses is ultimately about two things: love of God (Deut. 6:5) and love of neighbor (Lev. 19:18). This notion finds support in Exodus 19:3–6, which, as noted above, presents the covenant as intended to bring Israel into right relationship with YHWH so that they can be a blessing to the nations. The God- and neighbor-oriented nature of the law can also be seen in the Ten Commandments (Exod. 20:3–17; Deut. 5:7–21), in which the first four commandments are primarily oriented toward God, the latter six toward humans.[35]

---

33. E.g., Kenneth A. Kitchen, *Ancient Orient and Old Testament* (Chicago: InterVarsity, 1966), 96–98; Jon D. Levenson, *Sinai and Zion: An Entry into the Jewish Bible*, New Voices in Biblical Studies (San Francisco: Harper & Row, 1985), 37; Richter, *Epic of Eden*, 83–88; Gentry and Wellum, *Kingdom through Covenant*, 398–402.

34. Levenson, *Sinai and Zion*, 37.

35. This is according to the Protestant/Reformed numbering.

1. You shall have no other gods before me.
2. You shall not make for yourself an idol.
3. You shall not bear YHWH's name in vain.[36]
4. Remember the Sabbath day.
5. Honor your father and mother.
6. You shall not murder.
7. You shall not commit adultery.
8. You shall not steal.
9. You shall not give false testimony.
10. You shall not covet.

Jesus's teaching here is important because it suggests that, far from being a list of arbitrary regulations, the law and the works that it commands are meant to cultivate love of God and neighbor.

The greatest commandments correspond to (and likely gave rise to) the Christian concepts of "works of piety" (acts of love toward God) and "works of mercy" (acts of love toward neighbor). When we speak of doing works of piety and mercy, then, we are ultimately talking about fulfilling the greatest commandments, which Jesus not only identifies as the heart of the Old Testament law but also enjoins would-be disciples to keep if they wish to inherit eternal life (Luke 10:25–28; cf. Mark 10:17–19 par.).

Sabbath

One commandment that bears directly on the issue of good works is that of the Sabbath. In the Ten Commandments, God declares,

> [8] Remember the Sabbath day by keeping it holy. [9] Six days you shall labor and do all your work, [10] but the seventh day is a sabbath to the LORD

---

36. Carmen Joy Imes argues compellingly that the name command does not prohibit *taking* YHWH's name in vain (i.e., misusing it) but *bearing* YHWH's name in vain. Israel, in other words, must represent YHWH well. See Carmen Joy Imes, *Bearing YHWH's Name at Sinai: A Reexamination of the Name Command of the Decalogue*, Bulletin for Biblical Research Supplements 19 (University Park, PA: Eisenbrauns, 2018); Imes, *Bearing God's Name: Why Sinai Still Matters* (Downers Grove, IL: IVP Academic, 2019), 48–52. Understood in this way, the name command is closely related to the titles "treasured possession," "kingdom of priests," and "holy nation" in Exod. 19:5–6 (Imes, *Bearing God's Name*, 51) and also to the concept of the image of God.

your God. On it you shall not do any work, neither you, nor your son or daughter, nor your male or female servant, nor your animals, nor any foreigner residing in your towns. [11] For in six days the LORD made the heavens and the earth, the sea, and all that is in them, but he rested on the seventh day. Therefore the LORD blessed the Sabbath day and made it holy. (Exod. 20:8–11)

God here instructs Israel *not* to work on the Sabbath and grounds this in his own rest at the end of the creation week (Gen. 2:2–3). Moses reiterates this command in Deuteronomy, but there the purpose of the command is "so that your male and female servants may rest, as you do" (Deut. 5:14), and the reason given is that "you were slaves in Egypt and . . . the LORD your God brought you out of there with a mighty hand and an outstretched arm" (5:15). Sabbath-breaking constitutes a serious offense in the Old Testament that carry the death penalty (Exod. 31:14–15; 35:2; Num. 15:32–36).

To some interpreters, Sabbath presents a significant challenge to the idea that work might be good. Scott Hafemann, for example, describes Sabbath as "a symbolic statement that the week's work . . . is not humanity's rightful or ultimate calling."[37] In our view, this goes too far. Sabbath certainly places limits on human work, but this does not necessarily mean that work itself is fallen or lies outside of humanity's God-given purpose. As noted above, humans are made in the image of a working God, and work constitutes a part of Adam and Eve's prefall vocation. God institutes Sabbath not because *work* is corrupt but because *humans* are corrupt and make an idol of work when left to our own ends. Sabbath teaches Israel not that work is bad but rather that work is good only when done by faith in YHWH, trusting that he will provide for one's needs. Sabbath, then, poses no problem for the idea that work is part of humanity's rightful calling. Whether work constitutes part of humanity's ultimate calling in the fullest sense (i.e., in the new creation) will need to wait for our study of the New Testament in the following chapter.

The Limits of the Law

We have argued above that the law and the works that it requires are good. However, to say that the law is good is not to say that it constitutes

---

37. Hafemann, "Work," 12.

a complete antidote to human sinfulness. Indeed, the law bears witness to its own limits. In Deuteronomy, the final book of the Pentateuch, Moses reiterates the law to Israel as they stand at the edge of the promised land. Toward the end of the book, however, God tells Moses,

> [16] You are going to rest with your ancestors, and these people will soon prostitute themselves to the foreign gods of the land they are entering. They will forsake me and break the covenant I made with them. [17] And in that day I will become angry with them and forsake them; I will hide my face from them, and they will be destroyed. . . .
> [19] Now write down this song and teach it to the Israelites and have them sing it, so that it may be a witness for me against them. (Deut. 31:16–17, 19)

This song, known as the "Song of Moses," is recorded in Deuteronomy 32. True to form, it forecasts how Israel will eventually forsake God and how God will render judgment on Israel for their infidelity but will eventually restore his people. And this is precisely how the Old Testament plays out: Israel repeatedly rebels against YHWH, is sent into exile as a penalty for their sin, and returns from exile only by God's grace. In this way, the Pentateuch contains within itself the whole story of the Old Testament. What is striking is that in telling this story the Pentateuch itself acknowledges that the law, for all its goodness, is ultimately impotent to remedy Israel's sin problem. While the law reveals the character and will of God, it does not itself empower humans to do the good it commands. The law thus recognizes the need for a divine solution to human sin beyond itself.

The Heart of the Matter (David and the Psalms)

Good works continue to play an important role throughout the historical books, Psalms, and Wisdom literature. Joshua and Judges, for example, illustrate the dire consequences of *not* doing good works, as Israel refuses to drive the nations from the promised land completely (as God commanded them), is led astray by the same nations, and spirals downward into infidelity despite the efforts of the judges. Wisdom literature, too, is deeply concerned with good works, as it explores what it means to live wisely amid the complexities of life. Some representative statements give us an entry point into this literature; here we will limit ourselves to exploring the role of good works in the life and covenant of David and in Psalms, a book with which David is intimately connected.

A Man after God's Own Heart

Good works constitute one of the major differences between David and Saul, Israel's first king. Saul initially seems to have great promise: he is handsome and tall (1 Sam. 9:2) and leads Israel to victory over the Ammonites (11:1–11). However, when the Philistines draw near for battle and Samuel has not yet come to offer the prebattle burnt offering, Saul takes matters into his own hands and makes the sacrifice himself (13:8–9). Samuel then appears and condemns Saul for his disobedience: "You have done a foolish thing. . . . You have not kept the command the LORD your God gave you; if you had, he would have established your kingdom over Israel for all time. But now your kingdom will not endure; the LORD has sought out a man after his own heart and appointed him ruler of his people, because you have not kept the LORD's command" (13:13–14; cf. 10:8). Interpreters puzzle over why Saul receives such a severe penalty for this offense. Whatever else one might say on this front, the consequence certainly underscores how important it is for Israel's king to obey a direct command from Israel's God. It is also noteworthy that Saul does not repent when confronted with his sin. Perhaps if he had, things would have turned out differently.

Saul again disobeys the Lord in an encounter with the Amalekites two chapters later. The Lord commands Saul, "Attack the Amalekites and totally destroy all that belongs to them. Do not spare them; put to death men and women, children and infants, cattle and sheep, camels and donkeys" (15:3). However, Saul spares Agag, king of the Amalekites, and some of the best livestock. Samuel approaches Saul the next day, and Saul at first claims to have fulfilled the Lord's instructions (15:13). When Samuel asks about the sheep and oxen that he hears, Saul blames his soldiers for sparing the animals and says they are for a sacrifice to the Lord (15:14–15, 21). Samuel responds,

> [22] Does the LORD delight in burnt offerings and sacrifices
>   as much as in obeying the LORD?
> To obey is better than sacrifice,
>   and to heed is better than the fat of rams.

> ²³ For rebellion is like the sin of divination,
>   and arrogance like the evil of idolatry.
> Because you have rejected the word of the LORD,
>   he has rejected you as king. (15:22–23)

Saul does acknowledge his sin at this point and asks to be forgiven. However, it becomes evident that Saul desires not so much to repent as to save face before the people (15:25, 30). Samuel tells Saul that the Lord has rejected him as king, and in the following chapter he anoints David as king.

David provides an interesting counterpoint to Saul. Samuel describes David as "a man after [God's] own heart" (13:14). This seems to indicate that, unlike Saul, David will obey the Lord's will. Luke seems to interpret the phrase in this way in Acts when he has Paul say, "God testified concerning [David]: 'I have found David son of Jesse, a man after my own heart; he will do everything I want him to do'" (Acts 13:22). Indeed, 1 and 2 Kings and 2 Chronicles present David as an example of obedience that other kings should follow.[38] However, we also know that David commits a sin that—at least on the face of it—rivals those that cost Saul the kingdom: he sleeps with Bathsheba and murders her husband, Uriah, to cover it up (2 Sam. 11). How, then, is David any different from Saul, and why does he not lose his kingdom as Saul did? At least part of the answer seems to be that whereas Saul fails to repent of his sin (at all in 1 Sam. 13 and genuinely in 1 Sam. 15), David immediately acknowledges his sin when confronted about it and repents (2 Sam. 12:13; Ps. 51). It seems that the obedience God desires involves not only abstaining from sin but also heartfelt repentance if one does sin. David declares as much in his psalm of repentance, interestingly recalling Samuel's earlier indictment of Saul (1 Sam. 15:22):

> ¹⁶ You do not delight in sacrifice, or I would bring it;
>   you do not take pleasure in burnt offerings.
> ¹⁷ My sacrifice, O God, is a broken spirit;
>   a broken and contrite heart
>   you, God, will not despise. (Ps. 51:16–17)

---

38. See 1 Kings 3:6, 14; 9:4; 11:4, 6, 33, 38; 14:8; 15:3, 5, 11; 2 Kings 14:3; 16:2; 18:3; 22:2; 2 Chron. 7:17; 17:3–4; 28:1; 29:2; 34:2.

First Kings 15:5 bears witness to the overarching pattern of obedience that such a heart produced in David's life while also acknowledging the Bathsheba incident as a notable exception: "David had done what was right in the eyes of the LORD and had not failed to keep any of the LORD's commands all the days of his life—except in the case of Uriah the Hittite."

The Davidic Covenant

Good works also play an important role in the Davidic covenant. Second Samuel 7:11b–16 records key elements of this covenant:

> [11] The LORD declares to you [David] that the LORD himself will establish a house for you: [12] When your days are over and you rest with your ancestors, I will raise up your offspring to succeed you, your own flesh and blood, and I will establish his kingdom. [13] He is the one who will build a house for my Name, and I will establish the throne of his kingdom forever. [14] I will be his father, and he will be my son. When he does wrong, I will punish him with a rod wielded by men, with floggings inflicted by human hands. [15] But my love will never be taken away from him, as I took it away from Saul, whom I removed from before you. [16] Your house and your kingdom will endure forever before me; your throne will be established forever.

As noted above, scholars generally agree that David's covenant resembles the form of the royal grant more than the suzerain-vassal treaty. As a result, many interpreters view the Davidic covenant as unconditional. However, the covenant in fact contains both conditional and unconditional elements. On the one hand, God promises to establish the kingdom of one of David's descendants (i.e., Solomon), to forge a father-son relationship with him, and to give David an everlasting house, kingdom, and throne.[39] This much at least seems unconditional. Indeed, the Lord emphasizes that he will not remove his love from this Davidic king as he did from Saul (7:15). On the other hand, God expects obedience of the Davidic king, for he promises to discipline him when he does wrong (7:14; cf. Ps. 89:30–32).

---

39. In 2 Sam. 7:9–11, God makes several other promises to David that will be fulfilled in David's lifetime.

Interpretations of the Davidic covenant later in Scripture also underscore the covenant's conditional nature, at least as it applies to David's descendants. In 1 Kings, David exhorts Solomon, "Walk in obedience to [God], and keep his decrees and commands, his laws and regulations, as written in the Law of Moses. Do this so that . . . the LORD may keep his promise to me: '*If* your descendants watch how they live, and *if* they walk faithfully before me with all their heart and soul, you will never fail to have a successor on the throne of Israel'" (2:3–4). Similarly, the Lord tells Solomon, "*If* you follow my decrees, observe my laws and keep all my commands and obey them, I will fulfill through you the promise I gave to David your father" (6:12). And at the dedication of the temple, Solomon prays, "Now LORD, the God of Israel, keep for your servant David my father the promises you made to him when you said, 'You shall never fail to have a successor to sit before me on the throne of Israel, *if only* your descendants are careful in all they do to walk before me faithfully as you have done'" (8:25). Such examples could be easily multiplied.[40] The conditional and unconditional elements of the Davidic covenant interweave throughout the Old Testament narrative, as God punishes Davidic kings for infidelity (most notably in dividing Solomon's kingdom) but also shows mercy to them for David's sake.[41]

If any doubt about the conditional nature of the Davidic covenant remained, the exile and postexilic period settle the matter. The overarching infidelity of the Davidic dynasty eventually leads to the dethroning of the Davidic king and the exile of Judah. Even after Judah returns from exile, no Davidic king reigns through the end of the Old Testament period. Of course, God makes good on his promise to give David an everlasting house, kingdom, and throne through Jesus the Messiah. However, the fact remains that the Davidic throne sits empty for several centuries because of the infidelity of Davidic kings, and this indicates no failure on God's part precisely because the Davidic covenant is in some measure conditional.

Works and Worship in the Book of Psalms

Given the importance of good works in David's life and covenant, it is perhaps not surprising that good works also figure prominently in the

40. E.g., 1 Kings 9:4–9; 11:31–33; 2 Chron. 6:16; 7:17–18; Ps. 132:11–12.
41. E.g., 1 Kings 11:34, 39; 15:4; 2 Kings 8:19; 19:34; 2 Chron. 21:7.

Psalms, half of which are attributed to David.[42] Psalm 1, which functions as an introduction to the entire book, contrasts the way of the righteous with the way of the wicked, concluding that "the LORD watches over the way of the righteous, but the way of the wicked leads to destruction" (1:6). To some, this might seem like an odd way to begin a book of worship songs, but it reminds us that worship and good works are inextricably interwoven; true worship both flows from and cultivates righteous behavior. As Derek Kidner says, Psalm 1 "stands here as a faithful doorkeeper, confronting those who would be in 'the congregation of the righteous' . . . with the basic choice that alone gives reality to worship."[43]

The book of Psalms emphasizes the importance of good works in at least two ways. First, numerous psalms describe how one's behavior (righteous or wicked) impacts one's relationship with God and the verdict one will receive from God. Psalm 24, for example, declares,

> [3] Who may ascend the mountain of the LORD?
>   Who may stand in his holy place?
> [4] The one who has clean hands and a pure heart,
>   who does not trust in an idol
>   or swear by a false god.
> [5] They will receive blessing from the LORD
>   and vindication from God their Savior. (24:3–5)

Psalm 34 similarly counsels,

> [12] Whoever of you loves life
>   and desires to see many good days,
> [13] keep your tongue from evil
>   and your lips from telling lies.
> [14] Turn from evil and do good;
>   seek peace and pursue it.
> [15] The eyes of the LORD are on the righteous,
>   and his ears are attentive to their cry;

---

42. David appears in the ascriptions of seventy-three psalms, and the New Testament attributes two additional psalms to David (Ps. 2, cf. Acts 4:25; Ps. 95, cf. Heb. 4:7).

43. Derek Kidner, *Psalms 1–72: An Introduction and Commentary on Books I and II of the Psalms*, Tyndale Old Testament Commentaries (Downers Grove, IL: InterVarsity, 1973), 47.

¹⁶ but the face of the LORD is against those who do evil,
　　to blot out their name from the earth. (34:12–16)

Likewise, Psalm 37:

³⁷ Consider the blameless, observe the upright;
　　a future awaits those who seek peace.
³⁸ But all sinners will be destroyed;
　　there will be no future for the wicked. (37:37–38)

Psalm 62 provides perhaps the strongest statement in the book on the relationship between works and final judgment: "You reward everyone according to what they have done" (62:12; cf. 28:4).[44]

Second, the psalmist often appeals to (or looks back on) his own righteous behavior as a ground for his deliverance. Here are a few examples:

Let the LORD judge the peoples.
Vindicate me, LORD, *according to my righteousness,*
　　according to my integrity, O Most High. (7:8)

¹ Hear me, LORD, *my plea is just;*
　　listen to my cry.
Hear my prayer—
　　it does not rise from deceitful lips. . . .

³ Though you probe my heart,
　　though you examine me at night and test me,
you will find that *I have planned no evil;*
　　my mouth has not transgressed.
⁴ Though people tried to bribe me,
　　I have kept myself from the ways of the violent
　　through what your lips have commanded.
⁵ *My steps have held to your paths;*
　　my feet have not stumbled. (17:1, 3–5)

²⁰ The LORD has dealt with me *according to my righteousness;*
　　according to the cleanness of my hands he has rewarded me.
²¹ For *I have kept the ways of the* LORD;
　　I am not guilty of turning from my God.

44. For similar passages in this vein, see Pss. 5:3–7; 7:10–17; 11:5–7; 15:1–5; 28:3–5; 36:10–12; 41:1; 50:1–23; 58:10–11; 94:21–23; 125:4–5; 140:13.

²² All his laws are before me;
I have not turned away from his decrees.
²³ I have been blameless before him
and have kept myself from sin.
²⁴ The LORD has rewarded me according to my righteousness,
according to the cleanness of my hands in his sight. (18:20–24)⁴⁵

Note that the phrases that stand in parallel with "my righteousness" are "my integrity" (7:8) and "the cleanness of my hands" (18:20, 24). The righteousness that the psalmist appeals to, then, is not primarily a status of "righteous" that God grants to sinners (i.e., imputed righteousness) but rather a lived-out righteousness. The psalmist, in other words, has kept the Torah and believes that this covenant faithfulness constitutes grounds for his vindication. Such passages not only underscore the importance of righteous behavior; they also bear witness that such behavior is possible, not merely an unattainable ideal.

Of course, the psalms are also keenly aware of human sin. Psalm 14, for example, asserts, "All have turned away, all have become corrupt; there is no one who does good, not even one" (14:3). Paul cites this psalm to demonstrate that "Jews and Gentiles alike are all under the power of sin" (Rom. 3:9; cf. 3:10–12), so apparently it applies to God's people, not just unbelievers. Yet this does not mean that righteous living is a pipe dream. After all, the very next psalm begins,

¹ LORD, who may dwell in your sacred tent?
Who may live on your holy mountain?
² The one whose walk is blameless,
who does what is righteous,
who speaks the truth from their heart. (Ps. 15:1–2)

Thus, in order for anyone to dwell in God's presence, righteous behavior (not, according to Ps. 15, righteous status alone) must be possible. Yes, God's people do sin, and the psalms attest both to this reality and to God's provision for forgiveness at numerous points, not least in Psalm 51.⁴⁶ However, to say that God's people may sin is far different than saying

45. See further Pss. 26:1–12; 41:12.
46. See further Pss. 25:7, 11; 32; 41:4; 51; 85:1–3; 103:8–12.

that they must. The psalms are honest about our capacity for evil while also holding forth the possibility of a life that is truly righteous. And as noted above, the psalms present such a life of good works as essential to true worship.

Do Justice, Love Mercy (the Prophets)

The Prophets, too, have much to say about good works in the life of God's people. For the sake of space, we will here focus on three eighth-century prophets for whom good works play a major role: Isaiah, Amos, and Micah.

Isaiah

Isaiah opens with a forceful indictment of Judah:

> [2] Hear me, you heavens! Listen, earth!
>   For the LORD has spoken:
> "I reared children and brought them up,
>   but they have rebelled against me.
> [3] The ox knows its master,
>   the donkey its owner's manger,
> but Israel does not know,
>   my people do not understand."
>
> [4] Woe to the sinful nation,
>   a people whose guilt is great,
> a brood of evildoers,
>   children given to corruption! (Isa. 1:2–4a)

As we read on, we discover that Judah's sin is not that they have neglected to make sacrifices to YHWH or to observe his festivals. On the contrary, they are excelling on this front. The problem is that their performance of these rites is just that—a performance. They are going through the religious motions while failing to live righteously, and God is not pleased.

> [11] "The multitude of your sacrifices—
>   what are they to me?" says the LORD.

"I have more than enough of burnt offerings,
    of rams and the fat of fattened animals;
I have no pleasure
    in the blood of bulls and lambs and goats.
[12] When you come to appear before me,
    who has asked this of you,
    this trampling of my courts?
[13] Stop bringing meaningless offerings!
    Your incense is detestable to me.
New Moons, Sabbaths and convocations—
    I cannot bear your worthless assemblies.
[14] Your New Moon feasts and your appointed festivals
    I hate with all my being.
They have become a burden to me;
    I am weary of bearing them.
[15] When you spread out your hands in prayer,
    I hide my eyes from you;
even when you offer many prayers,
    I am not listening.
Your hands are full of blood!" (1:11–15)

To anyone familiar with the law of Moses, such statements would have been jolting, to say the least. Our offerings are meaningless? Our incense is detestable? God hates our feasts and festivals? But to one who had understood the true intent of the law, these pronouncements would have been less surprising. As noted above, the heart of the law is to love God with one's whole being and to love one's neighbor as oneself, and to rehearse numerous offerings and festivals while neglecting these weightier matters is not piety but pretense. God goes on to exhort Judah,

[16] Wash and make yourselves clean.
    Take your evil deeds out of my sight;
    stop doing wrong.
[17] Learn to do right; seek justice.
    Defend the oppressed.
Take up the cause of the fatherless;
    plead the case of the widow. (1:16–17)

Here we see that Judah's redemption will consist not only of being for-given (a change in status) but also of repentance (a change of behav-ior), particularly doing justice toward the fatherless and the widow, two neighbors that the law repeatedly commands Israel to love.[47]

Good works continue to play a major role in Isaiah's view of salvation throughout the rest of the book. In chapter 6, Isaiah receives a vision of the Lord and cries out, "Woe to me! . . . I am ruined! For I am a man of unclean lips, and I live among a people of unclean lips, and my eyes have seen the King, the LORD Almighty" (6:5). Isaiah's phrase "unclean lips" becomes clearer in light of Isaiah 29:13, where the Lord says, "These people come near to me with their mouth and honor me with their *lips*, but their hearts are far from me." Isaiah, in other words, recognizes that he is guilty of the same sort of hypocrisy for which he has condemned Judah (cf. Isa. 1–5). The Lord goes on not only to cleanse Isaiah's lips (6:6–7) but also to commission him as a messenger to Judah (6:8–13). John Oswalt comments,

> [Chapters] 1–5 have raised a serious problem. Sinful, arrogant Israel is going to be the holy people of God to whom the nations will come to learn of God (cf. 43:8–14; 49:5, 6; Ezek. 36:22–38). But how can this be? [Chapter] 6 provides the solution. Sinful Israel can become servant Israel when the experience of Isaiah becomes the experience of the nation. When the nation has seen itself against the backdrop of God's holiness and glory, when the nation has received God's gracious provision for sin, then she can speak for God to a hungry world.[48]

YHWH desires not only to forgive Israel but also to transform them so that both their lips and their lives honor him and they can finally fulfill his Abrahamic promise to bless the nations. Of course, Judah ignores Isaiah and as a result goes into exile. However, the latter part of the book (Isa. 40–66) looks forward to the redemption that God will accomplish for his people on the other side of exile. Central to this redemption is the Isaianic servant of the Lord, whose mission includes *both* dying for "the sins of many" (53:12) *and* making them into "oaks of righteousness, a planting of the LORD for the display of his splendor" (61:3).

47. Exod. 22:22–24; Deut. 10:18; 14:28–29; 16:11, 14; 24:17, 19–21; 26:12–13; 27:19.
48. John N. Oswalt, *The Book of Isaiah: Chapters 1–39*, New International Commentary on the Old Testament (Grand Rapids: Eerdmans, 1986), 174–75.

Amos

Amos develops some of the same themes found in Isaiah but places an even greater emphasis on the social dimension of the good works that God expects of his people. Amos prophesies to the Northern Kingdom of Israel during a period of prosperity under Jeroboam, son of Jehoash. Amos begins by calling down judgment on various places and peoples—Damascus, Gaza, Tyre, Edom, the Ammonites, Moab, Judah—with the formula "For three sins . . . even for four, I will not relent." But then he turns to Israel:

> [6] This is what the LORD says:
>
> "For three sins of Israel,
>> even for four, I will not relent.
> They sell the innocent for silver,
>> and the needy for a pair of sandals.
> [7] They trample on the heads of the poor
>> as on the dust of the ground
>> and deny justice to the oppressed.
> Father and son use the same girl
>> and so profane my holy name.
> [8] They lie down beside every altar
>> on garments taken in pledge.
> In the house of their god
>> they drink wine taken as fines." (Amos 2:6–8)

Notice that the sins here are primarily acts of oppression, transgressions of the law's command to "love your neighbor as yourself" (Lev. 19:18). Indeed, most of the sins for which Amos condemns Israel throughout the book might be labeled as sins of oppression.[49]

The oppressors, as might be expected, are the rich and powerful. Amos 4:1–2 declares,

> [1] Hear this word, you cows of Bashan on Mount Samaria,
>> you women who oppress the poor and crush the needy
>> and say to your husbands, "Bring us some drinks!"
> [2] The Sovereign LORD has sworn by his holiness:
>> "The time will surely come

---

49. E.g., Amos 4:1–3; 5:7, 11–13; 6:1–7; 8:4–6.

> when you will be taken away with hooks,
>   the last of you with fishhooks."

The "cows of Bashan" seem to be the wealthy, leading women of Samaria, whom Amos charges with injustice toward the poor. Amos also condemns the "notable men" of Samaria (6:1), who "lie on beds adorned with ivory" and feast on the finest fare as Israel descends into ruin due at least to their inaction and likely to their action as well (6:4–6).

Like Judah in the book of Isaiah, Israel has apparently kept up religious observances amid all this injustice, and YHWH is not impressed by their hypocrisy:

> [21] I hate, I despise your religious festivals;
>   your assemblies are a stench to me.
> [22] Even though you bring me burnt offerings and grain offerings,
>   I will not accept them.
> Though you bring choice fellowship offerings,
>   I will have no regard for them.
> [23] Away with the noise of your songs!
>   I will not listen to the music of your harps. (5:21–23)

Rather, YHWH declares, "Let justice roll on like a river, righteousness like a never-failing stream!" (5:24). On the one hand, this justice might look like true repentance on the part of Israel:

> [14] Seek good, not evil,
>   that you may live.
> Then the LORD God Almighty will be with you,
>   just as you say he is.
> [15] Hate evil, love good;
>   maintain justice in the courts. (5:14–15a)

But if Israel refuses to repent, Amos warns, there will be exile to pay (5:27; 6:7; 7:11, 17). In short, Amos sets two options before Israel: do justice or face God's judgment. For Amos, good works, particularly toward one's neighbor and even more particularly toward poor and underprivileged neighbors, are a necessary part of what it means to be in covenant relationship with the God of Israel.

Micah

Whereas Isaiah and Amos focus on Judah and Israel, respectively, Micah prophesies to both kingdoms with a particular focus on their capital cities, Samaria and Jerusalem (Mic. 1:1). The overarching story that Micah tells is largely the same as that told by Isaiah and Amos: Judah and Israel are wallowing in sin, and YHWH's judgment lies close at hand if they do not repent. The sins in view run the gamut, from idolatry (1:7) to coveting and defrauding (2:2, 8–9), to cheating and lying (6:11–12). Micah calls out two groups as particularly responsible for these transgressions. The first is the (false) prophets, who apparently are countering Micah's woeful warnings of judgment with a feel-good message that one can sin boldly without consequences.

> "Do not prophesy," their prophets say.
>   "Do not prophesy about these things;
>   disgrace will not overtake us." (2:6)

Micah declares that "the sun will set" for these would-be prophets who proclaim peace to anyone who will pay (3:5–7). "But as for me," he says,

> I am filled with power,
>   with the Spirit of the LORD,
>   and with justice and might,
> to declare to Jacob his transgression,
>   to Israel his sin. (3:8)

True prophets apparently care about good works; false prophets don't. The second group that Micah condemns is the leaders:

> ⁹ Hear this, you leaders of Jacob,
>   you rulers of Israel,
> who despise justice
>   and distort all that is right;
> ¹⁰ who build Zion with bloodshed,
>   and Jerusalem with wickedness. . . .
> ¹² Therefore because of you,
>   Zion will be plowed like a field,

Jerusalem will become a heap of rubble,
the temple hill a mound overgrown with thickets. (3:9–10, 12;
cf. 3:1–4)

These leaders think that they are immune to YHWH's judgment, but Micah warns that they will by no means escape it (3:4, 11).

Yet we should not assume that the perpetrators of Judah's and Israel's sins are limited to a few higher-ups. Micah also declares that "the faithful have been swept from the land; not one upright person remains" (7:2; cf. 6:12). This is perhaps hyperbole, but it is nonetheless telling. God's people as a whole have rebelled, and a reckoning is coming. Micah, of course, also looks forward to how the Lord will redeem his people and the nations in the latter days (e.g., 4:1–8; 5:2–4). But this future hope does not remove the reality of impending judgment and the need for national repentance. In the end, Micah leaves no doubt about the conduct that YHWH expects of his people:

He has shown you, O mortal, what is good.
And what does the LORD require of you?
To act justly and to love mercy
and to walk humbly with your God. (6:8)

Conclusion

From start to finish, the Old Testament presents good works as a natural element of right relationship with God. Genesis 1–2 portrays work as part of God's original intent for humans. The fall, of course, corrupts humans and our relationship to work, but the creation narratives suggest that the goal of God's redemptive project will not be to free humans *from* work but to free us *for* work—the good we were created to do. The rest of the Old Testament seems to confirm this hypothesis, as God calls Abraham and his descendants to inherit the Adamic commission of filling the earth with the image of God (Gen. 1:28). God defines his relationship with Abraham and his descendants through covenants (mutual, oath-bound commitments) that demonstrate his benevolence toward them but also communicate how he expects them to behave in order to be his image in the world. Our studies of David and the Psalms and of the Prophets above add some important nuances to the overarching picture of good works that the Pentateuch provides. Through the life of David, we discover that God desires obedience more than sacrifice and that to be "a man after [God's] own heart" (1 Sam. 13:14) means not only obeying God consistently but also repenting with "a broken and contrite heart" (Ps. 51:17) when one fails to do so. In the Psalms, we find not only that good works are possible (through the psalmists' appeals to their righteousness) but also that true worship is impossible without good works. The prophets develop this latter theme from the perspective of Israel's disobedience, emphasizing that Israel's and Judah's numerous religious observances are an abomination to YHWH because they emerge from hearts and hands that do injustice. In sum, the Old Testament presents good works not as opposed to God's grace but as an appropriate and expected response to it.

CHAPTER 3

The Greatest Commandments Fulfilled

Good Works in the New Testament

In the preceding chapter, we saw that the Old Testament presents good works as an important part of what it means for humans to be made in the image of God and, therefore, an important part of what it means for us to be remade (or redeemed) as the image of God. Here we will argue that the New Testament complements the overarching picture of good works that we find in the Old Testament. Despite the significant differences between the old and new covenants, the basic principle that good works constitute the appropriate and necessary response to God's grace remains unchanged. As noted above, the relevant material far exceeds the limits of this project, so here we will simply attempt to trace the major themes that emerge within the New Testament and to draw them together into a coherent whole.

Jesus and the Gospels

We begin where the New Testament begins—with Jesus and the Gospels. This might seem like an obvious place to start, but it is probably fair to say that Paul's Letters have exerted a far greater influence on how most Protestants today think about good works than Jesus's own words

and actions as recorded in the Gospels have. We need to make sense of
Paul, and we will below, but we will be able to do so better if we first
understand what Jesus did and taught.

The New Adam and His Work (Luke 1–4)

Luke presents Jesus as a new Adam who, like his primeval predeces-
sor, has a God-ordained mission.[1] Like Adam, Jesus owes his human
existence entirely to God's initiative (Gen. 2:7; Luke 1:35). Adam and Jesus
are also the only two figures in Luke-Acts who receive the title "son of
God" (1:35; 3:38). Indeed, Luke describes Adam as a "son of God" just before Jesus undergoes temptation, another point of similarity between the
two men (3:38; 4:1–13), and in Luke the two temptations in which Satan
refers to Jesus as "Son of God" come first and last (4:3, 9; cf. Matt. 4:1–11).
However, whereas Adam failed to believe God's word and succumbed to
temptation, Jesus quotes God's word and chooses to trust in his Father.
Luke notes that Jesus is "full of the Holy Spirit" (Luke 4:1) when he enters
the temptation and that he returns to Galilee "in the power of the Spirit"
(4:14), suggesting that Jesus overcomes Satan's temptation by the power
of the same Holy Spirit who initiated his conception (1:35).

Like the first Adam, the new Adam also has work to do. At the beginning of his ministry in the Gospel of Luke, Jesus enters a synagogue
and stands up to read. Someone hands him a scroll of Isaiah, and he
unrolls it and reads,

> [18] The Spirit of the Lord is on me,
>   because he has anointed me
>   to proclaim good news to the poor.
> He has sent me to proclaim freedom for the prisoners
>   and recovery of sight for the blind,
> to set the oppressed free,
> [19]   to proclaim the year of the Lord's favor. (Luke 4:18–19; cf. Isa.
>   61:1–2)[2]

---

1. This section and the following section adapt some material from the chapter "Holiness in
the Gospels and Acts," to be published in *Holiness: A Biblical, Historical, and Systematic Theology*, by
Matt Ayars, Christopher T. Bounds, and Caleb T. Friedeman (Downers Grove, IL: IVP Academic,
forthcoming). Used by permission.

2. On the differences between Luke 4:18–19 and Isa. 61:1–2 in the Septuagint, see Darrell L.
Bock, *Luke 1:1–9:50*, Baker Exegetical Commentary on the New Testament (Grand Rapids: Baker
Academic, 1994), 404–5.

Jesus rolls up the scroll, hands it back, sits down, and declares, "Today this scripture is fulfilled in your hearing" (4:21).

Luke seems to use this story to frame Jesus's public ministry as a fulfillment of Isaiah 61:1–2. Jesus is the Spirit-filled servant of the Lord from Isaiah 61, and he has come to *do* something: to proclaim good news to the poor, free the prisoners, and so forth. Of course, Jesus's climactic act of liberating the oppressed occurs in his death and resurrection, but these events are precisely the climax of a mission that began on a memorable day in the Nazareth synagogue. In the next few stories, Luke gives us snapshots of Jesus's Isaiah 61–themed ministry: Jesus casts a demon out of a man (Luke 4:31–35) and heals and casts demons out of many others (4:38–41). Asked by the crowds to stay, Jesus declares, "I must *proclaim the good news* of the kingdom of God to the other towns also, because that is why I was sent" (4:43), recalling the servant's mission in Isaiah 61:1. Language from Isaiah 61 continues to pop up in Luke's descriptions of Jesus's ministry:[3]

> The *blind* receive *sight*, the lame walk, those who have leprosy are cleansed, the deaf hear, the dead are raised, and *the good news* is proclaimed to the poor. (Luke 7:22)

> After this, Jesus traveled about from one town and village to another, *proclaiming the good news* of the kingdom of God. (8:1)

> The Law and the Prophets were proclaimed until John. Since that time, *the good news* of the kingdom of God is being *preached*, and everyone is forcing their way into it. (16:16)

> One day as Jesus was teaching the people in the temple courts and *proclaiming the good news* . . . (20:1)

And this Isaiah 61–themed mission is not for Jesus alone. As Jesus begins to call disciples to follow him (Luke 5:1–11, 27–28; 6:12–16), he is calling them to follow him *in fulfilling Isaiah 61*. Indeed, in Luke 9 Jesus sends out the Twelve to extend his ministry, and Luke notes that they

---

3. See also the uses of "the poor" in Luke 6:20; 14:13, 21; 18:22; 19:8. Luke 14:13 and 14:21 also mention "the blind."

"went from village to village, *proclaiming the good news* and healing people everywhere" (9:6). A chapter later, Jesus sends out seventy-two other disciples to heal the sick and proclaim the kingdom of God (10:9). Through these features of his narrative, Luke emphasizes that to follow Jesus, the new Adam and the true human, means to participate in his redemptive mission.

A Greater Righteousness (Matt. 5–7)

In the Sermon on the Mount, Jesus discusses the good works that he expects of his followers (Matt. 5–7). The sermon contains some of Jesus's most rigorous ethical teaching, and many interpreters have attempted to moderate its commands by interpreting them as an impossible ideal or instructions for a spiritual elite.[4] Yet Jesus introduces the sermon with the Beatitudes, a series of "blessed" statements that describe what it means to live well in light of God's coming kingdom. As Jonathan Pennington says, the Beatitudes are "invitations to the kind of life that will experience flourishing."[5] Such a beginning suggests that while the sermon may ask much of us, it is ultimately a gift meant to guide us into the good life—a life that accords with God's dawning end-time reign. And it is worth noting that Jesus not only commands this life of would-be followers but also lives it himself, so much so that Pope John Paul II calls the Beatitudes "a sort of *self-portrait of Christ.*"[6]

A central theme of the sermon is *righteousness*—and more particularly the righteousness Jesus expects of his disciples that is greater than that of the Pharisees and the teachers of the law.[7] Jesus introduces this concept in 5:17–20:

> [17] Do not think that I have come to abolish the Law or the Prophets; I have not come to abolish them but to fulfill them. [18] For truly I tell you, until

---

4. See the survey of views in Jonathan T. Pennington, *The Sermon on the Mount and Human Flourishing: A Theological Commentary* (Grand Rapids: Baker Academic, 2017), 5.

5. Pennington, *Sermon*, 54.

6. Pope John Paul II, *Veritatis Splendor* §16 (italics original), https://www.vatican.va/content/john-paul-ii/en/encyclicals/documents/hf_jp-ii_enc_06081993_veritatis-splendor.html. Earlier, E. Stanley Jones wrote, "This is not a sermon—it is a portrait, the portrait of Jesus himself, and of the Father and of the man-to-be" (*The Christ of the Mount: A Working Philosophy of Life* [New York: Abingdon, 1931], 27).

7. Pennington, *Sermon*, 87–91, 119–27, 132–33.

heaven and earth disappear, not the smallest letter, not the least stroke of a pen, will by any means disappear from the Law until everything is accomplished. [19] Therefore anyone who sets aside one of the least of these commands and teaches others accordingly will be called least in the kingdom of heaven, but whoever practices and teaches these commands will be called great in the kingdom of heaven. [20] For I tell you that *unless your righteousness surpasses that of the Pharisees and the teachers of the law, you will certainly not enter the kingdom of heaven.*

The context makes clear that by "righteousness" (5:20) Jesus is referring not to a righteous status that God credits to believers but to righteous behavior that his disciples must exhibit. But how could anyone live more righteously than the Pharisees or the teachers of the law? Jesus addresses this in 5:21–48 by giving six examples of what this greater righteousness looks like in relation to the law or contemporary Jewish teachings ("You have heard that it was said . . . But I tell you . . ."). In general, we may say that in these examples Jesus *intensifies* and *internalizes* the law, revealing its true intent. For instance, Jesus teaches that "You shall not commit adultery" (Exod. 20:14) prohibits not only adultery itself but also the lustful thoughts that give rise to such external behavior. While such teachings certainly constitute a high standard, we must resist the temptation to dismiss them as impossible or optional, for (as noted above) Jesus presents them precisely as examples of the righteousness without which one "will certainly not enter the kingdom of heaven" (Matt. 5:20).

Jesus continues to expound this "greater righteousness" in Matthew 6, where he introduces his teaching on giving to the needy, praying, and fasting by saying, "Be careful not to practice your *righteousness* in front of others to be seen by them. If you do, you will have no reward from your Father in heaven" (6:1). Once again, Jesus seems to use "righteousness" to refer to righteous behavior, and he teaches not only that one should practice personal piety but also that doing pious things with wrong intentions (i.e., to be seen by others) will not result in heavenly rewards.

The conclusion to the sermon (7:13–27) emphasizes the role of good works in final judgment. Jesus begins by warning his hearers, "Enter through the narrow gate. For wide is the gate and broad is the road that leads to destruction, and many enter through it. But small is the gate and narrow the road that leads to life, and only a few find it" (7:13–14). As Robert Gundry notes, "The narrowness of the small gate . . . represents the structures of the surpassing righteousness just taught by Jesus as a requirement for entering the kingdom."[8] Thus, when Jesus says, "Enter through the narrow gate" (7:13), he is exhorting his listeners to practice the greater righteousness that he has been explaining, for without it they will not enter eternal life.

Jesus goes on to discuss false prophets (7:15–20) and false disciples (7:21–23). False prophets, Jesus says, can be recognized by their "fruit": "Every good tree bears good fruit, but a bad tree bears bad fruit. A good tree cannot bear bad fruit, and a bad tree cannot bear good fruit. Every tree that does not bear good fruit is cut down and thrown into the fire. Thus, by their fruit you will recognize them" (7:17–20). R. T. France rightly comments that here "the idea is clearly that profession must be tested by practice."[9] And while it is false prophets who are specifically in view here, "the principle would apply equally to any Christian profession."[10] Indeed, Jesus goes on to declare regarding would-be disciples in general, "Not everyone who says to me, 'Lord, Lord,' will enter the kingdom of heaven, but only the one who does the will of my Father who is in heaven. Many will say to me on that day, 'Lord, Lord, did we not prophesy in your name and in your name drive out demons and in your name perform many miracles?' Then I will tell them plainly, 'I never knew you. Away from me, you evildoers!'" (7:21–23). Apparently, merely calling Jesus "Lord" and performing miraculous acts in his name do not qualify as doing the will of the Father (7:21). Jesus, it seems, desires something more: the greater righteousness that he has been teaching throughout the sermon.

Jesus concludes by setting two potential responses before his hearers: "Therefore everyone who hears these words of mine and puts them into practice is like a wise man who built his house on the rock. . . . But everyone who hears these words of mine and does not put them into

8. Robert H. Gundry, *Matthew: A Commentary on His Literary and Theological Art* (Grand Rapids: Eerdmans, 1982), 127.

9. R. T. France, *The Gospel according to Matthew: An Introduction and Commentary*, Tyndale New Testament Commentaries (Grand Rapids: Eerdmans, 1985), 147.

10. France, *Matthew*, 147. Matthew 3:10, where John the Baptist says something very similar to the Pharisees and Sadducees, also supports this broader application.

practice is like a foolish man who built his house on sand" (7:24, 26). The house built on the rock, of course, stands firm when the storms come, but the house built on the sand falls "with a great crash" (7:27). The "therefore" that links this passage to the preceding context confirms that "the collapse of the house built on sand refers to condemnation at the last judgment."[11] Jesus thus seems to present good works as necessary for one to enter the kingdom of heaven.

"What Must I Do to Inherit Eternal Life?"

On at least two occasions during his ministry, Jesus is asked, "What must I do to inherit eternal life?" In neither case does he answer "Nothing" or "Wrong question." Rather, he instructs the questioner to *do* something. The first instance comes in the prelude to the parable of the good Samaritan:

> [25] On one occasion an expert in the law stood up to test Jesus. "Teacher," he asked, "what must I do to inherit eternal life?"
> [26] "What is written in the Law?" he replied. "How do you read it?"
> [27] He answered, "'Love the Lord your God with all your heart and with all your soul and with all your strength and with all your mind'; and, 'Love your neighbor as yourself.'"
> [28] "You have answered correctly," Jesus replied. "Do this and you will live." (Luke 10:25–28)

Jesus shrewdly turns the question back on the expert in the law, and when he answers using Deuteronomy 6:5 and Leviticus 19:18 (the two commandments that Jesus elsewhere designates as the greatest ones that sum up all the others [Matt. 22:37–40; Mark 12:29–31]), Jesus agrees with him. The expert, wanting "to justify himself," then asks a further question: "And who is my neighbor?" (Luke 10:29). This, of course, is an important question, for if "neighbor" were to refer only to Torah-observant Israelites, Leviticus 19:18 would be much easier to fulfill, and eternal life much easier to inherit. Jesus, however, answers with a story in which a Samaritan shows mercy to a man (probably assumed to be a Jew) and so becomes his neighbor. He concludes by telling the expert, "Go and *do* likewise" (10:37), recalling his initial question, "What must I *do* . . . ?"

11. Gundry, *Matthew*, 133.

(10:25). If the expert wishes to inherit eternal life, in other words, he must love God and neighbor, including difficult-to-love Samaritans.

The second instance occurs in the story of the rich young ruler:

> [18] A certain ruler asked him, "Good teacher, what must I do to inherit eternal life?"
>
> [19] "Why do you call me good?" Jesus answered. "No one is good—except God alone. [20] You know the commandments: 'You shall not commit adultery, you shall not murder, you shall not steal, you shall not give false testimony, honor your father and mother.'" (Luke 18:18–20)

In the Lukan version, Jesus answers the man's question by quoting five of the six "horizontal" or neighbor-focused commands from the Ten Commandments, interestingly leaving out "You shall not covet" (cf. Matt. 19:18–19; Mark 10:19). When the man replies, "All these I have kept since I was a boy" (Luke 18:21), Jesus does not disagree but says, "You still lack one thing. Sell everything you have and give to the poor, and you will have treasure in heaven. Then come, follow me" (18:22). Here Jesus seems to imply that while the man may have kept some of the neighbor-oriented commandments, his wealth constitutes an idol that must be eliminated before he can fulfill the first four of the Ten Commandments and love God with his whole being. Luke tells us that "when [the man] heard this, he became very sad, because he was very wealthy" (18:23). Jesus goes on to teach that while it is difficult for the rich to enter the kingdom of God, "What is impossible with man is possible with God" (18:27). Indeed, in the very next chapter Luke illustrates the power of God to save the rich by recounting the salvation of Zacchaeus, who gives away a significant portion of his substantial fortune to follow Jesus (19:1–10).

Jesus's responses to the question, "What must I do to inherit eternal life?"—like the Sermon on the Mount—indicate that Jesus regards good works as important and even necessary for ultimate salvation. Jesus, the new Adam, has not only come to do good works; he also expects his disciples to follow in his footsteps.

Good Works and Final Judgment (Matt. 25:14–46)

Jesus explicitly addresses the relationship between good works and final judgment in two back-to-back teachings in Matthew 25. In the first, the parable of the talents, Jesus tells of a man who goes on a journey and entrusts his three servants with five talents, two talents, and one talent, respectively.[12] The first two servants "put [their master's] money to work" (25:16) and double it. The third servant, however, buries the master's money in the ground. The master returns after a long time and settles accounts with his servants. He commends the first two servants for their faithfulness and promises them, "I will put you in charge of many things" (25:21, 23). The third servant then approaches and explains that he knew his master was "a hard man" who would want a profit. "So," he says, "I was afraid and went out and hid your gold in the ground. See, here is what belongs to you" (25:25). The master rebukes him for his wickedness and laziness, reassigns his talent to the first servant, and commands that he be thrown "into the darkness, where there will be weeping and gnashing of teeth" (25:30).

As Ulrich Luz notes, Matthew presents the master in the parable as "the Jesus Christ who is absent but who will return."[13] The servants, of course, represent Christians. The first two symbolize disciples who have produced good fruit (cf. 7:16–20), the third those who have failed to. France rightly comments, "'Being ready' consists not only in keeping your slate clean, but in active, responsible, faithful service which produces results."[14] According to Jesus, the penalty for not producing such fruit is severe: the unfaithful servant is thrown into the place of "weeping and gnashing of teeth," which in Matthew's Gospel lies outside the kingdom of heaven (8:12; 13:42; 22:13; 24:51). Craig Keener sums up the parable's sobering conclusion well: "Disciples who neglect the resources entrusted to them in this life will be damned."[15]

Jesus moves directly to a second teaching on final judgment often referred to as the parable of the sheep and the goats: "When the Son

---

12. A talent is generally understood to be worth about six thousand denarii (one denarius being equal to a common laborer's daily wage). See Frederick W. Danker et al., *Greek-English Lexicon of the New Testament and Other Early Christian Literature*, 3rd ed. (Chicago: University of Chicago Press, 2000), 988; Johannes P. Louw and Eugene A. Nida, eds., *Greek-English Lexicon of the New Testament: Based on Semantic Domains*, 2nd ed. (New York: United Bible Societies, 1989), §6.82. One talent would therefore be equivalent to about twenty years' worth of a common laborer's wages—a significant sum. On the complexities of calculating the value of a talent, see D. A. Carson, "Matthew," in *The Expositor's Bible Commentary*, vol. 8 (Grand Rapids: Zondervan, 1984), 516.

13. Ulrich Luz, *Matthew: A Commentary*, trans. James E. Crouch, ed. Helmut Koester, 3 vols., Hermeneia (Minneapolis: Fortress, 2001–7), 3:255.

14. France, *Matthew*, 354.

15. Craig S. Keener, *A Commentary on the Gospel of Matthew* (Grand Rapids: Eerdmans, 1999), 601.

of Man comes in his glory, and all the angels with him, he will sit on his glorious throne. All the nations will be gathered before him, and he will separate the people one from another as a shepherd separates the sheep from the goats. He will put the sheep on his right and the goats on his left" (25:31–33). The King invites those on his right to inherit the kingdom, saying, "For I was hungry and you gave me something to eat, I was thirsty and you gave me something to drink, I was a stranger and you invited me in, I needed clothes and you clothed me, I was sick and you looked after me, I was in prison and you came to visit me" (25:35–36). The "sheep," now described as "the righteous" (25:37), ask the King when they saw him in any of these conditions. He replies, "Truly I tell you, whatever you did for one of the least of these brothers and sisters of mine, you did for me" (25:40). However, to the "goats," the King says, "Depart from me, you who are cursed, into the eternal fire prepared for the devil and his angels" (25:41), explaining that they failed to do for him the things that the righteous did. Like the "sheep," the "goats" inquire about when they ever saw the King hungry, thirsty, and so forth, and he answers, "Truly I tell you, whatever you did not do for one of the least of these, you did not do for me" (25:45). Jesus concludes, "Then they will go away to eternal punishment, but the righteous to eternal life" (25:46).

Two questions confront the reader of this story: (1) Who are "all the nations" (25:32) that are divided into "sheep" and "goats"? (2) Who are "the least of these" (25:40, 45)? With respect to the first question, the main options are

1. all Christians,
2. all non-Christians, or
3. all humans.[16]

Option 2, if correct, would mean that this passage does *not* directly describe the judgment of Christians (or, by extension, Jesus's expectations for Christians). However, this interpretation is open to several critiques. In the first place, the larger section (24:4–25:46) is an

16. For a more detailed survey, see W. D. Davies and Dale C. Allison, *A Critical and Exegetical Commentary on the Gospel according to Saint Matthew*, 3 vols., International Critical Commentary (Edinburgh: T&T Clark, 1988–97), 3:422.

exhortation aimed at Jesus's disciples,[17] and the part that directly precedes this passage explicitly deals with the judgment of said disciples (24:36–25:30). It seems improbable that Jesus would change course and discuss the judgment of non-Christians alone here (as option 2 requires). Furthermore, Jesus has described just this sort of sifting of true from false disciples at several points earlier in the Gospel,[18] so it would be odd for his disciples not to be in view at all here. We are therefore left with option 1 (all Christians) or option 3 (all humans). Two factors tip the scales in favor of option 3: (1) Jesus seems to envision a universal judgment according to works earlier in Matthew when he says, "The Son of Man is going to come in his Father's glory with his angels, and then he will reward each person according to what they have done" (16:27);[19] (2) elsewhere in Matthew "all the nations" includes non-Christians (24:9, 14; 28:19).[20] But whether one takes option 1 or option 3, the key point is that Jesus's disciples, not merely unbelievers, are being judged.

The main options for how to interpret "the least of these" are

1. Christian missionaries or leaders in need,
2. all Christians in need, or
3. all humans in need.[21]

Options 1 and 2 draw support from 10:40–42, where Jesus says to the Twelve before he sends them out,

[40] Anyone who welcomes *you* welcomes *me*, and anyone who welcomes me welcomes the one who sent me. [41] Whoever welcomes a prophet as a prophet will receive a prophet's reward, and whoever welcomes a

---

17. Davies and Allison, *Matthew*, 3:422.

18. E.g., Matt. 7:13–27; 13:24–30, 36–43, 47–50.

19. Note the similarity between the Son of Man coming "in his Father's glory with his angels" (16:27) and "in his glory, and all the angels with him" (25:31).

20. Davies and Allison, *Matthew*, 3:422. The authors also note that this phrase "manifestly includes Christians elsewhere in the NT," citing Acts 15:17; Rom. 15:11; 16:26; Rev. 12:5 (422n27). A potential objection to options 2 and 3 is that both leave open the possibility that someone might be saved based on works of mercy alone apart from an explicit profession of faith in Christ. We discuss this matter below.

21. For a more detailed survey, see Davies and Allison, *Matthew*, 3:428–29. Davies and Allison do not include the "in need" qualifier for options 1 and 2 above, but it seems contextually appropriate.

righteous person as a righteous person will receive a righteous person's reward. [42] And if anyone gives even a cup of cold water to one of these *little ones* who is my disciple, truly I tell you, that person will certainly not lose their reward.

Here, "Anyone who welcomes *you* welcomes *me*" provides a conceptual parallel to "Whatever you did for *one of the least of these* . . . , you did for *me*" (25:40; cf. 25:45). The Greek adjective for "least" (*elachistos*) in "the least of these" is also a superlative of the word for "little ones" (*mikros*) in 10:42.[22] Two other factors also favor the idea that "the least of these" are Christians of some sort: (1) Jesus uses "little ones" to describe his disciples earlier in Matthew (18:6, 10, 14); (2) Jesus calls the least of these his "brothers and sisters" (25:40), and he elsewhere uses this language of his disciples (12:48–50; 28:10).

However, other teachings of Jesus problematize interpreting "the least of these" as only needy Christians (or some subset thereof). For example, in Matthew 5:43–48 Jesus teaches that "Love your neighbor" (Lev. 19:18) includes one's enemies. In this passage, Jesus declares, "If you love those who love you, what reward will you get? Are not even the tax collectors doing that? And if you greet only your own people, what are you doing more than others? Do not even pagans do that?" (Matt. 5:46–47). This teaching resonates strongly with the parable of the good Samaritan, which also focuses on Leviticus 19:18 and expands "neighbor" to include even tough-to-love Samaritans. Similarly, in Matthew 7:12 Jesus says, "In everything, do to others what you would have them do to you, for this sums up the Law and the Prophets." The command to "do to others" seems intentionally broad, referring not just to other disciples but to other people in general. Such teachings make it difficult to believe that in Matthew 25 Jesus intends to say that people will be judged merely on how they have treated needy Christians, as if one could safely ignore needy non-Christians. In our view, the safest interpretation (both exegetically and existentially) is the broadest one: "the least of these" refers to needy humans in general.[23]

22. *Elachistos* is an irregular superlative of *mikros*; the regular superlative is *mikrotatos*.
23. For additional arguments in favor of this view, see C. E. B Cranfield, "Who Are Christ's Brothers (Matthew 25.40)?," in *On Romans and Other New Testament Essays* (Edinburgh: T&T Clark, 1998), 125–35.

Therefore, in Matthew 25:31–46 Jesus seems to be saying that all people will be judged based on how they have responded to him as personified in the needy. Two clarifying comments may be helpful at this point. First, one potential objection to this interpretation is that it allows the possibility that one might be saved through good deeds apart from faith in Christ. We would argue that such a universalist interpretation is neither correct nor necessary. The rest of the New Testament (including Matthew to some degree) is clear that one can be saved only by faith in Christ,[24] and in our view the canonical context must shape our reading of this passage. In addition, the universalist reading described above is necessary only if one assumes that Matthew 25:31–46 provides a complete picture of final judgment. In our view, it is much more likely that this passage describes one element of final judgment—judgment according to works—and that people will also be judged based on whether they have received Jesus as Lord.

Second, one might disagree with our interpretation of "the least of these" above and still agree about the ultimate significance of Matthew 25:31–46. For our present purposes, the main point is that good works play an important role in final judgment: Jesus will judge all people based on their good works toward the needy (whether Christians or people in general). Martin Luther captures this well when he says, "Beware! God will not ask you at your death and at the Last Day how much you have left in your will, whether you have given so and so much to churches . . . he will say to you, 'I was hungry, and you gave me no food; I was naked, and you did not clothe me' [Matt. 25:42–43]. Take these words to heart! The important thing is whether you have given to your neighbor and treated him well."[25] Jesus's teaching therefore constitutes a sober warning that works of mercy are not an optional extra in the Christian life but rather an integral part of it.

24. E.g., Matt. 28:18–20; John 14:6; 20:30–31; Acts 2:21, 38; 4:12; 10:43, 48; 19:4–5; 22:16; Rom. 3:21–26.

25. Martin Luther, *Trade and Usury*, in *Christian in Society II*, Luther's Works 45 (Philadelphia: Fortress, 1962), 286, quoted in Samuel Torvend, *Luther and the Hungry Poor: Gathered Fragments* (Minneapolis: Fortress, 2008), 81. Luther also says, "We, too, when we show some kindness to the least in the kingdom of God, receive Christ himself in a hospitable manner when he comes to us in the person of his poor" (Luther, *Lectures on Genesis: Chapters 15–20*, Luther's Works 3 [St. Louis: Concordia, 1961], 184, quoted in Torvend, *Luther and the Hungry Poor*, 85).

The Early Church in Acts

The early church seems to have taken Jesus's teaching on good works seriously, for good works occupy a prominent place in the church's life in Acts. Below we will briefly explore both how Luke frames these good works and their specific content.

The Frame: Jesus-Shaped Witness (Acts 1:1–8)

Luke introduces Acts by saying, "In my *former book*, Theophilus, I wrote about all that Jesus began to do and to teach . . ." (Acts 1:1).[26] The "former book" is, of course, Luke's Gospel, which is addressed to the same Theophilus (Luke 1:3). By describing his Gospel as all that Jesus *began* to do and to teach, Luke implies that Acts recounts what Jesus *continued* to do and to teach. However, Jesus ascends to heaven a few verses into the book (Acts 1:9), and he appears as an actor only occasionally (e.g., 2:33; 9:4–5, 10–12, 15–16; 22:7–8, 10; 26:14–18), so in what sense can Acts be about *Jesus's* continued work? The most likely answer is that Luke views the "acts" of Jesus's followers as an extension of Jesus's own mission. This hypothesis finds support in Acts 9:34, where Peter says to Aeneas, a man who has been paralyzed for eight years, "*Jesus Christ* heals you. Get up and roll up your mat." Clearly, Peter is the immediate agent of this healing, but he nonetheless attributes the deed to Jesus, who is apparently at work through him.

Acts 1:8 provides insight into why Luke sees the works of the early church as an extension of Jesus's mission. Jesus tells his disciples, "You will receive power when the Holy Spirit comes on you; and you will be my witnesses in Jerusalem, and in all Judea and Samaria, and to the ends of the earth." Acts 1:8 constitutes the blueprint for the rest of the book, for when the Holy Spirit comes upon the disciples at Pentecost, their witness begins in Jerusalem (2:1–8:1a), spreads to Judea and Samaria (8:1b–11:18), and continues toward the ends of the earth (11:19–28:31). Two aspects of this verse are key. First, Jesus's words about the Holy Spirit coming on his disciples recall what Gabriel said to Mary about Jesus's conception:

---

26. This section adapts some material from the chapter "Holiness in the Gospels and Acts," to be published in *Holiness: A Biblical, Historical, and Systematic Theology*, by Matt Ayars, Christopher T. Bounds, and Caleb T. Friedeman (Downers Grove, IL: IVP Academic, forthcoming). Used by permission.

The Holy Spirit *will come on* [*epeleusetai*, from *eperchomai*] you, and the power of the Most High will overshadow you. So the holy one to be born will be called the Son of God. (Luke 1:35)

You will receive power when the Holy Spirit *comes on* [*epelthontos*, from *eperchomai*] you; and you will be my witnesses in Jerusalem, and in all Judea and Samaria, and to the ends of the earth. (Acts 1:8)

These two passages are the only places in the entire New Testament where the Holy Spirit is said to "come on" (*eperchomai*) someone or something. It therefore seems that Luke has created a parallel between Jesus's conception and the origin of the church. But why? To answer this question, we must consider the significance of Jesus's Spirit-initiated conception. Note that Luke links Jesus's conception to his status as the Son of God: "*So* the holy one to be born will be called the Son of God" (Luke 1:35). This makes more sense when we read on to Jesus's genealogy (3:23–38), where Luke calls Adam, too, a "son of God" (3:38). What do Adam and Jesus have in common? Both owe their existence entirely to God's initiative. God creates Adam from dust, and God conceives Jesus in the womb of a virgin. The virginal conception therefore marks Jesus out as a new Adam. But as noted above, this new Adam is different, for whereas the first Adam succumbed to temptation, Jesus conquers temptation and lives in obedience to the Father by the power of the same Spirit who conceived him. By creating a parallel between Jesus's Spirit-initiated conception and the church's Spirit-initiated origin, Luke seems to imply a similarity between the two. We might put the point this way: *just as the Spirit came upon Mary to conceive Jesus, a new Adam, the Spirit now comes upon Jesus's disciples to conceive the church, a group of people who will (like Jesus) manifest a new way of being human.* As we will see below, the church's Jesus-shaped pattern of life in Acts seems to bear this out.

The second noteworthy aspect of Acts 1:8 is that Jesus's words "You will be my witnesses" allude to Isaiah 43, where YHWH declares to Israel, "You are my witnesses" (43:10, 12). But in Isaiah there is a problem: Israel is a blind and deaf witness (43:8). They have become like the idols they have worshiped and are unable to testify to the nations that YHWH alone is God.[27] In order for Israel to be the witnesses that YHWH

27. E.g., Isa. 6:8–10; 8:16–9:2; 42:6–7.

desires, YHWH will have to redeem them from their sinful state. Thus, when Jesus tells his disciples, "You will be my witnesses" (Acts 1:8), he seems to be saying that the coming of the Holy Spirit (predicated upon his death, resurrection, and ascension) constitutes the redemptive act that will transform the disciples into witnesses who will at long last fulfill Israel's mission to represent (image!) YHWH to the nations. And how will they do this? By living lives that are shaped like the life of Jesus—lives initiated and empowered by the Spirit and obedient to the will of the Father. Acts, then, envisions good works as an integral part of what it means to be a Christian.

Good Works in the Early Church

As Acts 1:1–8 would lead us to expect, Jesus-shaped good works constitute the life rhythm of the early church in Acts. We may divide these good works into two basic categories: works of piety (directed toward God) and works of mercy (directed toward neighbor). Works of piety that appear in Acts include

- prayer,[28]
- devotion to the apostles' teaching,[29]
- breaking of bread (i.e., the Lord's Supper),[30] and
- singing.[31]

The most prominent of these by far is prayer. This is interesting, for Luke emphasizes the role of prayer in Jesus's life more than any of the other Gospel writers do.[32] The early church's practice of prayer thus seems to mirror Jesus's own life. Similarly, the early church's practice

28. Acts 1:14; 2:42; 3:1; 4:24–31; 6:4, 6; 7:59; 8:15, 24; 9:11, 40; 10:9; 11:5; 12:5, 12; 13:3; 14:23; 16:25; 20:36; 21:5; 22:17; 28:8.
29. Acts 2:42; 5:42; 15:35; 18:11; 20:7 (cf. 20:20; 21:28; 28:31).
30. Acts 2:42, 46; 20:7, 11 (cf. 27:35).
31. Acts 16:25.
32. Luke 3:21; 5:16; 6:12; 9:18, 28–29; 10:21; 11:1–4; 22:32, 41–42, 44–45; 23:34, 46. For Jesus praying in the other Gospels, see Matt. 6:9–13; 11:25–26; 14:23; 19:13; 26:39, 42–43; Mark 1:35; 6:46; 14:32, 35–36, 39; John 11:41–42; 12:27–28; 17:1–26. Luke alone mentions Jesus praying before four key events: Jesus's baptism (Luke 3:21; cf. Matt. 3:16; Mark 1:10), Peter's confession (Luke 9:18; cf. Matt. 16:13; Mark 8:27), the transfiguration (Luke 9:28–29; cf. Matt. 17:1; Mark 9:2), and teaching the Lord's Prayer (Luke 11:1; cf. Matt. 6:7).

of breaking bread is modeled on Jesus's actions at the Last Supper (Luke 22:14–23). The first Christians therefore not only do works of piety; they do works of piety that are patterned on the life of Jesus.

Luke also presents the early church as engaging in works of mercy. These include

- proclaiming the good news,[33]
- performing signs and wonders,[34]
- healing the sick,[35]
- casting out unclean spirits,[36]
- sharing of possessions,[37] and
- providing food for widows.[38]

Here we find numerous parallels to Jesus's ministry in the Gospel of Luke. Proclaiming the good news is, of course, the first action listed in Isaiah 61:1–2, the passage that Jesus claims as his mission statement at the outset of his public ministry (Luke 4:16–21). And while Luke's Gospel does not use the language of "signs and wonders" to describe Jesus's actions, Luke does have Peter describe Jesus as "a man accredited by God to you by miracles, *wonders and signs*" in his Pentecost message (Acts 2:22). These wonders and signs presumably refer to Jesus's supernatural actions such as healing and casting out demons—two other elements of Jesus's ministry that the early church reprises.[39] The first Christians' sharing of possessions and care for widows likewise recall Jesus's Isaiah 61-themed mission to the poor (see above) and his teachings concerning the poor.[40] Thus the early church's works of mercy, like its works of piety, are substantially patterned on the life of Christ.[41]

33. Acts 5:42; 8:4, 12, 25, 35, 40; 10:36; 11:20; 13:32; 14:7, 15, 21; 15:7, 35; 16:10; 17:18; 20:24.
34. Acts 2:43; 4:16, 22, 30; 5:12; 6:8; 8:6, 13; 14:3; 15:12; 19:11.
35. Acts 3:6–8; 5:15–16; 19:11–12; 28:8–9.
36. Acts 5:16; 8:6–7; 16:18; 19:11–12.
37. Acts 2:44–45; 4:32–37; 11:29–30. Luke's note that "there were no needy persons among" the early Christians (Acts 4:34) alludes to Deut. 15:4 ("There need be no poor people among you").
38. Acts 6:1–7.
39. Acts 4:16, 22 use the language of "sign" (*sēmeion*) to describe the healing of a lame man. Acts 8:6 uses the same language to describe both exorcisms and healings (cf. 8:7).
40. E.g., Luke 6:20–21; 7:22; 12:33; 14:12–14; 16:19–31; 18:22.
41. The parallels discussed above constitute only a small portion of those between Jesus in Luke and believers in Acts. For a fuller discussion, see James R. Edwards, "Parallels and Patterns between Luke and Acts," *Bulletin for Biblical Research* 27, no. 4 (2017): 485–501.

Acts therefore confirms what the Gospels have already intimated: good works are central to the Christian life. In the introduction to Acts, Luke portrays the life of the early church as an extension of Jesus's own life and mission, and he develops this thesis in the body of his work by recounting the Jesus-shaped actions of the first Christians.

Paul on Faith and Works

In the eyes of many Protestants, Paul's doctrine of justification by faith excludes good works from contributing in any way to salvation. However, as we have seen above, Jesus teaches that good works are necessary for salvation, and Luke forges a strong link between good works and Christian identity in Acts. The unified witness of the Gospels and Acts on this point should make us question whether Paul really denies any relationship between good works and salvation. And it is not only the Gospels and Acts that problematize this popular reading of Paul; Paul himself affirms a judgment according to works.[42] We must, then, examine Paul's teaching on justification by faith and judgment according to works to see how he develops each of these ideas and relates them to each other. But first we need to examine our presuppositions regarding two key terms: "grace" and "faith."

Rethinking Grace and Faith in Paul's Letters

One of the perennial challenges in biblical interpretation is making sure that we are defining Scripture's words and phrases in the same way that the biblical authors do. This task is especially important in the case of terms such as "grace" and "faith," which play a pivotal role in Paul's teaching about salvation. We think we know what these words mean, and perhaps we do to a degree. But what if we have unwittingly smuggled certain assumptions into them that cause us to prioritize some parts of Paul's theology (e.g., justification by faith) and ignore others (e.g., judgment according to works)? Or what if these same (re)definitions cause us to find tensions and paradoxes in parts of Paul's theology that he thought were completely coherent? Take Ephesians 2:8–10, for example:

42. The most explicit texts are Rom. 2:6; 2 Cor. 11:15; 2 Tim. 4:14. See further below.

[8] For it is by grace you have been saved, through faith—and this is not from yourselves, it is the gift of God— [9] not by works, so that no one can boast. [10] For we are God's handiwork, created in Christ Jesus to do good works, which God prepared in advance for us to do.[43]

Many Protestants quote Ephesians 2:8–9 to demonstrate that good works are not necessary for salvation. However, one must not forget 2:10, where Paul states that Christians are "created in Christ Jesus to do good works, which God prepared in advance for us to do." Once aware of this verse, one might (1) respond that the good works, while important, are not strictly necessary for salvation (a dubious claim), or (2) brush the issue aside as a Pauline paradox. But what if Paul conceived of grace and faith in ways that would allow for him to affirm in the same breath that salvation is "not by works" and that believers are "created . . . to do good works"? This is the possibility that we wish to explore below.

"Grace," according to one common definition, means "unmerited favor." This is not wrong, but it tells only part of the story. In Paul's Letters, "grace" typically translates the Greek word *charis*, which occurs one hundred times in the Pauline corpus. *Charis* was not an exclusively religious term but was used of both divine and human gifts. For example, it played a major role in the patronage system that constituted the foundation of Greco-Roman culture. According to David deSilva, "In a world in which wealth and property were concentrated into the hands of a very small percentage of the population, the majority of people often found themselves in need of assistance in one form or another and therefore had to seek the patronage of someone who was better placed in the world than himself or herself."[44] The better-placed party was called the "patron," the needier party the "client." Within this system, *charis* could refer either to the patron's benevolent attitude or

43. Here and below we treat all thirteen letters attributed to Paul in the New Testament as authentic. However, a decision against the authenticity of Ephesians or other letters would not significantly alter our conclusions, for whether Paul wrote all thirteen letters or not, they are part of the New Testament and must therefore be incorporated into a New Testament theology of good works.

44. David A. deSilva, "Patronage," in *Dictionary of New Testament Background*, ed. Craig A. Evans and Stanley E. Porter (Downers Grove, IL: InterVarsity, 2000), 767. For a more detailed discussion of patronage, see David A. deSilva, *Honor, Patronage, Kinship and Purity: Unlocking New Testament Culture* (Downers Grove, IL: InterVarsity, 2000), 95–156.

action toward the client (grace, favor) or to the client's response, "the necessary and appropriate return for favor shown"[45] (gratitude, thanks). What is important to recognize is that in the patronage system *charis* was reciprocal. Both patrons and clients gave gifts expecting a response, and this did not make the gifts any less gracious.

John Barclay has shed further light on Paul's notion of grace in his seminal book *Paul and the Gift*.[46] One of Barclay's major contributions is that he outlines six "perfections" of gift/grace that describe the various ways that one might define the essence of a gift:[47]

1. *Superabundance*: the gift is large, significant, or permanent.
2. *Singularity*: "the giver's sole and exclusive mode of operation is benevolence or goodness."
3. *Priority*: the gift is given "always prior to the initiative of the recipient."
4. *Incongruity*: the gift is "given without condition, that is, without regard for the worth of the recipient."
5. *Efficacy*: the gift "fully achieves what it was designed to do."
6. *Non-circularity*: the gift "escapes reciprocity" (i.e., the giver receives nothing in return).

These perfections provide a rubric of sorts for analyzing uses of "grace" by Paul and other authors. For our purposes, two of them—incongruity and non-circularity—are particularly important. With these two perfections, Barclay draws an important distinction between two things that many of us in the modern Western world have conflated. We often assume that God's grace is necessarily both incongruous (given to unworthy recipients) and nonreciprocal (expects no response). But is this how Paul conceived of grace? There is good reason to think that it is not. Through an analysis of Galatians and Romans, Barclay argues compellingly that "Paul perfects the incongruity of the gift (given to the unworthy) but he does *not* perfect its non-circularity (expecting nothing in return). The divine gift in Christ was *unconditioned* (based on

---

45. DeSilva, "Patronage," 768.
46. John M. G. Barclay, *Paul and the Gift* (Grand Rapids: Eerdmans, 2015).
47. Barclay, *Paul and the Gift*, 70–75.

no prior conditions) but it is not *unconditional* (carrying no subsequent demands)."[48] Barclay, we submit, is correct. Once one relinquishes the presupposition that grace must necessarily be nonreciprocal, all sorts of pieces in the puzzle of Paul's theology that previously did not fit begin to fall into place. Ephesians 2:8–10 is just one example. When Paul says that salvation is "by grace . . . through faith . . . not by works" and goes on to assert that believers are "created . . . to do good works," he is not being inconsistent or illogical. He is simply affirming that God's gift is both incongruous (given to those who are not worthy) and reciprocal (expects an appropriate response).

The notion of appropriate response brings us to our second word of interest: "faith." One of the difficulties that confronts the English reader is that Paul's language of faith is somewhat broader than the words that most English Bibles translate as "faith" and its cognates. Paul uses (1) the noun *pistis* ("faith"), (2) the verb *pisteuō* ("believe"), and (3) the adjective *pistos* ("faithful"), which share the root *pist-*. However, the English words "faith" and "believe" look very different, so it is easy to miss that the Greek words behind these two words (*pistis* and *pisteuō*, respectively) are closely related. Another difficulty is that the words "faith," "belief," and cognates are often used very differently in a twenty-first-century Western context than in Paul's Letters. "I believe in God" in a modern American setting often means simply that the speaker is not an atheist, not that he or she has any sort of relationship with or expresses devotion to a particular God in any meaningful sense. Such belief or faith is certainly a far cry from what Paul means when he says that the righteousness of God "is given through faith [*dia pisteōs*] in Jesus Christ to all who believe [*pisteuontas*]" (Rom. 3:22).

What, then, does Paul mean by the language of faith? To discuss all the ways that Paul uses faith language would require a book of its own.[49] Since here we are interested in justifying or saving faith and how this relates to good works, we will focus on Romans 4, Paul's most extensive

---

48. Barclay, *Paul and the Gift*, 500 (italics original). Barclay is discussing Rom. 5–6 here, but the statement is characteristic of his overarching thesis.

49. For a recent treatment, see Nijay K. Gupta, *Paul and the Language of Faith* (Grand Rapids: Eerdmans, 2020). Gupta identifies three meanings of *pistis* in Paul's writings: believing faith (cognitively active), obeying faith (relationally active), and trusting faith (volitionally active), with trusting faith as a middle ground of sorts between the other two meanings (9–13).

discussion of faith as it relates to justification.[50] At the outset, Paul cites Abraham as an example of faith:

> ¹ What then shall we say was gained by Abraham, our forefather according to the flesh? ² For if Abraham was justified by works, he has something to boast about, but not before God. ³ For what does the Scripture say? "Abraham believed [*episteusen*] God, and it was counted to him as righteousness" [Gen. 15:6]. ⁴ Now to the one who works, his wages are not counted as a gift but as his due. ⁵ And to the one who does not work but believes [*pisteuonti*] in him who justifies the ungodly, his faith [*pistis*] is counted as righteousness. (Rom. 4:1–5 ESV)

Three observations are key for understanding Paul's concept of justifying faith. First, Paul contrasts faith with works.[51] Paul's problem with works seems to be that they attempt to earn or merit righteousness (4:4), undermining the incongruous nature of God's gift. Faith, by contrast, seems to be the act of receiving God's gift precisely as something that is unearned and unmerited.

Second, Paul uses faith language to refer to a human action in response to God: "Abraham *believed* [*episteusen*] God" (4:3). But this brings up an interesting question: If believing / having faith is an action (something one does), how is it not a "work"? We suggest that the answer is found in the contrast between faith and works noted above. Paul's problem with "works" is not that they are actions but that they reject the gracious nature of God's gift by attempting to earn or merit it. Believing, on the other hand, is the act of receiving God's gift as something one does not deserve.[52] The difference between works and faith, then, is

50. On the relationship between justification and ultimate salvation, see below.

51. Paul contrasts faith with both "works" (e.g., Rom. 4:2, 6) and "works of the law" (e.g., Rom. 3:20, 28). Interpreters debate whether Paul takes issue primarily with "works *of the law*" (for which "works" would be a shorthand) or with "works" in general (of which "works of the law" would be a subset). In our view, the latter is more likely. On this point, see Douglas J. Moo, *A Theology of Paul and His Letters: The Gift of the New Realm in Christ*, Biblical Theology of the New Testament (Grand Rapids: Zondervan Academic, 2021), 435–39, 522.

52. Some interpreters deny that believing is something that one does (e.g., Moo, *Theology of Paul*, 522). In our view, it is better to acknowledge that believing is something that one does but to distinguish between actions aimed at self-justification ("works") and actions that receive and respond to a divine gift ("faith"). Gupta says of faith in Galatians, "Paul does *not* intend for πίστις [*pistis*] to refer to nonwork, a kind of passive reliance on Christ. Paul uses πίστις in reference to the core relational dynamic of the covenant, the nature of a covenantal bond that expects fidelity and mutuality with trust at its core" (*Paul and the Language of Faith*, 143 [italics original]; cf. 139–40). Gupta argues more

not one of doing versus not doing, but one of achieving versus receiving. Yet we must be careful at this point not to understand "receiving" in a nonreciprocal sense. In our discussion of grace above, we noted that in the Greco-Roman world gifts were typically given expecting a response. To receive a gift from a patron meant that one had become a client and needed to reciprocate loyalty to the patron. (This is similar to the concept of covenant that we examined in the preceding chapter.) Interestingly, "faith" (Greek *pistis*; Latin *fides*) was used in the patronage system to refer to both a client's trust in and loyalty toward a patron.[53] In light of this background and the way that Paul develops the reciprocity of God's grace, should we then understand *pistis* and *pisteuō* in Romans 4:1–5 and elsewhere in the sense of both *faith* (belief or trust) and *faithfulness* (obedience, loyalty, allegiance)? Some scholars have argued that we should.[54] While it is possible that Paul does intend both meanings in some cases, he does not seem to interpret Abraham's faith in this way in Romans 4, since he is clear that Abraham's initial justification was not based on his later faithfulness (e.g., in being circumcised [4:9–12]). In our view, it is best to say that justifying faith *is* an attitude of trust that necessarily *produces* faithfulness or obedience.

Third, Abraham's faith has an object: "Abraham believed *God*" (4:3). In the context of Genesis 15, Abraham's belief is likely focused on God's promise that his offspring would be as numerous as the stars (15:5). For Paul's readers, the object of their faith is Jesus the Messiah, the climax of all God's promises. The fact that Paul gives faith an object is important, for it reminds us that faith itself has the power to save no one; it is faith in God and/or in Christ that saves. Douglas Moo puts it well: "Faith possesses the power to justify not in itself but as the agency by which we are joined to Christ."[55]

Thus, when we understand grace and faith on Paul's terms, we find that there is no necessary tension between the idea that salvation is "by grace . . . through faith . . . not by works" and that believers are "created

---

broadly that "no one in the ancient Hellenistic world would have thought of πίστις as kinetically passive (as in nonactive)" (183).

53. DeSilva, *Honor, Patronage, Kinship and Purity*, 115.

54. E.g., Matthew W. Bates, *Salvation by Allegiance Alone: Rethinking Faith, Works, and the Gospel of Jesus the King* (Grand Rapids: Baker Academic, 2017); Bates, *Gospel Allegiance: What Faith in Jesus Misses for Salvation in Christ* (Grand Rapids: Brazos, 2019).

55. Moo, *Theology of Paul*, 523.

. . . to do good works" (Eph. 2:8–10). For Paul, to say that salvation is "by grace" means that salvation is a gift, and to say that it is "through faith" means that one must receive it as a gift, trusting in the character and ability of the Giver. Salvation is "not by works" because it is an incongruous gift, something that is not (and indeed, cannot be) earned or merited. But God's gift is also meant to produce good works—a transformed life—in those who receive it. Such good works are consistent with the incongruous nature of the gift because they are a natural and necessary outflow of faith and may be the means by which God works in saving grace.

Justification by Faith and Judgment according to Works

Having recalibrated our understanding of grace and faith in Paul's thought, we are now prepared to see how Paul develops the ideas of justification by faith and judgment according to works and relates these to each other.

Justification, like faith, is a Pauline concept that involves a family of Greek words that do not easily translate into English in a uniform way. In Paul's Letters, we find the following words related to the concept of justification:

- *dikaiosynē* ("righteousness")—58 times
- *dikaioō* ("justify")—27 times
- *dikaios* ("just," "righteous")—17 times[56]

These words share a common *dikai-* root. However, to render them adequately in English we must employ at least two roots: "just-" and "right-." The interplay between these *dikai-* words can be seen in Romans 3:25–26, where Paul says, "God presented Christ as a sacrifice of atonement . . . to demonstrate his righteousness [*dikaiosynēs*] at the present time, so as to be just [*dikaion*] and the one who justifies [*dikaiounta*] those who have faith in Jesus." The relationship between righteousness (*dikaiosynē*) and the act of justifying (*dikaioō*) also makes sense of why Paul uses Abraham as an example of justification by faith.

---

56. Paul uses other *dikai-* words as well: *dikaiōma* ("righteous decree/requirement"), *dikaiōs* ("justly," "rightly"), *dikaiōsis* ("justification"), *dikaiokrisia* ("righteous judgment").

"Abraham believed God, and it was credited to him as righteousness [*eis dikaiosynēn*]" (4:3, quoting Gen. 15:6) is, for Paul, a declaration that Abraham was made right with or justified before God.

Paul presents justification by faith as the foundation of God's solution to human sinfulness. This can be seen particularly in Romans 1:18–4:25. Paul opens the body of his letter to the Romans by painting a dismal picture of human sin (1:18–3:20), concluding, "There is no one righteous, not even one" (3:10). In 3:21–4:25, Paul turns to God's solution to this problem:

> [21] But now apart from the law the righteousness [*dikaiosynē*] of God has been made known, to which the Law and the Prophets testify. [22] This righteousness [*dikaiosynē*] is given through faith [*pisteōs*] in Jesus Christ to all who believe [*pisteuontas*]. There is no difference between Jew and Gentile, [23] for all have sinned and fall short of the glory of God, [24] and all are justified [*dikaioumenoi*] freely by his grace through the redemption that came by Christ Jesus. (3:21–24)

Paul goes on to explain and substantiate this claim in Romans 4 by appealing to the example of Abraham in Genesis 15:6. Here we find that Abraham's faith was "credited to him as righteousness" (Rom. 4:3). The language of "crediting" is important, for it suggests that what has changed is not Abraham's character but his status. Justification, then, seems to refer to a declaration that grants someone a status of "righteous" before God. It is "forensic" (pertaining to a judicial decision), for it grants a sinner the status of "righteous" before the person has attained a righteous character.[57] But if justification by faith is distinct from sanctification, it must not be separated from it. Paul's central subject in Romans is arguably the gospel (1:1–2, 16–17; 16:25), and if the gospel consisted only of justification by faith (1:18–4:25), Romans would have been a much shorter letter. After discussing justification by faith, Paul goes on to describe the new life that the justified get to live (5:1–8:39). If justification by faith as the solution to human sin (1:18–4:25) constitutes the *foundation* of the gospel, life in Christ by the Spirit (5:1–8:39) constitutes its *fullness*, and both are essential.

---

57. On the forensic nature of justification, see N. T. Wright, *Justification: God's Plan and Paul's Vision* (Downers Grove, IL: IVP Academic, 2009), 90–91; Moo, *Theology of Paul*, 479–86.

Paul portrays justification as having both present and future dimensions. On the one hand, he can speak of justification as something that has already happened in the present:

> Therefore, since *we have been justified* [*dikaiōthentes*] through faith, we have peace with God through our Lord Jesus Christ. (Rom. 5:1)

> Since *we have now been justified* [*dikaiōthentes*] by his blood, how much more shall we be saved from God's wrath through him! (Rom. 5:9)

> But you were washed, you were sanctified, *you were justified* [*edikaiōthēte*] in the name of the Lord Jesus Christ and by the Spirit of our God. (1 Cor. 6:11)

> [God our Savior] saved us . . . so that, *having been justified* [*dikaiōthentes*] by his grace, we might become heirs having the hope of eternal life. (Titus 3:5, 7)

On the other hand, Paul can also speak of justification as a future event:

> [4] You who are trying to be justified [*dikaiousthe*] by the law have been alienated from Christ; you have fallen away from grace. [5] For through the Spirit we eagerly await by faith the righteousness [*dikaiosynēs*] for which we hope. (Gal. 5:4–5)

Moo argues compellingly that "righteousness" here refers to "vindication in the judgment,"[58] and the context makes clear that this judgment is still future. Similarly, in 1 Corinthians Paul seems to envision a future divine verdict that applies both to him and to others:

> [3] But with me it is a very small thing that I should be judged by you or by any human court. In fact, I do not even judge myself. [4] For I am not aware of anything against myself, but I am not thereby acquitted [*dedikaiōmai*]. It is the Lord who judges me. [5] Therefore do not pronounce judgment before the time, before the Lord comes. . . . Then each one will receive his commendation from God. (4:3–5 ESV)

---

58. Moo, *Theology of Paul*, 80; cf. 488–89. The correlation between *dikaiousthe* (Gal. 5:4) and *dikaiosynēs* (5:5) also supports this interpretation.

Finally, in Romans Paul declares,

> [13] It is not those who hear the law who are righteous [*dikaioi*] in God's sight, but it is those who obey the law who *will be declared righteous* [*dikaiōthēsontai*]. . . . [16] This will take place on the day when God judges people's secrets through Jesus Christ, as my gospel declares. (2:13, 16)

One might argue that the justification here concerns only nonbelievers, but this seems unlikely when we correlate this passage with those above, as well as Paul's teaching about judgment according to works—to which we now turn.

Paul's notion of a future justification is closely linked with (and perhaps identical to) the judgment according to works that he also affirms.[59] The most explicit texts are as follows:

> God "will repay each person according to what they have done [*kata ta erga autou*]." (Rom. 2:6, quoting Ps. 62:12 or Prov. 24:12)

> It is not surprising, then, if [Satan's] servants also masquerade as servants of righteousness. Their end will be what their actions deserve [*kata ta erga autōn*]. (2 Cor. 11:15)

> Alexander the metalworker did me a great deal of harm. The Lord will repay him for what he has done [*kata ta erga autou*]. (2 Tim. 4:14)

Each of these passage uses the phrase *kata ta erga autou/autōn*—literally, "according to his/their works." The word for "works" (*erga* [singular, *ergon*]) is the same one that Paul employs when he says that "a person is not justified by the works [*ex ergōn*] of the law" (Gal. 2:16) and that salvation is "not by works [*ex ergōn*]" (Eph. 2:9). But to whom does this judgment according to works apply? As Moo notes,

> A judgment that involves ultimate condemnation for unbelievers and the wicked is not hard to integrate into Paul's larger teaching. However, Paul also makes clear that believers must face this day of judgment as well (see Rom 14:10; 1 Cor 4:5; 2 Cor 5:10). . . . Paul can also cite the day

---

59. Moo, *Theology of Paul*, 488–90.

of judgment as a basis for his exhortation to believers, warning them of the consequences for them on that day should their lives not measure up to God's expectations of them (Rom 8:12–13; 1 Cor 3:10–15[?]; 10:5–10; 2 Cor 5:10; Gal 6:7–9).[60]

One way to reconcile justification by faith with the idea that believers will be judged according to their works is to suggest that the latter determines only the degrees of reward that believers will receive, not whether they will enter eternal life.[61] However, this solution does not do justice to statements such as "If you live according to the flesh, you will *die*" (Rom. 8:13) or "Whoever sows to please their flesh, from the flesh will reap *destruction*; whoever sows to please the Spirit, from the Spirit will reap *eternal life*" (Gal. 6:8).[62] Similarly, it is difficult to believe that when Paul exhorts the Philippians, "Work out your salvation with fear and trembling" (Phil. 2:12), the "fear and trembling" is merely trepidation over having one's eternal reward downgraded slightly. Furthermore, it is unclear what greater or lesser rewards would even mean in the new creation. Another solution is to treat judgment according to works as merely a public manifestation of what was already declared in initial justification.[63] Yet this does not square with Moo's observation that Paul uses final judgment as a basis for his warnings to *believers* (who by definition have already been justified). If Paul thinks that every believer will necessarily receive the verdict of "righteous" at the final judgment regardless of what they have done, why would he warn believers to ready themselves for final judgment? And how could Paul possibly describe this as judgment "according to works"?

We suggest a simpler solution: Paul (like Jesus) believes that good works are necessary for salvation and that God will judge all people—

60. Moo, *Theology of Paul*, 490 (brackets original).
61. One text often cited to support this view is 1 Cor. 3:12–15, where Paul speaks of Christian leaders' work being tested, with some receiving a reward and others suffering loss yet being saved. However, Craig Blomberg argues compellingly that the implied object of "suffer loss" (3:15) is not "reward" (3:14) but the nearer "work" (3:15a ESV). The reward of more faithful Christian leaders, then, is "nothing more or less than knowing that they did spend substantial time on building things that would last into eternity" ("Degrees of Reward in the Kingdom of Heaven?," *Journal of the Evangelical Theological Society* 35, no. 2 [1992]: 165). Blomberg also provides broader biblical objections to the "degrees of reward" view of judgment according to works.
62. See Moo, *Theology of Paul*, 490.
63. E.g., Dane C. Ortlund, "Justified by Faith, Judged according to Works: Another Look at a Pauline Paradox," *Journal of the Evangelical Theological Society* 52, no. 2 (2009): 336.

believers included—according to their works (Rom. 2:6). Does this undermine salvation as a gift? By no means. As noted above, when Paul says that we are saved "by grace . . . through faith . . . not by works" (Eph. 2:8–9), this means that salvation is an unmerited gift that must be received as such, *not* that no subsequent response is required. Paul expects Christians to grow in holiness throughout their lives so that on the day of judgment they are "righteous" not only in status but also in reality. As Barclay says (commenting on Rom. 2), "In his eschatological scenario, Paul describes *congruity* rather than *incongruity*: he foresees a final judgment in which the righteous are rewarded and the unrighteous are condemned."[64] For Paul, God's gift is *not* noncircular but is meant to transform believers' lives (not merely their statuses) and expects a response. Thus, "Judgment 'according to works' does not entail a new and incompatible principle of soteriology; it indicates that the incongruous gift has had its intended effect in embedding new standards of worth in the practice of those it transforms."[65]

We conclude this section with two points. First, our reading of Paul given above is fully Protestant. We affirm that justification is by grace through faith and not by works and that it is forensic. If we have found a stronger emphasis on good works in Paul's writings than some recent Protestant interpreters have, this is not because we have forsaken the Reformation foundations but because we have approached Paul with different categories that better reflect Paul's first-century context and allow us to reconcile seemingly disparate elements of Paul's theology. Second, our interpretation not only allows Paul to agree with himself; it also brings him into harmony with the Old Testament and Jesus, not to mention James and Revelation (see below). A strong doctrine of final justification / judgment according to works therefore not only allows for a coherent Pauline theology; it is essential for a coherent biblical theology.

64. Barclay, *Paul and the Gift*, 493 (italics original). Barclay rightly grants that grace remains incongruous throughout the Christian life in that "everything that can be said about Christian action, obedience, and obligation arises from this generative basis" (517). Yet this is far different from a common understanding of Luther's *simul iustus et peccator* (at the same time righteous and a sinner), for "what began as a morally incongruous gift will be completed as a morally congruous gift" (518).

65. Barclay, *Paul and the Gift*, 569.

James on Faith and Works

It is no secret that James places a significant emphasis on good works. Indeed, one of the perennial issues in New Testament theology has been how to reconcile James's assertions that Abraham was "justified by works" (James 2:21 ESV) and that "faith apart from works is dead" (2:26 ESV) with Paul's doctrine of justification by faith.[66] As noted above, one of the benefits of our reading of Paul is that it leaves far less to be reconciled than some have thought. As a result, our discussion of James can be brief, simply showing the conceptual similarities between James and Paul and explaining one apparent verbal contradiction.

James discusses the relationship between faith and works explicitly in 2:14–26. He begins by saying,

> [14] What good is it, my brothers, if someone says he has faith but does not have works? Can that faith save him? [15] If a brother or sister is poorly clothed and lacking in daily food, [16] and one of you says to them, "Go in peace, be warmed and filled," without giving them the things needed for the body, what good is that? [17] So also faith by itself, if it does not have works, is dead. (2:14–17 ESV)

Having asserted that works are necessary for true faith, James goes on to counter a potential objection:[67]

> [18] But someone will say, "You have faith and I have works." Show me your faith apart from your works, and I will show you my faith by my works. [19] You believe that God is one; you do well. Even the demons believe—and shudder! [20] Do you want to be shown, you foolish person, that faith apart from works is useless? (2:18–20 ESV)

So far James has said nothing that Paul would dispute; both writers agree that true faith produces good works. But James now appeals

---

66. Throughout James 2:14–26, the NIV avoids translating *erga* (and other plural forms of *ergon*) as "works," instead using "deeds," "action(s)," "what [someone] did," and so forth. This translation choice is unfortunate because it obscures the fact that James is using the same language that is usually rendered as "works" in Paul's writings (even by the NIV).

67. There is disagreement about whether the imagined speaker in James 2:18a is agreeing with or objecting to James's argument (and if the latter, how). In our view, the best interpretation is that this person is "objecting to James' argument by claiming that different people may have different 'gifts': one may have faith and another may have works" (Douglas J. Moo, *The Letter of James: An Introduction and Commentary*, Tyndale New Testament Commentaries [Grand Rapids: Eerdmans, 1985], 105).

to Abraham to prove his point, and it is here that a potential conflict arises. We can observe the issue by placing James's teaching alongside Romans 4:1–5.[68]

James 2:21–24	Romans 4:1–5
[21] Was not *Abraham our father justified by works* when he offered up his son Isaac on the altar? [22] You see that faith was active along with his works, and faith was completed by his works; [23] and the *Scripture* was fulfilled that says, *"Abraham believed God, and it was counted to him as righteousness"*—and he was called a friend of God. [24] You see that *a person is justified by works and not by faith alone.* (ESV)	[1] What then shall we say was gained by *Abraham, our forefather* according to the flesh? [2] For if Abraham *was justified by works*, he has something to boast about, but not before God. [3] For what does the *Scripture* say? *"Abraham believed God, and it was counted to him as righteousness."* [4] Now to the one who works, his wages are not counted as a gift but as his due. [5] And to *the one who does not work but believes* in him who justifies the ungodly, *his faith is counted as righteousness.* (ESV)

Both James and Paul use Abraham as an example and quote Genesis 15:6. Yet Paul clearly affirms that a person is justified by faith and *not* by works, whereas James argues that "a person is justified by works and not by faith alone" (James 2:24). How can both be right? Of the solutions that interpreters have proposed, two are most promising. First, it is possible that James and Paul are using "faith" in different ways. According to Frank Thielman, "James defines 'faith' in 2:14–26 as mere verbal and intellectual assent."[69] (Note the emphasis on saying versus doing in 2:14–17 and James's statement in 2:19 that "even the demons believe [*pisteuousin*].") Paul, however, "describes Abraham's faith as an unwavering trust in God ([Rom.] 4:19), free of doubt (4:20), and full of conviction that, as improbable as it seemed that God could keep his promises, he would keep them nevertheless (4:21)."[70] If Paul views good works as the natural and necessary outflow of faith, then he would agree with James that "a person is justified by works and not by [mere verbal and intellectual assent] alone" (James 2:24 ESV).

Second, Paul and James may be speaking of different aspects of justification. In Romans 4, Paul focuses on Abraham's initial justification

68. Frank Thielman uses a similar chart in his *Theology of the New Testament: A Canonical and Synthetic Approach* (Grand Rapids: Zondervan, 2005), 506.

69. Thielman, *Theology of the New Testament*, 508.

70. Thielman, *Theology of the New Testament*, 509.

that took place in Genesis 15:6 before he was circumcised (Rom. 4:9–13). James cites Genesis 15:6, but this is not the justification that he is interested in. He argues that Abraham was justified by works when he offered Isaac on the altar, and that this act *completed* and *fulfilled* his faith in Genesis 15:6 (James 2:21–23; cf. Gen. 22:9–10). It therefore seems likely that Paul is speaking of initial justification, but James is speaking of final (or at least some subsequent) justification.[71] And in light of what Paul says about final justification / judgment according to works (see above), we have every reason to believe that he would agree with James on this point.

These two solutions are not incompatible, but in our view, the latter is most compelling, because it draws on and makes sense of how James uses Genesis 15 and 22. James, then, does not deny the Pauline doctrine of (initial) justification by faith. Rather, he emphasizes that one's faith must produce good works if one wishes to receive the verdict of "righteous" in the final judgment (something that Paul, too, would affirm). Within New Testament theology, James stands as an important witness to the necessity of good works for ultimate salvation and against (mis)readings of Paul that would minimize the importance of good works.

Revelation on Good Works

Revelation, the climax of the canon, has much to say about the role of good works in salvation. We will here focus on the role that good works play in (1) final judgment and (2) God's final intent.

Judgment according to Works in Revelation

The book of Revelation, like Paul's Letters, describes the final judgment as being "according to works":

> [12] And I saw the dead, great and small, standing before the throne, and books were opened. Another book was opened, which is the book of life.

---

71. See John Wesley, "Minutes of Some Late Conversations," in *The Works of John Wesley*, 14 vols. (London: Wesleyan Methodist Book Room, 1872), 8:277; Moo, *James*, 109; Ralph P. Martin, *James*, Word Biblical Commentary 48 (Waco: Word, 1988), 91. We owe the Wesley reference to Moo.

The dead were judged according to what they had done [*kata ta erga autōn*] as recorded in the books. ¹³ The sea gave up the dead that were in it, and death and Hades gave up the dead that were in them, and each person was judged according to what they had done [*kata ta erga autōn*]. (20:12–13)

Twice John describes people as being judged *kata ta erga autōn*—literally, "according to their works." One might argue that the people judged according to their works here are not believers, but earlier in Revelation, Jesus warns the church at Thyatira, "I will repay each of you according to your deeds [*kata ta erga hymōn*]" (2:23), so the idea that Christians are excused from this judgment seems unlikely.

Furthermore, Revelation elsewhere treats good works as necessary for salvation. Jesus's messages to the churches in Revelation 2–3 provide numerous examples of this. Jesus tells the church in Ephesus, "Consider how far you have fallen! Repent and do the things you did at first. If you do not repent, I will come to you and remove your lampstand from its place" (2:5). The lampstand here symbolizes a church (1:20), so Jesus is in effect threatening to remove their status as one of his churches. Similarly, Jesus says to the church in Sardis,

⁴ You have a few people . . . who have not soiled their clothes. They will walk with me, dressed in white, for they are worthy. ⁵ The one who is victorious will, like them, be dressed in white. I will never blot out the name of that person from the book of life, but will acknowledge that name before my Father and his angels. (3:4–5)

The soiling of clothes here is a metaphor for sinful behavior; as Jesus tells this church earlier, "I know your deeds; you have a reputation of being alive, but you are dead" (3:1b). And Jesus's promise *not* to blot the name of the victorious one out of the book of life strongly implies that he *will* blot out the names of those who continue in sin; that is, they will not be saved (cf. 13:8; 17:8; 20:12, 15).

Revelation 19:8 likewise describes how the bride of the Lamb is given "fine linen, bright and clean" to wear. John then explains, "Fine linen stands for the righteous acts of God's holy people." Note that John does not say that the bride is clothed with *Christ's* righteous acts, but with the righteous acts *of God's holy people*. Yet even here John preserves the gracious character of salvation: this linen is *given* to the bride. God's people, in other words, have received his gift and have responded appropriately.

Good Works and God's Final Intent

Revelation presents good works as part of God's final intent. John's vision of the new creation in Revelation 21–22 focuses more on the creation itself than on what God's people will do in it. However, several features suggest that human activity will not be restricted to "something like what happens in church on Sunday morning."[72] First, the new creation includes elements from the garden of Eden: a river (22:1; cf. Gen. 2:10–14) and the tree of life (22:2; cf. Gen. 2:9). The echoes of Eden in the new creation suggest that, barring an explicit notice to the contrary, we should assume continuity between God's original intent (where work is regarded as good) and his final intent.

Second, John's use of Isaiah in Revelation 21 suggests that human activity in the new creation will consist of more than participating in an eternal worship service. The "new heaven and new earth" that John sees (Rev. 21:1) recall the new creation of which Isaiah prophesied:

> See, I will create
> new heavens and a new earth.
> The former things will not be remembered,
> nor will they come to mind. (Isa. 65:17)

> "As the new heavens and the new earth that I make will endure before me," declares the LORD, "so will your name and descendants endure." (Isa. 66:22)

Isaiah interestingly describes God's people working in this new creation:[73]

> 21 They will *build houses* and dwell in them;
> they will *plant vineyards* and eat their fruit.

---

72. Andy Crouch, *Culture Making: Recovering Our Creative Calling* (Downers Grove, IL: IVP Books, 2008), 173.

73. See Theology of Work Project, *Theology of Work Bible Commentary: One-Volume Edition* (Peabody, MA: Hendrickson, 2016), 938–39.

²² No longer will they build houses and others live in them,
    or plant and others eat.
For as the days of a tree,
    so will be the days of my people;
my chosen ones will long enjoy
    the *work of their hands*. (65:21–22)

According to Isaiah, in the new creation, work is not abolished but perfected; God's people will be able to "enjoy the work of their hands," free from the injustice that plagues the present age.

John says of the new Jerusalem,[74]

²³ The city does not need the sun or the moon to shine on it, for the glory of God gives it light, and the Lamb is its lamp. ²⁴ The nations will walk by its light, and the kings of the earth will bring their splendor into it. ²⁵ On no day will its gates ever be shut, for there will be no night there. ²⁶ The glory and honor of the nations will be brought into it. (Rev. 21:23–26)

Verse 23 echoes Isaiah 60:19:

The sun will no more be your light by day,
    nor will the brightness of the moon shine on you,
for the Lord will be your everlasting light,
    and your God will be your glory.

Verses 24–26 likewise allude to earlier parts of Isaiah 60:

³ *Nations will come to your light,*
    and kings to the brightness of your dawn. . . .

⁶ Herds of camels will cover your land,
    young camels of Midian and Ephah.
And all from Sheba will come,
    bearing gold and incense
    and proclaiming the praise of the Lord.
⁷ All Kedar's flocks will be gathered to you,
    the rams of Nebaioth will serve you;

---

74. The observations about John's allusions to Isaiah 60 below are drawn from Crouch, *Culture Making*, 166–67.

they will be accepted as offerings on my altar,
> and I will adorn my glorious temple. . . .

⁹ Surely the islands look to me;
> in the lead are the ships of Tarshish,
bringing your children from afar,
> with their silver and gold,
to the honor of the LORD your God,
> the Holy One of Israel,
for he has endowed you with *splendor*. . . .

¹¹ Your gates will always stand open,
> *they will never be shut, day or night,*
so that people may bring you *the wealth of the nations—*
> *their kings* led in triumphal procession. . . .

¹³ The glory of Lebanon will come to you,
> the juniper, the fir and the cypress together,
to adorn my sanctuary;
> and I will glorify the place for my feet. (60:3, 6–7, 9, 11, 13)

Here "the glory and honor of the nations" (Rev. 21:26) are the animals, silver, gold, wood, and so forth that are brought into the new Jerusalem "to adorn [the LORD's] sanctuary" (Isa. 60:13).[75] But who will tend these animals and craft these materials so they can be used in the temple (which for John is the whole new creation)? Presumably, God's people. Indeed, Richard Mouw and Andy Crouch suggest that "the glory and honor of the nations" represent not only the specific creatures and materials mentioned in Isaiah 60 but also the best of the nations' cultural goods more broadly.[76] Building on this interpretation, Crouch comments,

> Much of the glory and honor of the nations, whether epic poetry or baroque fugues or fine cuisine, can be realized only when people "perform" it—when singers sing, chefs cook and dancers dance. . . . It seems likely to me that part of the activity of eternity will be endlessly creative improvisions upon the "glory and honor of the nations"—human beings using

75. See Crouch, *Culture Making*, 167.
76. Richard J. Mouw, *When the Kings Come Marching In: Isaiah and the New Jerusalem* (Grand Rapids: Eerdmans, 2002), 29–30; Crouch, *Culture Making*, 167–69.

their creative capacities to their fullest to explore the depth and breadth of all that human beings made in their vocations as cocreators with God.[77]

Third, John explicitly mentions two actions that God's people will perform in the new creation:

> [3] The throne of God and of the Lamb will be in the city, and his servants will *serve* him. . . . [5] They will not need the light of a lamp or the light of the sun, for the Lord God will give them light. And they will *reign* for ever and ever. (Rev. 22:3, 5)

The verb for "serve" here (*latreuō*) typically refers to performing religious rites (e.g., priestly service) in biblical Greek.[78] However, we must also remember that John envisions the whole new creation as a temple in the shape of the holy of holies (21:16, 22), so *latreuō* would be a natural way to describe any human activity in the new creation (whether "worship" narrowly conceived or "work"). And whatever we make of "serve," "reign" certainly cannot be reduced to singing, praying, and other activities normally associated with worship services. Rather, it would encompass the wide range of activities involved in exercising God's dominion over the new creation, like Adam and Eve's role in the original creation.

Together, these three factors—the echoes of Eden, John's use of Isaiah 60 and 65–66, and the description of God's people serving and reigning with him—suggest that good works are part of God's final and eternal intent for his people. In the new creation, we will have the privilege of doing good to the glory of God, free of all the anxiety and pain that accompany work in the present. By doing good in the present, then, we experience a foretaste of the goodness of the age to come.

Conclusion

The diverse New Testament documents examined above reveal a remarkably unified perspective on the role of good works in salvation. One

77. Crouch, *Culture Making*, 173–74.
78. Danker et al., *Greek-English Lexicon*, 587; Louw and Nida, *Greek-English Lexicon*, §53.14; Johan Lust, Erik Eynikel, and Katrin Hauspie, eds., *Greek-English Lexicon of the Septuagint*, rev. ed., 2 vols. (Stuttgart: Deutsche Bibelgesellschaft, 2003), 2:278.

can perhaps best appreciate this unity by undertaking a brief thought experiment: Imagine that you are a historian studying Christian origins, but the only New Testament documents that have survived are the Gospels, Acts, James, and Revelation. What would you conclude about the role of good works in early Christian thinking about salvation? From the Gospels and Acts, you might conclude that early Christians thought that a cataclysmic event had occurred with Jesus's life, death, resurrection, and ascension and the coming of the Holy Spirit, such that followers of Jesus were empowered (and expected) to live Jesus-shaped lives in the present. From James, you might determine that some early Christians did not live this way and had to be reminded that saying or thinking the right things but doing the wrong ones would not end well on judgment day. From Revelation, you might get more of the same, along with a sense that the first Christians were motivated to live well in the present by a vision of a new creation in which all things, including human work(s), would be fully redeemed. But the underlying message that you would derive from all these documents would be that good works were considered necessary, such that no Jesus-follower should expect to be saved without them.

Such a thought experiment demonstrates the extent to which a certain reading of Paul's writings has caused many modern Christians to de-emphasize works in the New Testament's view of salvation. But as we have seen above, the "works optional" interpretation of Paul is not compelling even as a reading of Paul, and it is even less compelling when we take the rest of the New Testament into account. Paul, of course, places his own accents on the incongruity of grace and the necessity of faith, but he also affirms with Jesus and the other New Testament authors that good works are necessary for salvation.

From Genesis to Revelation, then, we find that Scripture depicts good works as being an essential part of God's intent—original, redemptive, and final—for humans. And this is good news, for it means that God desires not only to declare us "righteous" but also to make us righteous in the here and now so that our lives become a true testament to his saving power.

CHAPTER 4

Holiness as Love of God and Love of Neighbor

Toward a Theology of Good Works

T o this point, we have seen that a positive doctrine of good works is deeply rooted in classical Protestant (as well as, of course, patristic and medieval) theology, and we have seen further that such commitments to the reality, goodness, urgency, and necessity of good works are anchored in Holy Scripture. The Reformers and confessionally aligned scholastic theologians of the major Protestant traditions are convinced that good works are both possible and necessary for those who are justified, regenerate, and sanctified, and they challenge those who follow Christ to good deeds of piety and mercy. And they do so because of the clear and compelling biblical witness to the fact that God's people are created and called to be "zealous for good works" (Titus 2:14 ESV).

We now have the basic elements for a theology of good works, one that is grounded in the goodness of God and motivated by the gracious work of the Father, Son, and Holy Spirit. In what follows, we sketch, albeit with broad strokes, the major affirmations of such a theology.

The God Who Works for and with Us: Trinity and Creation

Scripture informs us that "the LORD is good" (e.g., Ps. 100:5), exhorts us to "give thanks to the LORD, for he is good" (e.g., Pss. 106:1; 107:1), and invites us to "taste and see that the LORD is good" (Ps. 34:8). The biblical witness to the goodness of God is pervasive; it runs broad and deep. Accordingly, Christians have understood goodness to be absolutely fundamental to the doctrine of God. God does not just happen to be good; God is not arbitrarily or contingently good. No, to the contrary, God is wholly good. God is perfectly good. God is necessarily good. God is, in line with the doctrine of divine simplicity, not in any way compromised by internal tension or anything that is not wholly and perfectly good— God can be said to be goodness itself.

This divine goodness can further be understood in terms of holy love. While in God holiness and love are not really different components or elements that are somehow more fundamental than God and of which God is composed, nonetheless we can helpfully think of God's nature in terms of holiness and love. When we say that God is holy, we refer to the sheer otherness and transcendence of God. Holiness is, in the language made famous by Rudolph Otto, the *mysterium tremendum et fascinans* (a mystery that both frightens and fascinates); it is what simultaneously both attracts and repels finite and fallen creatures. It is inherently attractive and luminously beautiful, but it is also dangerous and terrifying to those who are opposed to it. Holiness also refers, in addition to the sheer otherness or transcendence of God, to God's complete and untarnished moral purity. God "is light, and in him there is no darkness at all" (1 John 1:5). God is essentially holy—perfectly and fully and necessarily holy. "Holy, holy, holy is the LORD Almighty; the whole earth is full of his glory" (Isa. 6:3).

God is love (1 John 4:8, 16). Love for someone includes three elements: a desire for the good of the beloved, a desire for union with the beloved, and a delight in the beloved.[1] To be sure, God is loving toward creation: "God so loved the world . . ." (John 3:16). But the love with which God loves the world is nothing arbitrary, for the love with which God loves the world is grounded in the love that God just *is*. God is essentially loving—perfectly and fully and necessarily loving. Indeed, Christians have long understood the biblical affirmation that "God is love" in robustly trinitarian terms: the God whose nature is love is the

---

1. See Petrus van Mastricht, *Theoretico-Practica Theologia*, 2nd ed. (Utrecht, 1698), 2.2.24, p. 237; ET, *Theoretical-Practical Theology*, vol. 2, *Faith in the Triune God*, trans. Todd M. Rester, ed. Joel R. Beeke (Grand Rapids: Reformation Heritage Books, 2019), 503.

triune God whose own life consists of perfect and perfectly pure fellowship between Father, Son, and Holy Spirit. In the window into the intratrinitarian life of the triune God opened by Jesus in his famous "high-priestly" prayer to his Father, we catch a precious glimpse of their eternal relationship of holy love, for there Jesus refers to the love that they shared "before the foundation of the world" (John 17:24 ESV).

So when Christians affirm that God is *good*, the claim is not that God is simply better behaved than creatures or that God partakes of something called "goodness" that is somehow exterior to the divine life. No, the claim is that God is wholly good, necessarily good, perfectly good. The claim is that God's own life is the life of purest and perfect holy love shared between the Father, the Son, and the Holy Spirit. God is light, and in him is no darkness at all—none whatsoever. And God is love, for his own life is the communion of perfect giving and receiving shared between the three divine persons.

Christian theology takes the goodness of God—the moral perfection and holy love of the triune God—to be absolute bedrock. This is who God just is; God is good. And it informs and motivates all that God does. Thus God creates to extend and share goodness with creatures; God sustains and provides to share that goodness with creatures; and God redeems fallen and sinful creatures so that they might be restored to knowledge of that goodness and share in that holy love. As John of Damascus puts it, "God's goodness is revealed in that He did not disregard the frailty of His own handiwork, but was moved with compassion for him in his fall, and stretched forth His hand back to him. . . . In His goodness and justice He made him, who had become through his sins the slave of death, himself once more conqueror and rescued."[2]

God creates from his essential goodness; he creates to share holy love. Thus God's own work in creation is good, and the creation is recognized and declared as such by God (Gen. 1:31). So what Christian theologians have historically referred to as the *opera ad intra*, the works of God that are interior to the divine life (the generation of the Son and the procession of the Spirit), are good. And the works of God *ad extra* in creation, providence, and redemption are also good. They are motivated

---

2. John of Damascus, *The Orthodox Faith* 3.1, in *A Select Library of Nicene and Post-Nicene Fathers of the Christian Church*, 2nd series, ed. Philip Schaff and Henry Wace, 14 vols. (Grand Rapids: Eerdmans, 1988–91), 9:45.

by God's own goodness, and they express and extend that goodness. Indeed, classical Christian teaching maintains that God not only upholds or sustains creaturely agents in existence but also gives them the power to do things and indeed in some sense "concurs" with their actions. Crucial here is the distinction between *primary* and *secondary* causality, for God, as the primary causal agent, works through other agents as secondary causes. Thus when creatures act, they do not do so independently of God. But neither is God the only causal agent, for genuinely free creatures perform actions in the world that are rightly said to be their own. God *conserves* the universe and its creatures in existence, and were it not for God's moment-by-moment sustaining action in caring for the creation, the universe and its creatures would cease to exist. Similarly, God *concurs* with creaturely action, for God not only upholds everything in existence but also grants causal powers to creatures.

God gives causal powers to human creatures who are free, and some events that occur are rightly said to be contingent. In other words, such events might or might not take place. Some events and actions are contingent, and some of these contingent actions are free.[3] God sustains and provides causal powers, but God does not determine all outcomes. Therefore, when God creates humans who are free and morally responsible, he does not make some course of action inevitable. As John of Damascus says, "God knows all things beforehand, yet He does not predetermine all things."[4] And as it turns out, humans misappropriate the good abilities that God has given, and they abandon the good works to which they are called to pursue evil deeds.

Creatures of Godly Vocation: Theological Anthropology

God's creation is pronounced "good" by the perfectly good Creator. But it is not pronounced "very good" until God makes creatures in the divine image. These creatures—humans—are said to be made in the divine image and likeness. The statement that they bear the image of God

3. For further discussion, see Michael J. Dodds, *Unlocking Divine Action: Contemporary Science and Thomas Aquinas* (Washington, DC: Catholic University of America Press, 2012).
4. John of Damascus, *The Orthodox Faith* 2.30, in Schaff and Wace, *Nicene and Post-Nicene Fathers*, 9:42.

comes even before they are made. God does not look at them and only then recognize that they resemble him; to the contrary, the pronouncement comes first and signals divine intentionality (Gen. 1:26). And then, immediately following the creation of the humans, God declares that they bear the sacred image (Gen. 1:27).

As we have seen, (at least) part of what it means for humans to be image-bearers is related to what is sometimes referred to as the "functional" account of the image of God. On this view, being in the image of God is closely related to what God actually says in both the preliminary pronouncement and the subsequent declaration "Let them have dominion . . ." (Gen. 1:26, 28 ESV). The theological context for this command points us toward the multiple relationships given to humans: "vertically," they are related to their Creator, while "horizontally," they are related to one another and to the rest of creation. To be in God's image entails the vocation to care for one another and, indeed, the entirety of creation. To be in God's image brings with it both the responsibility to be rightly related to the Creator and the responsibility to be rightly related to one another and the rest of creation. In other words, to be in God's image brings with it the responsibility for both "works of piety" and "works of mercy."

As we have seen, the biblical story moves very quickly to tragedy, for the fall of humankind unleashes ruin and devastation on creation. We were made for communion with God and loving fellowship with and care for one another, and we were given a responsibility to care for all of creation. Sin is the action of turning away from those proper relationships; it is the rejection of God's goodness and good purposes for us. It is expressed in many ways: sometimes we turn away from God and then turn away from one another in selfishness, sometimes we turn away from God and turn on one another in violent destruction, and always sinners turn to their own way. Sins are committed against God, neighbor, and self. Sins can be committed in culpable ignorance or willful rebellion. Some sins are sins of commission; they are actions that we take. But others are sins of omission, for sometimes we are negligent in actions we should perform. Sins are expressed as greed or avarice, as envy and rage, as pride and vainglory, as gluttony and lust. Notably for our purposes in this study, sin can be expressed not only as outright and volitionally intense acts of rebellion but also as sloth.

In other words, we can sin not only by what we do but also by what we leave undone. As Rebecca Konyndyk DeYoung says, sloth is "apathy— comfortable indifference to duty and neglect of others' needs."[5] It is sin "not merely because it makes us lazy but because of the lack of love that lies behind that laziness."[6]

We can summarize the doctrine of sin in this way:

> Sin is whatever is opposed to God's will, as that will reflects God's holy character and as that will is expressed by God's commands. Sin is funda- mentally opposed to nature and reason, and it is ultimately opposed to God. The results of sin are catastrophic—sin wreaks havoc on our relation- ships with God, with one another, and the rest of creation. It is universal in human history and manifests itself in various cultural expressions. It wrecks human lives, and it leaves us broken and vulnerable. It also leaves us needing grace and longing for redemption.[7]

God for Us, God with Us: Union with Christ and Life in the Spirit

The redemption for which we long has been provided by God, and the grace that we need has indeed been lavished freely on wayward and rebellious sinners. As we have seen, God begins this process of redemp- tion by making a series of promises or covenants. These covenants are established by the gracious initiative of God, and they provide oppor- tunity for response. These covenants also come with obligations, for while God's grace is *unconditioned*, it is not, strictly speaking, *uncondi- tional*.[8] God calls and then makes a covenant with Abram (Gen. 12:1–3; 15:1–20), and in this covenant he promises not only to bless Abram and his descendants but also to bless the entire creation through him. God repeats, extends, and expands this promise when he makes a covenant with Moses (Exod. 19:1–6); here God reminds his people of his gracious work on their behalf, and he tells them that because the entire earth belongs to him, he is making them to be a "kingdom of priests" and a

---

5. Rebecca Konyndyk DeYoung, *Glittering Vices: A New Look at the Seven Deadly Sins and Their Remedies*, 2nd ed. (Grand Rapids: Brazos, 2020), 89.

6. DeYoung, *Glittering Vices*, 89.

7. Thomas H. McCall, *Against God and Nature: The Doctrine of Sin*, Foundations of Evangelical Theology (Wheaton: Crossway, 2019), 21.

8. The distinction is from John M. G. Barclay, *Paul and the Gift* (Grand Rapids: Eerdmans, 2015), 500.

"holy people" (Exod. 19:6). They are, accordingly, to represent God to the nations and the peoples of the world to God. And they are to fulfill this role—to be a "priestly kingdom"—precisely by sharing and reflecting God's character of holy love to their neighbors.

Similarly, the Davidic covenant (2 Sam. 7:1–17) specifies that the divine promises will be fulfilled in the house and lineage of David, for the coming Redeemer will be a "son of David." And God's action through the Davidic kingdom will bring about a new covenant:

> "The days are coming," declares the LORD, "when I will make a new covenant with the people of Israel and with the people of Judah. It will not be like the covenant I made with their ancestors when I took them by the hand to lead them out of Egypt, because they broke my covenant, though I was a husband to them," declares the LORD. "This is the covenant I will make. . . . I will put my law in their minds and write it on their hearts. I will be their God, and they will be my people. No longer will they teach their neighbor, or say to one another, 'Know the LORD,' because they will all know me, from the least of them to the greatest," declares the LORD. "For I will forgive their wickedness and will remember their sins no more." (Jer. 31:31–34)

This covenant has been fulfilled in the person and work of Jesus Christ. This is evident on the very first page of the New Testament, for the genealogy that begins Matthew's Gospel both identifies Jesus Christ as "the son of David, the son of Abraham" (Matt. 1:1) and also informs us that he is called "Immanuel," which means "God with us" (Matt. 1:23), and is named "Jesus" because he will "save his people from their sins" (Matt. 1:21). Jesus is the "climax of the covenant."[9] As such, he comes as "Prophet, Priest, and King." He comes to teach his people and to embody an example of how to bring glory to God by his good works and substitutionary death. For "Christ suffered for you, leaving you an example, that you should follow in his steps" (1 Pet. 2:21); therefore, followers of Jesus "ought to walk in the same way in which he walked" (1 John 2:6 ESV). He comes to provide the final sacrifice for the sins of the people. God "made him who had no sin to be a sin offering, so that in him we might become the

---

9. N. T. Wright, *The Climax of the Covenant: Christ and the Law in Pauline Theology* (Minneapolis: Fortress, 1993).

righteousness of God" (2 Cor. 5:21 NIV mg.). He "suffered once for sins, the righteous for the unrighteous, to bring you to God" (1 Pet. 3:18). Giving his life as a "ransom for many" (Mark 10:45), he comes to defeat sin, death, and the devil. "Since the children have flesh and blood, he too shared in their humanity so that by his death he might break the power of him who holds the power of death—that is, the devil—and free those who all their lives were held in slavery" (Heb. 2:14–15). For "the reason the Son of God appeared was to destroy the devil's work" (1 John 3:8).

Christ came to do good works on behalf of his people. But while he indeed does perform such good works for others, so also he calls those who are redeemed by him to do good works. Significantly, he insists that love of God and love of neighbor cannot be separated. When asked which commandment in the law is the greatest, Jesus does not hesitate: "'Love the Lord your God with all your heart and with all your soul and with all your mind.' This is the greatest and first commandment" (Matt. 22:37–38). But while there was only one question and Jesus has already answered it, he will not rest content until he adds, "And the second is like it: 'Love your neighbor as yourself'" (22:39). And then he clarifies further, "All the Law and the Prophets hang on these two commandments" (22:40). It is interesting to note that, in the dialogue as presented in the Gospel, Jesus is only asked one question. The interlocutor wants to know only about the most important question. But while the questioner might be satisfied to separate the two, Jesus is not. To the contrary, he refuses to allow these to be divided or separated. He clearly distinguishes them, and he leaves no room for doubt: love for God is primary and ultimate. But he just as clearly refuses to allow consideration of love for God without also adding that love of neighbor is vitally important and essential to discipleship.

Note carefully Jesus's clarifying remark: all the Law and the Prophets are based upon these two commandments, and all the Law and the Prophets can be summed up accordingly. The first and greatest commandment echoes the first table of the Decalogue, while the second commandment summarizes and encapsulates the second table. Likewise, the first table is reflected directly in the actions of "works of piety," and the second is concerned with "works of mercy." And who is the "neighbor" to whom these works of mercy are to be given? Jesus makes the answer to this question unmistakably clear as well; when asked this question, he tells a story about a man who was attacked, robbed, and beaten. In this story, two religious leaders and authorities ignore the broken victim, whereas a "Samaritan" is "moved with pity" and takes sacrificial steps to help (Luke 10:33–34). Jesus asks, "Which of these three do you think was a neighbor to the man who fell into the hands of the robbers?" (10:36). When the respondent correctly answers, "The one who had mercy on him," Jesus tells him, "Go and do likewise" (10:37).

But Christ does not merely call us to emulate his example, for his relation to those saved by him runs much deeper. Paul's characteristic language for this relation is "union with Christ." Paul's language in the second chapter of Galatians is especially striking. Here he makes it clear that no one is justified by doing the "works of the law" (v. 16), but he also goes on to say, "I have been crucified with Christ and I no longer live, but Christ lives in me. The life I now live in the body, I live by faith in the Son of God, who loved me and gave himself for me" (vv. 19–20). Paul is not talking about some mystical union that destroys or undoes personal identity.[10] But neither is he referring only to an inspiring example seen at a distance. No, he is talking about a close interpersonal bond or union with Christ, one that deeply transforms the persons in it.

Recent work on "joint attention" is relevant here. "Joint attention" refers to the mutual closeness and shared attention that two persons share in close relation to each other. Somewhat like how a mother immediately and intuitively shares the thoughts and feelings of her young child who is being bullied or terrorized, or how two lovers come to share a deep connection to mutual delights and joys, so too those joined in union with Christ come to know and share Christ's affections and passions. In other words, the one joined in union with Christ comes to know and share, however imperfectly, the feelings of love and wrath, kindness and empathy, joy and sorrow that are experienced by Christ himself. It is to share the compassion and passion of Christ for those who are weighed down and distressed by sin. It is to hate what Christ hates and love what Christ loves. It is not to lose one's personal identity, but it is to have that personal identity reshaped and reclaimed and ultimately perfected by the presence and power of Christ.[11] Thus when

10. For further discussion, see Thomas H. McCall, *Analytic Christology and the Theological Interpretation of the New Testament* (Oxford: Oxford University Press, 2021), 7–38.
11. This paragraph echoes McCall, *Analytic Christology*, 35.

we are told that we are God's handiwork, "created in Christ Jesus to do good works" (Eph. 2:10), we are being called into union with Christ. We are not being commanded to do something to impress Christ. Nor are we even being called merely to emulate Christ (although there is truth to such a claim). Instead, we are being called into union with Christ's work—not only to do good works for him, but also to do good works *with* him.

It is vitally important for any fully Christian account of good works to realize that Christ does not merely provide an example. Nor does he simply call us into solidarity with him in his sufferings on behalf of others (as remarkable as that is). No, there is much more: Christ said that it was better for his disciples that he goes away because he will send another "Paraclete" (John 16:5–15). This Paraclete, whom Christ will send, is the Holy Spirit, and he will "prove the world to be in the wrong about sin and righteousness and judgment" and lead his people into truth while bringing glory to the Son and Father (John 16:8–14). This coming of the Spirit happens at Pentecost and brings profound consequences: the Spirit empowers for witness and service, and the gospel is proclaimed with force and lived with world-changing power (Acts 2).

What does all this have to do with good works? As it turns out, Christology and pneumatology matter immensely for a properly Christian understanding of the doctrine of good works. It is clear from Scripture, both the Old Testament and the New, that God's people are called and commanded to love God wholeheartedly and their neighbors similarly. But in no sense are the people of God thrown back upon themselves and simply told to go do good deeds. And in no sense is there any possibility that salvation is to be merited or earned by those good works. In other words, to understand the first and greatest commandment and the second commandment as exhortations to make oneself better in hopes that God will be suitably impressed and favorable is to completely misunderstand the theology. No, no indeed! Rather than simply issue commands and wait for results, God takes drastic action on our behalf. God, in the person of the Son, actually enters the finite and fallen world as human. God the Son, incarnate as Jesus Christ, suffers and dies, and then he rises again in power and newness of life. In doing so, he both "breaks the power of canceled sin" and "sets the prisoner free."[12] He both provides an empowering example and defeats the sin that enslaves. He invites people into union with himself, and by that union he fundamentally transforms them into his own likeness. Upon his ascension, he sends the Holy Spirit to cleanse and empower his people for worship and service.

So when God's people live out their faith in good works of piety and good works of mercy, they do so in union and communion with the triune God. They do not do so as enemies who hope for leniency. They do so not merely as servants dutifully fulfilling obligations in hopes of reward. To the contrary, when God's people live into their faith in good works of piety, they are joining into the communion of the triune God. When they worship, they are, by virtue of their union with Christ and represented by his continuing priesthood, included in the fellowship of the Father, Son, and Spirit.[13] And when they serve their neighbors in good works of mercy, they are joining in the mission of the triune God to extend God's grace and share God's goodness in the world. They do so as people who are filled with and empowered by the Spirit of life.

Working Out Our Own Salvation: The *Via Salutis* and the Christian Life

Prevenient Grace and the Perennial Struggle with Pelagianism

As we have seen, the theologians of the classical Protestant confessions are deeply concerned not only about losing the doctrine of good works but also about abusing it. They are exercised to avoid any notion that salvation can be earned or merited. And for good reason, for the temptation toward Pelagianism is both strong and perennial. Associated with the fourth-century theologian Pelagius, who insisted on the importance of moral responsibility and who rejected the doctrines of original sin, Pelagianism can be summarized as (1) the denial of original sin (with respect not only to the guilt of original sin but also to any residual corrupting impact on the affections and volition of the human agent), along with (2) the denial of the need for any grace that exerts a "special

12. Charles Wesley, "O for a Thousand Tongues," in *Hymns for Praise and Worship* (Nappanee, IN: Evangel, 1984), no. 81.

13. See further James B. Torrance, *Worship, Community and the Triune God of Grace* (Downers Grove, IL: InterVarsity, 1997).

pressure" on the human will and (3) the accompanying insistence that we somehow initiate and cause our own salvation by exercising our faith and performing good works.[14] Similarly, what is sometimes known as semi-Pelagianism is the belief that the beginning of human salvation is (or, at least in some cases, may be) from humans rather than God, for while we are deeply wounded, at least some human agents are not so deeply damaged to the point that we cannot at least initiate the salvation that God may then bring to completion.[15]

Lutheran, Anglican, and Reformed (including Remonstrant, or Arminian) theologians alike resist and reject the lure of Pelagianism, and they warn against thinking of good works in a Pelagian or semi-Pelagian manner. And for good reason. Human sinners are "not able to serve the Lord, for he is a holy God" (Josh. 24:19 ESV). They are "dead in . . . transgressions and sins" (Eph. 2:1). John Barclay is correct when he says, "Paul has diagnosed the human condition as senseless (Rom. 1:21), hardened, and incapable of repentance (Rom. 2:5)."[16]

Moreover, the Christian gospel gives us the resources to avoid such traps. For as we have seen, the good news about good works is that God has acted initially and preveniently so that we might respond. In other words, God has done good works in Christ so that we might be able to do good works in union with Christ as we are filled with the Holy Spirit. So while it is true that God's people are called and commanded to do good works, it is also true that any truly Christian doctrine of good works is about grace from first to last.

But how, more precisely, are good works related to salvation? In this section, we will explore the doctrine of good works in relation to the entire "way [or "order"] of salvation"—the *via salutis*. In doing so, we must emphasize how vitally important it is to recognize that the doctrine of salvation is broader than the doctrine of justification. Justification

14. We draw this summary from McCall, *Against God and Nature*, 299. The phrase "special pressure" is drawn from J. N. D. Kelly, *Early Christian Doctrines*, 2nd ed. (New York: Harper & Row, 1960), 359.

15. The label "semi-Pelagian" is problematic from the perspective of historical theology. We use it here only for convenience. For further discussion, see Irena Backus and Aza Goudriaan, "'Semipelagianism': The Origins of the Term and Its Passage into the History of Heresy," *Journal of Ecclesiastical History* 65, no. 1 (2014): 25–46; Owen Chadwick, *John Cassian*, 2nd ed. (Cambridge: Cambridge University Press, 1968), 127; Thomas H. McCall and Keith D. Stanglin, *Jacob Arminius: Theologian of Grace* (Oxford: Oxford University Press, 2012), 157–64.

16. John M. G. Barclay, *Paul and the Gift* (Grand Rapids: Eerdmans, 2015), 463–64.

is an essential element of salvation, but it is not the whole or sum of it. To the contrary, while it is an essential element, it is only one such element. The doctrine of justification continues to attract a great deal of attention at various levels, both popular and scholarly. Such attention may be entirely appropriate and completely warranted, but it should not distract us from the broader and deeper aspects of salvation. It is important to underscore this point because it is not uncommon in evangelical theology to conflate justification with salvation. As an example, recall the claims of Millard Erickson when he says, "Salvation is not by works. A person is declared righteous in the sight of God, not because of having done good works but because of having believed."[17] Erickson insists that good works are only the evidence of saving faith but have no role to play beyond that. When considering biblical passages that would seem to teach the necessity of good works for salvation, Erickson says that when such passages are "seen in their context and in relation to texts that speak of justification by faith," they "do not teach that works are a means of receiving salvation."[18] Erickson's statement tracks well with historic Protestant teaching on justification in this respect: with the confessional Protestants, he is insisting that justification is by grace through faith rather than works. But notice that his statement departs rather sharply from historic Protestant teaching by subtly equating justification with salvation *simpliciter*: "salvation" is being "declared righteous." And when Erickson denies that works are a "means of receiving salvation," he is diametrically opposed to important strands of classical Reformed doctrine. For as we have seen, major Reformed theologians of the tradition explicitly affirm that good works are necessary for salvation precisely as a means of receiving it. And such works of piety and mercy are indeed necessary. As John Davenant puts it, "It is impossible to reach the goal of salvation when the pursuit of good works is altogether evaded and rejected."[19] With this reminder to take a broader view of salvation in mind, let us now turn to a closer look at good works in relation to important elements of the order of salvation.

17. Millard J. Erickson, *Christian Theology*, 3rd ed. (Grand Rapids: Baker Academic, 2013), 938.

18. Erickson, *Christian Theology*, 940; cf. Michael F. Bird, *Evangelical Theology: A Biblical and Systematic Introduction* (Grand Rapids: Zondervan, 2013), 569–70.

19. John Davenant, *A Treatise on Justification; or, The Disputatio de Justitia Habituali et Actuali; Together with Translations of the "Determinationes" of the Same Prelate, by the Rev. Josiah Allport*, vol. 1 (London: Hamilton, Adams, 1844), 302.

Justice and Judgment: Good Works and the Doctrine of Justification

We begin with the doctrine of justification. According to traditional Protestant teaching, it is common to affirm that justification concerns the legal status of sinners before a holy God. The connotations are legal or forensic. Justification concerns the imputation of righteousness from Christ to sinners. The work is instantaneous, and it is what God in Christ does *for* the sinner. The Westminster Shorter Catechism defines justification as "an act of God's free grace, wherein he pardons all our sins, and accepts us as righteous in his sight, only for the righteousness imputed to us, and received by faith alone."[20] John Calvin explains that justification is "the acceptance with which God receives us into his favor as if we were righteous; and we say that this justification consists in the forgiveness of sins and the imputation of the righteousness of Christ."[21] With respect to justification, John Wesley says that he believes "just as Mr. Calvin does. . . . I do not differ from him a hair's breadth."[22] He says further, "Faith is the necessary condition of justification"—indeed, it is the "*only necessary* condition" of it.[23] He repeatedly, clearly, and explicitly says that justification is the legal declaration by God in which the sinner is acquitted of sin, and he insists that this gracious work of God is accessed by the faith that produces union with Christ.[24] He says, "I believe in justification by faith alone, as much as I believe there is a God."[25] On these points Wesley is right in line with the declaration made by the Anglican Thirty-Nine Articles and the Methodist Articles of Religion: "We are accounted righteous before God only for the merit of our Lord and Savior Jesus Christ by faith, and not for our works or deservings. Wherefore, that we are justified by faith only is a most wholesome doctrine and very full of comfort."[26]

---

20. The Westminster Shorter Catechism, Q. 33, in *The Evangelical Protestant Creeds, with Translations*, vol. 3 of *The Creeds of Christendom: With a History and Critical Notes,* ed. Philip Schaff (Grand Rapids: Baker Academic, 2007), 683.

21. John Calvin, *Institutes of the Christian Religion,* trans. Henry Beveridge, 2 vols. (Grand Rapids: Eerdmans, 1989), 3.11, p. 2:38.

22. John Wesley, "Letter to John Newton," quoted in Kenneth J. Collins, *The Scripture Way of Salvation: The Heart of John Wesley's Theology* (Nashville: Abingdon, 1997), 67.

23. John Wesley, "Justification by Faith," in *Wesley's 52 Standard Sermons,* ed. N. Burwash (Salem, OH: Schmul, 1988), 49.

24. See the discussion in Collins, *Scripture Way of Salvation,* 69–100.

25. John Wesley, "Remarks on a Defense of Aspasio Vindicated," quoted in Collins, *Scripture Way of Salvation,* 95.

26. Compare "The Thirty-Nine Articles of the Church of England," art. 11, with "The Methodist Articles of Religion," art. 9, in Schaff, *Evangelical Protestant Creeds,* 494, 809.

Where do good works come into view? Recall Francis Turretin's distinctions: good works are "related to justification not *antecedently, efficiently,* and *meritoriously,* but consequently and declaratively."[27] Good works, as such, are not antecedent to justification. In other words, such activities do not come before God's justifying activity (for good deeds by the unconverted do not come from proper motivations and thus are not, strictly speaking, good works). Good works are not "efficient" to justification. No human exercises efficient causality with respect to justification; put bluntly, no one can be the effective causal agent of one's own justification. Nor are good works in any way meritorious for justification. Simply put, no one earns justification.

So much for good works related negatively to justification. Now that we know what is not done by the performance of good works, what can we say truthfully and positively about good works in relation to justification? Turretin says that we should affirm that good works are related to justification *consequently* and *declaratively.* They are related *consequently,* for good works are the necessary consequence of genuinely justifying faith. One cannot have such faith without having good works follow from it. Just as a good tree produces good fruit (rather than bad fruit or no fruit at all), so also a justified person is active in works of piety and mercy. Moreover, such works are related to justification *declaratively,* for good works are the herald of Christ's righteousness that has been accredited or imputed to repentant and believing sinners.

Turretin provides a helpful summary of the relation of good works to the doctrine of justification. Good works do not merit justification. Such activities, no matter how sincere or frenetic, do not somehow serve as an efficient cause of justification. Nor do such good works somehow obligate God to pronounce the sinner righteous. To the contrary, justification is always by grace and only by grace. Sinners are justified by what God has done for them in Christ, and all good works will flow from that and testify to the reality of the good work that God has done on behalf of sinners, who cannot save themselves. At the same time, however, such works of piety and mercy—love of God and love of neighbor—really do follow from such genuine and lively faith. The technical language of the

---

27. Francis Turretin, *Institutes of Elenctic Theology,* trans. George Musgrave Giger, ed. James T. Dennison Jr., 3 vols. (Phillipsburg, NJ: P&R, 1994), 2:705 (italics added). Turretin's Latin original, *Institutio Theologiae Elencticae,* was published in three parts in Geneva, between 1679 and 1685.

scholastics helps us immensely in our understanding of justification in relation to good works: such works are vitally important, but they follow from justification and bear witness to it.

New Life in Christ: Good Works and the Doctrine of Regeneration

We can reason similarly about the doctrine of regeneration or the "new birth." Whereas the doctrine of justification considers the legal standing of the sinner before God, with the doctrine of regeneration the language shifts from forensic accounting and legal pronouncements to the family. Here we are talking about newness of life and entrance into the filial relationships that bind and sustain. And here again we can say that regeneration, as the point of entry into new life, is not related to good works according to merit. No one gives life to themselves, and no one earns the right to be born. To the contrary, good works play no role whatsoever in the new birth with respect to efficient causality or meritorious credit. Instead, we should see good works as the genuine and normal consequence of regeneration. Just as new birth is the celebration of new life that is active and growing, so also good works are the visible and tangible sign of regeneration.

Filled with the Spirit: Good Works and the Doctrine of Sanctification

The situation is very different when we consider the doctrine of sanctification. Theologically, sanctification refers to the work that God does within the believer. Whereas justification concerns legal status and refers to forensic righteousness that is imputed, sanctification is concerned with the person and refers to real or actual righteousness that is infused or imparted and is thus inherent in the believer. Whereas the pronouncement of justification is instantaneous, the work of sanctification is progressive and ongoing (though marked by singularly important punctiliar moments). Whereas justification refers to the work of Christ *for* the believer, sanctification refers to the work of the Holy Spirit to apply the benefits of Christ's sacrificial death and victorious resurrection *in* the life of the believer.

It is true that various Protestant theologies harbor long-standing and important disagreements about sanctification. And it would be problematic to overlook these differences. But it would also be a mistake to ignore or downplay the very important common ground shared by Lutheran, Reformed, Anglican, and Wesleyan understandings of sanctification. All reject any notion that sanctification is somehow an optional add-on feature of salvation—as if to really be saved is merely to be justified. All affirm that when God saves a person, not only is the person's legal status changed, but so is the *person*. All reject views that reduce salvation to justification, and all affirm that salvation brings decisive transformation. All believe that salvation turns sinners into saints.

This commitment to the reality and necessity of sanctification is evident in Anglican theology (and, of course, in the Wesleyan reception and development of that theology). For instance, Thomas Cranmer (1489–1556) says that the genuine faith of justification is always accompanied by repentance and holiness. Any so-called faith that does not produce the good works that are the fruit of holiness is "a dead, devilish, counterfeit, and feigned faith."[28] Any notion that justifying faith renders sanctification irrelevant or that frees us "from doing all good works" is a "phantasy," and if anyone holds or defends this position, they "trifle with God, and deceive themselves."[29] Similarly, Richard Hooker (1554–1600) teaches that sanctification is "that baptism with heavenly fire which both illumineth and inflameth. This worketh in man that knowledge of God and that love unto things divine whereupon our eternal felicity endureth."[30] This sanctification is necessary, for "Pelagius urged labour for the attainment of eternal life without necessity of God's grace; if we teach grace without the necessity of man's labour, we use one error as a nail to drive out another."[31]

The Reformed theological tradition holds a very similar position. For theologians such as John Calvin, the basis and foundation of salvation is union with Christ. Union with Christ is the root, and from it various branches extend. When we are joined by faith in union with Christ, his legal benefits are extended to us: we are justified by faith as

---

28. Thomas Cranmer, "Homily of Salvation," in *The Works of Thomas Cranmer*, ed. John Edmund Cox, 2 vols. (Cambridge: Cambridge University Press, 1846), 2:133.

29. Thomas Cranmer, "A Short Declaration of the True, Lively, and Christian Faith," in Cox, *Works of Thomas Cranmer*, 2:136.

30. Richard Hooker, "Sanctifying Grace," in *Golden Words: A Selection of Eloquent Extracts from the Writings of the Most Eminent Divines of the Fifteenth, Sixteenth, and Seventeenth Centuries* (London: Ward, Lock, & Tyler, 1863), 288.

31. Hooker, "Sanctifying Grace," 289.

his righteousness is imputed to us. And when we are joined by faith in union with Christ, other benefits are extended as well: this same union not only changes our legal status—it also changes *us*. The transformation goes so deep that it is rightly said to be "of the soul itself."[32] While it is to be distinguished from justification, sanctification can never be truly separated. As Calvin says, while sinners "are justified freely by faith alone, yet that holiness of life, real holiness, as it is called, is inseparable from the free imputation of righteousness."[33] "Do we not see," he asks, "that the Lord justifies his people freely, and at the same time renews them in true holiness by the sanctification of the Spirit?"[34] The Lord, he reminds us, has promised to "purge us from all iniquity and defilement."[35] Other Reformed theologians defend views that are very similar. For instance, Johannes Wollebius (1589–1629) and Amandus Polanus (1561–1610) maintain that sanctification demands our cooperation with God's prevenient and operating grace, and they insist as well that it addresses the entire person by cleansing the intellect, will, and affections.[36] Zacharias Ursinus (1534–83) similarly defends the doctrine that one can never be justified without also being sanctified.[37] Johannes Heidegger (1633–98) even says that sanctification is our greatest need (*sanctificationis summa necessitas est*).[38] Petrus van Mastricht (1630–1706) and Lucas Trelcatius Jr. (1573–1607) agree that sanctification is nothing less than necessary.[39] We can summarize the salient points: For the Reformed theological tradition, sanctification is a very present and beautiful reality. It is also an essential element of salvation; it is necessary for salvation. So if salvation necessarily includes sanctification, and if good works are necessary for sanctification, then it follows that good works are necessary for salvation. The Reformed do not hesitate to draw this conclusion.

32. Calvin, *Institutes* 3.3, p. 1:513.
33. Calvin, *Institutes* 3.3, p. 1:509.
34. Calvin, *Institutes* 3.3, p. 1:525.
35. Calvin, *Institutes* 3.3, p. 1:520.
36. E.g., Johannes Wollebius, *Christianae Theologiae Compendium* (Basel, 1634), 1.31.3–9, pp. 258–59; Amandus Polanus, *Syntagma Theologiae Christianae* (Basel, 1609), 6.36–37, pp. 2933–3030.
37. See the discussion in Heinrich Heppe, *Reformed Dogmatics: Set Out and Illustrated from the Sources*, ed. Ernst Bizer, trans. G. T. Thomson (London: Allen & Unwin, 1950), 566.
38. Johannes Heidegger, *Corpus Theologiae Christianae* (Zurich, 1700), 23.7, p. 314.
39. E.g., Petrus van Mastricht, *Theoretico-Practica Theologica*, 2nd ed. (Utrecht, 1698), 6.13.7, p. 745; Lucas Trelcatius Jr., *Disputatio Theologica de Justificatione Hominis Coram Deo* 20 (Leiden, 1604), 386.

Sometimes the Lutheran position is taken to be opposed to such an emphasis on sanctification, and sometimes Lutheran theology is understood to reject the claim that sanctification is necessary for salvation. Gerhard Forde, a Lutheran theologian who has been very influential in the latter twentieth and early twenty-first centuries, asserts that sanctification is only "the art of getting used to justification."[40] He regards talk of sanctification as problematic; it is at any rate "dangerous" and in some cases can produce a "disaster."[41] He thinks that to admit the necessity or reality of "cooperation" with grace threatens the gospel, for then "*everything* eventually depends on the human contribution."[42] Rather than encouraging the development of a doctrine of sanctification, Forde trumpets Luther's famous dictum that we are *simul justus et peccator* (at the same time righteous and a sinner), and he boldly endorses Luther's infamous advice to his colleague Philip Melanchthon, "Be a sinner and sin boldly, but believe even more boldly and rejoice in Christ."[43]

But to read Luther this way is to misunderstand him profoundly. It is one thing to say that if—in our best efforts to follow Jesus in lives of wholehearted discipleship—we fall short of God's standard of righteousness and realize that even our good works are still tainted by selfishness and sin, we should not despair but should press forward toward the mark. That is one sense of "sin boldly, but believe even more boldly and rejoice in Christ." But it is another thing entirely to simply shrug off Christ's call to discipleship with a nonchalant or even defiant attitude. That is a very different sense of "sin boldly, but believe even more boldly." And Luther quite clearly intends something much more like the former. He says, "Good works follow faith, renewal, and forgiveness. Whatever is still sinful or imperfect in those works will not be accounted as sin or defect, for the sake of . . . Christ. The whole man, in respect both of his person and of his works, shall be accounted and shall be righteous and holy through the pure grace and mercy" of our

---

40. Gerhard Forde, "The Lutheran View," in *Christian Spirituality: Five Views*, ed. Donald L. Alexander (Downers Grove, IL: InterVarsity, 1988), 13.

41. Forde, "Lutheran View," 15; Gerhard Forde, "The Christian Life," in *Christian Dogmatics*, ed. Carl Braaten and Robert W. Jenson, 2 vols. (Minneapolis: Fortress, 1984), 2:396.

42. Forde, "Christian Life," 2:406–7 (italics in original).

43. Forde, "Christian Life," 2:438–39; Forde, "Lutheran View," 23–27.

Lord.[44] Luther is clearly not endorsing any stance of nonchalance or defiance. When he refers to what is sinful and imperfect, he is talking about remaining imperfections in our best efforts to follow Christ in obedience and loyalty. His view of salvation encompasses not only being "accounted" righteous but also truly being *made* righteous. For the grace that saves not only justifies but also truly makes holy.

According to Luther, there is "no such Christ that died for sinners who do not, after the forgiveness of sins, desist from sins and lead a new life."[45] Christians are truly and rightly called "a Christian holy people."[46] Indeed, those who are rightly called "Christians" are those who "have the Holy Spirit" who "sanctifies them daily, not only through the forgiveness of sins acquired for them by Christ, but also through the abolition, the purging, the mortification of sins, on the basis of which they are called a holy people."[47] For the historic Lutheran tradition as well as other Protestant confessions, sanctification is both a precious promise and a beautiful reality.

Again, how is all this related to the doctrine of good works? What do good works have to do with sanctification? It is helpful again to recall Turretin's summary: good works are "related to sanctification constitutively because they constitute and promote it."[48] It is at this point that the common Reformed insistence that good works are a *means* of salvation is appropriate. For it is by doing good works of piety—private, family, and public or corporate worship of God—that we are transformed. If there is a sense in which it is true that we become what we worship, then it is in our worship that we are made more like God. It is in our adoration of God, in our humble posture as worshipers before God, that we come to know God better and are drawn deeper into the triune life of holy love. It is in the confessions of our shortcomings and sins that we contemplate the greatness of our Savior and the gloriousness of our salvation. It is in the proclamation of the Word in preaching that we encounter the good news of the good works that God has done for us

---

44. Martin Luther, Smalcald Articles 3.13, in *Martin Luther's Basic Theological Writings*, ed. Timothy Lull (Minneapolis: Fortress, 1989), 534.

45. Martin Luther, "On the Councils and the Church," *Luther's Works*, vol. 41, *Church and Ministry III* (St. Louis: Concordia; Philadelphia: Fortress, 1970), 114.

46. Luther, "On the Councils and the Church," 143.

47. Luther, "On the Councils and the Church," 143–44.

48. Turretin, *Institutes*, 2:705.

in Christ, that we hear again the good news of the good works to which we are called, that we are reminded again of the presence of the Holy Spirit to heal and to hold, to cleanse and to empower for service. It is in the celebration of the Eucharist that we encounter Christ and live ever further into the mystery of godliness. And it is also by doing good works of mercy—service to our neighbors—that we are transformed. It is in acts of service that we are reminded both of our needs and of our reliance on grace. It is in the self-giving to which we are called that we see the one who gave himself for us. It is in the presence of those who are needy—sometimes especially in the presence of the needy who are not deserving—that we experience grace by both giving and receiving it.

So good works are a means (or "medium") of God's sanctifying work; indeed, they can rightly be considered instrumental causes that God uses to transform his people. And as sanctification is an essential element of salvation, we can and should conclude that good works are means and even causes of salvation.

Life Everlasting: Good Works and the Doctrine of Glorification

Recall once again Francis Turretin's statement: good works "are related to glorification antecedently and ordinatively because they are related to it as the means to the end; yea, as the beginning to the complement because grace is glory begun, as glory is grace consummated."[49] He says that good works are *antecedent* to glorification. Good works are done before the time of glorification. And he adds that they are *ordained* by God. More specifically, they are ordained by God as the *means* by which glorification happens. They are used by God to shape and mold the redeemed person into the full likeness of Christ. In this sense, they are like the tools or instruments—indeed, akin to an instrumental cause—by which God does this great work.

In no sense, then, are good works meritorious. They are not the currency by which one earns salvation. No amount of good deeds removes the need for grace. The divine pronouncement of justification is by grace alone through faith alone. Nonetheless, in the God-ordained order (or "way") of salvation, good works are the instrument by which God's people are transformed to love holiness and live righteously. Good

49. Turretin, *Institutes*, 2:705.

works are not, as Turretin says, meant to return us to life under the bondage of legalism; to the contrary, they are necessary "because we live by the gospel."[50]

A Kingdom of Priests and a Holy People: The Church as the Community of Good Works

The church is the community called to God. It is the community of those who belong to the covenant; it is the people redeemed by God and called to live in holiness. It is the community of faith, the people who are called to be "zealous for good works" (Titus 2:14 ESV). Peter identifies the church as the people of God by recalling language used in the old covenant: "But you are a chosen people, a royal priesthood, a holy nation, God's special possession, that you may declare the praises of him who called you out of darkness into his marvelous light. Once you were not a people, but now you are the people of God; once you had not received mercy, but now you have received mercy" (1 Pet. 2:9–10). Here we see points that are central to ecclesiology. The doctrine of election is here: "Once you were not a people, but now you are the people of God." The doctrine of priesthood is here: God has chosen this people to represent himself to the world and the world to himself. The doctrine of holiness is here, for those who are chosen by God to serve as his priestly representatives in the world are said to be "holy." In other words, they represent, in visible, tangible, living form, not only divine "otherness" but also the divine moral purity. God's people are, then, "one holy, catholic, and apostolic" church.[51] They are a holy people who are called and commissioned to represent God and God's intentions for the world through their worship and service.

They proclaim the goodness of God and the goodness of God's intentions for the world through their good works of piety. Through their worship, as both the "gathered church" and the "scattered church," the people of God honor God and love the Lord their God with all their heart, soul, and strength. In their celebration of the Eucharist, they recall and receive once again the giving of Christ on their behalf. In the

---

50. Turretin, *Institutes*, 2:705.
51. The Nicene Creed, in *The Book of Concord: The Confessions of the Evangelical Lutheran Church*, ed. Robert Kolb and Timothy J. Wengert (Minneapolis: Fortress, 2000), 23.

proclamation of the Word in preaching, they again and again recount the goodness of God in action on behalf of those who have rebelled against their Creator.

And God's people proclaim the goodness of God and the goodness of God's intentions for the world through their good works of mercy. For through their active and engaged service to others, they demonstrate in tangible and powerful ways the mercy and justice of the Holy One. When they act in intentional acts of self-giving love—serving in soup kitchens and prisons, giving gladly and sacrificially, standing against injustice and on behalf of the oppressed and vulnerable, speaking for those who have no voice, receiving immigrants and refugees with hospitality, honoring those whose lives are deemed inferior or "useless"— they show what it means to be a "holy people" who are "God's own." It is precisely through such good works of mercy and justice that they serve to represent God to the world. Good works, then, are not accidental to the nature and mission of the church. To the contrary, good works of mercy and good works of piety are nothing less than essential.

From Goodness to Goodness: Eschatological Reflections on Good Works

Protology, the study of "first things" (the doctrine of creation), is closely related in Christian theology to eschatology, the study of "last things." As we have seen, God's plan from the beginning is for his people to be those who do good works. The doctrine of good works is grounded in protology, for God creates and commissions the creatures made in his image to worship him and serve one another. And it comes to fullness in eschatology, for here we see the telos, or "end," of good works.

Judgment and Damnation

On one hand, we must take full account of the serious and even dire warnings given in Scripture. Let us turn again to a consideration of the teaching of Jesus about the final judgment. In his famous parable of the talents, Jesus recounts the story of someone who goes away and leaves three servants with various resources. Two of the servants are industrious, while the third is timid and fearful and simply buries the resource. When the master returns, he commends the first two but judges the third for his wickedness and indolence. He commands that this servant be "thrown into darkness, where there will be weeping and gnashing of teeth" (Matt. 25:30). According to Matthew, this realm lies outside the kingdom of heaven (Matt. 8:12; 13:42; 22:13; 24:51). Craig Keener's summary puts the matter starkly: "Disciples who neglect the resources entrusted to them in this life will be damned."[52]

Jesus has more to say: "When the Son of Man comes in his glory, and all the angels with him, he will sit on his glorious throne. All the nations will be gathered before him, and he will separate the people from one another as a shepherd separates the sheep from the goats. He will put the sheep on his right and the goats on his left" (Matt. 25:31–33). The ones on the "right," the "sheep," are invited to inherit the kingdom. The judgment that he pronounces does not focus on their beliefs. Nor does he say anything about imputation. Instead, he focuses directly on their actions: "For I was hungry and you gave me something to eat, I was thirsty and you gave me something to drink, I was a stranger and you invited me in, I needed clothes and you clothed me, I was sick and you looked after me, I was in prison and you came to visit me" (Matt. 25:35–36). The righteous (the "sheep") are confused, and they respond with questions; they want to know when they did these things to Christ. His answer is striking: "Truly I tell you, whatever you did for one of the least of these brothers and sisters of mine, you did for me" (Matt. 25:40).

Jesus then divides the two groups. To the "goats" he says, "Depart from me, you who are cursed, into the eternal fire prepared for the devil and his angels" (Matt. 25:41). When they want to know why this is happening, he again says that they did not do *for him* the things that the righteous ("sheep") did for him. Again, when they want to know when they missed opportunities to do this for him, he tells them, "Whatever you did not do for one of the least of these, you did not do for me" (Matt. 25:45). His conclusion is bracing: "Then they will go away to eternal punishment, but the righteous to eternal life" (Matt. 25:46).

The picture of judgment offered in the apocalyptic vision of John coheres closely to the teachings of Jesus (and Paul). Here we see Jesus pronouncing judgment on the basis of actions; he tells the church at

---

52. Craig S. Keener, *A Commentary on the Gospel of Matthew* (Grand Rapids: Eerdmans, 1999), 601.

Thyatira that they will be judged "according to [their] deeds" (*kata ta erga hymōn*; Rev. 2:23). And here we see that the final judgment will be "according to works": "And I saw the dead, great and small, standing before the throne, and books were opened. Another book was opened, which is the book of life. The dead were judged according to what they had done [*kata ta erga autōn*] as recorded in the books. The sea gave up the dead that were in it, and death and Hades gave up the dead that were in them, and each person was judged according to what they had done [*kata ta erga autōn*]" (Rev. 20:12–13).

Present Grace and Future Glory

On the other hand, we also cannot afford to miss the richness and beauty of what is to come. The new creation is depicted in terms that evoke the original setting of Eden, and the echoes of Eden in the new creation suggest that humans will also be the priests and guardians of it as well.[53] John's Revelation indicates two distinct but closely related actions that God's people will be doing in the eschaton: they will *serve* and they will *reign* with Christ. For "the throne of God and of the Lamb will be in the city, and his servants will *serve* him. . . . They will not need the light of a lamp or the light of the sun, for the Lord God will give them light. And they will *reign* for ever and ever" (Rev. 22:3, 5).

While eschatology is about the future, of course, it is not *only* about the future. For the future impinges on the present, and Christians live into the future by anticipating the new creation in the present. To live into the future as Christians is not to attempt to earn salvation; instead, it is to receive all the fullness of the grace that not only justifies but also truly transforms.

Conclusion

The doctrine of good works is not something ancillary to the main body of Christian teaching. It is not and cannot be reduced to a mere add-on feature to Christian theology. To the contrary, it is woven into the very fabric of Christian doctrine; it is a substantial and important element

53. For helpful discussion, see Richard J. Mouw, *When the Kings Come Marching In: Isaiah and the New Jerusalem* (Grand Rapids: Eerdmans, 2002).

of any robustly theological understanding of God and all things considered in relation to God.

When we explore theology proper, we see that God is the God whose life is active. To use a distinctly modern theological idiom, God's very being is in his act; to use a much older way of speaking, the divine life is *actus purus*.[54] God's internal life in the Trinity is a life of self-giving, holy love shared between Father, Son, and Holy Spirit, and what the tradition has termed the *opera ad intra* refers to the eternal and necessary movement of life and love within God. God's work "outside of God," the *opera ad extra*, is not eternal and necessary but instead is contingent and utterly gratuitous. By his actions in creation and providence, God both sustains the universe and its creatures and grants and upholds the causal powers of creatures. Good works are, ultimately, what God does so that creatures may be able to join him in his work.

Turning to theological anthropology, we see that humans are created and commissioned to exercise good works under the authority of God and on behalf of creation. Sin results in the rupture of right relationships; it is the abdication of that responsibility and rebellion against the Creator, who is ultimately sovereign. It is both sloth, or the neglect of good works, and open mutiny in the performance of evil actions.

The good news about good works is that the triune God has worked graciously on behalf of undeserving sinners. The Son, incarnate as Jesus Christ, has performed good deeds (the "active obedience" of Christ) and suffered in the place of sinners (the "passive obedience" of Christ) so that those very sinners who are enemies of God might be rescued from sin and reconciled to him. The Holy Spirit, sent by the Son and active in the church and the world, is now working to complete and fulfill the mission of the triune God. The good news about the doctrine of good works is that it is the story of triune grace—God active in and for sinners in the world, working in it through Christmas and Pentecost to transform those very sinners into children of God and coheirs with Christ.

The doctrine of salvation spells out this triune gospel in more detail. Here we learn that good works testify to the reality of justification; they follow it and flow from it like good fruit grows on a healthy tree. We learn that good works both testify to the divine work of sanctification

---

54. The first is often attributed to Karl Barth; the second occurs throughout the Latin scholastic theological tradition.

and actually act as an instrument (i.e., "instrumental cause") or means of that sanctification, for God continues to transform his people precisely by their works of worship and acts of service to their neighbors. And we learn from our study of soteriology that good works prepare God's people for glorification, for "without holiness no one shall see the Lord" (Heb. 12:14).

The doctrines of the church and the last things remind us that this is just what it means to be God's people: to belong to God is to share and reflect God's holy character; it is to be a people who are truly "zealous for good works" (Titus 2:14 ESV). This is the end for which we were made, and it is to this end that God will take us.

Any properly *Protestant* doctrine—indeed, any *biblical* doctrine—of good works will not hesitate to affirm that good works are truly necessary. Works of piety and works of mercy are necessary. Worshiping God is not optional for Christians, and neither is serving neighbors. To be a Christian simply is to love God with all your heart, mind, and strength and your neighbor as yourself. But the fullness of the good news about good works is not that such works are necessary. Instead, it is that such good works are possible, for God has worked in Christ and the Holy Spirit so that we might truly love and live out that love.

CHAPTER 5

The Working Church

Case Studies in Living Faith

S haring lunch with a friend from India, I (Matt) asked what has become a common inquiry when speaking with people from other parts of the country or world: "What is the biggest barrier to the spread of the gospel where you live?" He didn't have to ponder long: "Our biggest problem is audiovisual." Realizing that my thoughts immediately went to technology, he quickly smiled and explained, "What they *hear* us preaching to them is not *seen* in our lives." From the beginning of this volume, we have attempted to address a crisis to which there is ample solution in God's Word and sound theology. The problem is that truth claims are far too often not accompanied by merciful action reflective of the God of those truths—of mission, of justice, and of holy benevolence. The biblical data and the best theological reflection on that data clearly point to the solution: the answer to this crisis is a collective witness wherein local churches provide at least as much "visual" as "audio" by turning their attention to the hurting and unchurched members of their communities.

But how does missional intention, biblically and theologically ordered toward a working faith, actually happen in and through local congregations? The richest source of that information lies with the pastors of churches whose members are not only committed to "works of piety" but also embody "works of mercy." So we include in this volume case studies of congregations that are effectively reaching their communities. These case studies demonstrate what has happened in different contexts and communities and with diverse leadership and doctrinal approaches; nonetheless, they also demonstrate what can happen when works of mercy are taken seriously by a local body of believers and compassion is released outward to places of significant human need. These examples provide helpful, qualitative information that can spark further conversation and possible replication. The best laboratory is personal experience, and what worked in these congregations is potentially transferable to other situations and locales. Hopefully there will be fodder here for further research, both formal and practical.

We showcase four such congregations in the current chapter and utilize a sampling of additional ministry leaders in the next, as we discuss principles for churches that earnestly desire to do "works of mercy." All of the congregations surveyed take works of piety seriously (as do most Protestant congregations that worship together), diligently engage in Bible study and prayer, and integrate these emphases in the worshiping community as well as in small groups and families. We emphasize works of mercy because, inasmuch as there is a dispute over good works, it doesn't tend to be about the works of piety that are universally subscribed to across the denominational and theological spectrum.

John Wesley, addressing these categories in his sermon "The Scripture Way of Salvation," listed the means of grace—those practices by which believers are strengthened and affirmed in their faith:

> "But what good works are those, the practice of which you affirm to be necessary to sanctification?" First, all works of piety; such as public prayer, family prayer, and praying in our closet; receiving the Supper of the Lord; searching the Scriptures, by hearing, reading, meditating; and using such a measure of fasting or abstinence as our bodily health allows.
>
> Secondly, all works of mercy; whether they relate to the bodies or souls of men; such as feeding the hungry, clothing the naked, entertaining the stranger, visiting those that are in prison, or sick, or variously afflicted; such as the endeavouring to instruct the ignorant, to awaken the stupid sinner, to quicken the lukewarm, to confirm the wavering, to comfort the feebleminded, to succour the tempted, or contribute in any manner to the saving of souls from death. This is the repentance, and these the

fruits meet for repentance, which are necessary to full sanctification. This is the way wherein God hath appointed his children to wait for complete salvation.[1]

Notice that the works of mercy mentioned here by Wesley blend evangelism and compassionate ministry. He addresses the physical needs ("the hungry, . . . the naked, . . . the stranger, . . . those that are in prison, . . . sick, . . . afflicted"), clearly underscoring compassionate outreach. But he doesn't neglect the spiritual destitution of "the ignorant, . . . the stupid sinner, . . . the lukewarm, . . . the wavering, . . . the feebleminded, . . . the tempted, . . . souls." Wesley himself put a special emphasis on works of mercy, as he notes elsewhere.

In his sermon "On Zeal," he writes,

> Thus should he show his zeal for works of piety; *but much more for works of mercy*; seeing "God will have mercy and not sacrifice," that is, rather than sacrifice. Whenever, therefore, one interferes with the other, works of mercy are to be preferred. *Even reading, hearing, prayer are to be omitted, or to be postponed, "at charity's almighty call"*; when we are called to relieve the distress of our neighbour, whether in body or soul.[2]

Wesley poses four provocative questions:

> But are you *more zealous for works of mercy*, than even for works of piety? Do you follow the example of your Lord, and prefer mercy even before sacrifice? Do you use all diligence in feeding the hungry, clothing the naked, visiting them that are sick and in prison? And, above all else, do you use every means in your power to save souls from death?[3]

Also conspicuous in the importance of works of mercy to salvation itself was Wesley's sermon "On Visiting the Sick." Here he notes the importance of understanding works of mercy as nonnegotiable means of grace:

1. John Wesley, "The Scripture Way of Salvation," in *Sermons II: 34–70*, ed. Albert C. Outler, vol. 2 of *The Works of John Wesley*, bicentennial ed. (Nashville: Abingdon, 1985), 166.
2. John Wesley, "On Zeal," in *Sermons III: 71–114*, ed. Albert C. Outler, vol. 3 of *The Works of John Wesley*, bicentennial ed. (Nashville: Abingdon, 1986), 314 (italics added).
3. Wesley, "On Zeal," 319 (italics added).

Surely there are works of mercy, as well as works of piety, which are real means of grace. They are more especially such to those that perform them with a single eye. And *those that neglect them, do not receive the grace which otherwise they might. Yea, and they lose, by a continued neglect, the grace which they had received.*[4]

That last phrase—"lose . . . the grace which they had received"—clearly insinuates that works of mercy are a necessary discipline in order to maintain one's salvation. Works of mercy afford supremely practical benefits as well. If you do not see the sick with your own eyes (not just sending help but sending yourself), Wesley says, "you lose a means of grace; you lose an excellent means of increasing your thankfulness to God, who saves you from this pain and sickness, and continues your health and strength; as well as of increasing your sympathy with the afflicted, your benevolence, and all social affections."[5]

Churches that prioritize works of mercy (both compassionate and evangelistic) in weekly and intentional outreach were far too rare in Wesley's day, as they are now. It takes constant teaching and persuasion, scheduling structured opportunities, and leadership that leads by example and emphasis. For lack of these, inertia sets in for, alas, "works" are work. We make the case that they are the stuff of abundant life but also of sacrifice and constant effort. But even if the case can be made that such churches are rare, there are always glorious exceptions to the inertia rule, and these are examples that we hope inspire. For this reason, we sought out congregations that purposefully and successfully practiced these "means" in corporate commitment, as a focus of their disciple-making objectives. They include different challenges in different contexts, but all are trying to live out a commitment to good works as they seek to respond to God's grace with works of piety and mercy.

The first of the four churches is DaySpring Community Church, where I (Matt) am founding pastor and Caleb has served as associate pastor. It seems appropriate that readers should have the opportunity to observe what authors of a book on this topic have actually done themselves and, in Matt's case, are doing in an existing congregation.

---

4. John Wesley, "On Visiting the Sick," in *Sermons III: 71–114*, 385 (italics added).
5. Wesley, "On Visiting the Sick," 387.

DaySpring Community Church

Location: Clinton, Mississippi
Denomination: Church of the Nazarene
Age: Birthed October 2000
Pastor: Matt Friedeman
Size: 250

DaySpring Community Church launched in October 2000 in a skating rink in Clinton, Mississippi. As the founding pastor, I (Matt) was somewhat known in the community through a daily talk radio show and weekly newspaper column.

At the first public Sunday service, 167 people were in attendance, accompanied by all the excitement and hard work that goes into a grand opening of a church plant. After the service, a first-time visitor approached me and asked, "When are we going to start our abortion clinic ministry?" I inwardly winced. On the radio, I had frequently proclaimed that pastors who wanted to end the atrocity of abortion—or any other ills or injustices that plagued their cities—were morally obligated to lead the way through personal involvement. It was a safe position when I wasn't actually a pastor. Faced with an expectant prospective parishioner, it suddenly dawned on me that I now *was* officially clergy and was being challenged to live up to my words. The next week found us outside the local clinic holding signs, singing hymns, and offering prayer and help in the women's perceived crisis. Little did we know that this would become a decades-long outreach to women considering abortion and their unborn children. From the first Sunday, putting feet to faith became a core value of the new church.[6]

The Vision and the Mission

Each Sunday the congregation recites DaySpring's mission statement as a part of corporate worship: "DaySpring exists to excite men and women, boys and girls, about a life-changing relationship with Jesus and to release these disciples for ministry in this community and around

6. Twenty-two years later, the clinic that we stood in front of for a majority of those years closed—the very clinic involved in *Dobbs v. Jackson Women's Health Organization*, which ended *Roe v. Wade* and closed the clinic, the only one in Mississippi.

the world for the glory of God." Being released to ministries outside the four walls of the church is fundamental to DaySpring's identity.

"The Habits of a DaySpringer" delineate the aspirational hope of every member in living out a corporate commitment to spiritual growth and intentional outreach:

- daily time in the Word of God
- daily personal and spousal prayer
- a tithe of 10 percent of our total income
- regular participation in an *internal* and an *external* (compassionate) ministry sponsored by the church
- regular participation in a DaySpring small group
- sharing our faith with our friends, relatives, associates, and neighbors and to the ends of the world

Members regularly affirm these statements together, many are able to embrace them wholly, and board members and staff are required to personally incorporate these disciplines into their lives.

Works of Piety

The "Habits" above compose the main body of works of piety that DaySpring hopes for the personal lives of their people. Add to that a challenge to regularly fast (that is, to skip one or two meals per day) on Wednesdays and Fridays and especially during Lent for particular ministries, the unchurched, and "prodigals" (loved ones who have left the church). DaySpring thus tries to fortify a spiritual backbone for substantial works of mercy.

Exposing people to the Word is also critical to DaySpring's outward-bound movement. Preaching often reflects a missional, outward-bound hermeneutic.[7] DaySpringers are urged to "run to the sound of the pain" in the community and are reminded, "If we make disciples by sitting around and talking, we shouldn't be surprised when our disciples sit around and talk." Movement to persons on the "margins" has always

---

7. Regular, foundational passages include "I will make you a great nation, and I will bless you . . . so that you will be a blessing. . . . And in you all the families of the earth shall be blessed" (Gen. 12:2–3 ESV) and "Go therefore and make disciples of all the nations" (Matt. 28:19 ESV).

been part of the congregational DNA and a persistent congregational concern.

Small groups have served as an integral part of congregational life since DaySpring's inception, as a means of imparting biblical knowledge, cultivating community, and fostering accountability. Teaching within these groups may focus on application of a given week's sermon or the study of a particular biblical book. Some groups have adopted what is referred to at DaySpring as the "5Q method of discipleship," based on five questions that can be applied to any biblical passage:

1. What does God want to say to us through this text?
2. From the passage, how can we praise God?
3. What does the Lord want me to do or change?
4. How can I testify and give thanks for how the Lord has helped me?
5. How can we pray for one another today using this teaching from God's Word?

This method is designed to make Bible study more than what might be irreverently described as a "content dump," instead moving from revealed truth to life change and intercessory prayer to support that change.[8] Key to the 5Q method of discipleship and consistent with DaySpring's philosophy of "Don't just study—do!" is the application step. Group members identify specific actions or changes inspired by Scripture. Often, one member of the group will record these commitments so that participants can give a progress report the following week. The accountability element transitions these gatherings from the written Word to the Word lived out in the attitudes and actions of believers.

Works of Mercy

The intentional emphasis on putting feet to faith has resulted in an ever-expanding engagement of DaySpringers in outreach beyond the four walls of the church. The first ministry was sidewalk counseling at one of the local abortion clinics. Shortly after that, the church began a

---

8. Matt Friedeman, *The 5Q Method of Discipleship: Five Questions That Will Change Your Life* (Jackson, MS: Teleios, 2021).

prison ministry. Through the years, the list of external ministries has proliferated. The impetus has not been primarily from staff; rather, the expansion has grown out of members' responses to the needs around them. Outreach ministries have included the following:

- *Pro-life ministry.* DaySpringers offered help and hope to women in crisis outside the state's only remaining abortion clinic. Resources ranging from physician referrals to baby items to free sonograms were available to expectant mothers who often felt as though they had no options. Church members have volunteered at the local crisis pregnancy center. One DaySpringer who experienced the trauma of abortion has helped other women find hope and healing after an abortion through a program called Surrendering the Secret.

- *Prison ministry.* Weekly Bible studies and church services are held at both men's and women's prison facilities in Hinds County, where DaySpring also provides Bibles and other Christian materials to inmates. DaySpring laypeople have also led monthly worship services at the local detention center.

- *Celebrate Recovery.* This Bible-based 12-step program provides help and healing for hurts, habits, and hang-ups. DaySpringers provide a weekly meal followed by worship, a message, and small accountability groups.

- *Adoption of a local inner-city elementary school.* Volunteers help with Book Buddies, a program to assist struggling readers. A Princess Club for girls (which won an award from the governor of Mississippi) taught etiquette and provided a strong moral foundation. DaySpring volunteers lead a weekly after-school Good News Club on the school campus.

- *Nursing home ministry.* Weekly visitation and church services are offered at several local facilities.

- *Light into Darkness strip club ministry.* Some DaySpringers provide home-baked goodies while others deliver these treats to local clubs, where they befriend female employees, build relationships, pray for them, and, when requested, assist in finding employment beyond the strip club.

- *Tutoring ministry for children from a nearby apartment complex.* Building bridges of friendship to neighborhood children and families developed into bringing the children to church and then providing an after-school tutoring ministry to multiple ages.

How DaySpring Does It

Church leadership encourages members to look for ways to share a regular, compassionate touch with the community. As laypeople develop ministry skills and passion, it has become evident to everyone that it is not necessary, nor even preferable, for a pastor to be overseeing the effort. The diverse gifts and expertise of a Spirit-led body of believers are a far more potent force for kingdom work.

To further reinforce the emphasis on outward-bound ministry, in each Sunday service the church's outreach impact is highlighted. During the announcement time a chart is displayed that lists the external ministries of the church, the number of church members who participated in them the previous week, and how many outside the church were reached. A typical chart might look like this:

"DaySpring Released . . ."

Ministry	# of DaySpringers	# Reached
Men's Penal Farm	8	80 (6 commitments)
Women's Penal Farm	4	30
Elementary School	8	80
Bible Club	17	75
Nursing Home	7	20
Veterans Home	4	15
Strip Club	2	15
Celebrate Recovery	8	30

DaySpring doesn't publicly display other metrics (like attendance and giving), not because they don't matter but because the primary emphasis is on ministry to the lost and hurting. As a result, being released for ministry has become the identifying mark of DaySpring. Before joining the church, potential members participate in the DaySpring 101 seminar, which not only explains the doctrinal and organizational aspects of the church but also highlights individual and corporate commitments to spiritual growth, fellowship, and service within and beyond the congregation.

This ministry engagement cuts across all age groups. Parents are encouraged to take their children with them when serving in the community. DaySpring youth are invested in the life of the church, participating fully in the "Habits," including youth group and an intensive discipleship program called Carpe Diem. Teens have become an integral part of the life of the church through internal ministries ranging from nursery to children's ministry to worship team to audiovisual ministry, along with vital participation in outreach opportunities where their age allows. They also plan and execute a weeklong summer event called GOlocal, where they engage in community ministry. Children serve as ushers, taking up the offering and readily assisting with setting up chairs and other tasks. The hope is that DaySpringers of all ages see themselves as doers of the Word and not hearers only.

A few years ago, when DaySpring launched a daughter church, young adults from DaySpring's college and career group served as the primary members of the church plant team. DaySpring's vision is for *more*: more of God's work in and through us—to plant more churches, start more ministries that both evangelize and reach the needy, inspire more people to go to the mission fields of the world (DaySpring has had up to twelve overseas missionaries at any one time), and involve more DaySpringers in outreach.

While it can be challenging, this approach to ministry provides many moments of celebration and encouragement. More than a thousand babies were saved at the abortion clinic in the past two decades, and thousands of prisoners have committed their lives to Christ through the prison ministry, having been baptized and continuing to be discipled in the incarceration facilities.

The most visible testimony to the power of expressed love and outreach are DaySpring members who have come to the church through the mercy expressed to them in these outreach ministries, whose lives have been transformed and who now serve as vital ministry partners and valuable church leaders. One of the most inspirational of these is that of DaySpring's executive pastor, who was befriended by DaySpring in prison as he served his time as a felon and who, today, has a dynamic relationship with the Lord and is thus compelled to share that love with others in and beyond the church. And his story is not unlike many in the church; that is, they were sought out and cared for in their various sinful and desperate predicaments, and having found faith, hope, and love in Christ, they understand that the proper response is to similarly seek out and care for needy and hurting people.

Tierra Prometida

Location: Mexico City, Mexico
Denomination: Unaffiliated (a network of 60 church plants)
Age: Birthed 1996
Pastor: Roberto Stevenson
Size: 8,000 in main campus attendance (2,000 in the church plants)

Tierra Prometida (Spanish for "Promised Land") in Mexico City had no ordinary beginning.[9] Pastor Aurelio Gómez Velázquez had spent forty-one years in the Franciscan priesthood when he began holding evangelistic meetings that eventually attracted thousands of people but also drew a skeptical response from the Catholic hierarchy in Mexico City. After an eventual parting of ways, when Velázquez announced that his meetings were no longer Catholic, only five hundred or so of the most steadfast remained. But from that beginning, a church was planted.

Velázquez met a young church planter and street evangelist, Roberto Stevenson, and invited him to be part of the fledgling ministry. Stevenson himself had an inauspicious beginning. Imprisoned in his native United States for drug possession and sales, he came to faith and was discipled in prison by Black Pentecostals. After his release, he married, attended Bible college, and with his family moved to Mexico as a missionary.

On his deathbed, Velázquez named the American, Stevenson, as his successor—to the shock of more than a few in the church. The choice, while initially unexpected, was soon acknowledged as prescient. The

9. Roberto Stevenson, interview by Matt Friedeman, video call, December 13, 2021. Subsequent Stevenson quotations are from that interview.

church enjoyed amazing growth; some sixty churches in and beyond Mexico now stand as outposts of the original vision of Velázquez and the remarkable spiritual leadership of Stevenson.

The Vision and the Mission

The vision and mission of Tierra Prometida is distributed in print to both the congregation and visitors. The topic is also regularly addressed from the pulpit to keep the critical emphases of the church before the congregants.

Vision

1. Love the Lord our God with all our heart, soul, and mind, and love our neighbor as ourself (Matt. 22:36–38).
2. Be a Christ-centered, Spirit-filled, missionary church that takes seriously in word and deed the command to make disciples in Mexico and in all the nations (Matt. 28:18–20).
3. Disciple and train every member of the church so that they can live a life of holiness and service in the power of the Holy Spirit.

Mission—How We Do It

1. Develop an intimate relationship with God through praise, prayer, and the reading and study of the Bible.
2. Equip those whom God has called to send them out, planting churches to be an instrument of God's kingdom.
3. Use the economic resources of our businesses to support the vision of the church.[10]
4. Provide activities and opportunities for every member and every generation to be involved in serving the Lord, in works of mercy.[11]

Works of Piety

Stevenson especially promotes prayer, noting, "Prayerlessness is one of the areas where my church—all churches—need to repent and then

---

10. The congregation owns several small businesses, including a prominent water-bottling enterprise, that are quite profitable and that help underwrite the expenses of the church.

11. These vision and mission statements are translations of a handout provided by Tierra Prometida.

grow." Prayer, he says, is a hallmark of the church, and the pastor is intentional about advocating both consistency and passion in corporate prayer. There is a similar emphasis on personal Bible study: "We at every point of our life together exalt the Bible as the Word of God, and so we need to read it, study it, practice it. Everyone needs to be regularly and habitually into it." Fasting is advocated and practiced, as is participation in small groups. Stevenson reports that after a recent teaching emphasis on discipleship groups, "we went from one hundred small groups to many times that—taking off [like] wildfire."

One of Wesley's key works of piety—the Eucharist—has created an interesting issue for Stevenson. Often in Latin American countries there is significant theological tension between Catholics and evangelicals. Many of Stevenson's parishioners are former Catholics who are now evangelicals with a different approach to matters of faith. Stevenson explains, "Involvement with the Lord's Supper for us has meant a once-a-month emphasis in church. But this has been a big transition from weekly and sometimes daily 'mass' to practice once a month." After some theological wrangling, the congregation eventually found a balance between former traditions and scriptural mandates by establishing a monthly celebration of this sacrament.

Works of Mercy

Involvement in the practice of ministry has been a notable mark of the church and its daughter congregations. Slogans such as "If you are a Christian, you are in ministry" appear on screens in the worship area. This goes for ministries within and beyond the congregation. "Bathroom-cleaning ministry is not differentiated from pulpit preaching," says Stevenson. "They are *all* ministries. We don't even like the 'clergy'/'laity' verbiage. We are together; we are in ministry."

In regard to compassionate ministry, nearly all such outreach at Tierra Prometida has been congregationally instigated and led. Prison ministry started because a female minister wanted to reach her incarcerated father. Stevenson became enthused with what was happening through this ministry and is now a regular participant in leading studies at the maximum-security facility in Mexico City. Another major emphasis is ministry in the indigenous villages, providing dental and

medical care, haircuts, and other services. Stevenson notes that many
from the mother church enjoy joining the smaller churches when they
can; doing so forges an important link back to the original congregation. When compassionate ministries are provided with consistency
and care, this outreach often results in the establishment of another
daughter church.

These outreaches have been born out of recognizing felt needs within
the church and in surrounding communities. "We say, 'If you see a need,
fill it,'" explains the pastor. Below are some examples of ministries:

- *Counseling for domestic violence*
- *Prison ministry*. Tierra ministers in a local maximum-security
  facility.
- *Prison aftercare*. Tierra has come to realize the need for aftercare
  for those who are released after many years behind bars. The
  church maintains a small dormitory on the church property and
  has provided jobs for dozens of former convicts.
- *Ministry to families of long-term prisoners*. Done especially at Christ-
  mastime, this is described as "incredibly fruitful." Some of this
  takes place as church members supply bottled water, gospel tracts,
  and prayer to families lined up outside the facility, waiting to see
  their incarcerated family members.
- *Drivers, dentists, doctors—monthly medical missions to villages*. "Everybody gets behind this because it is demonstrably helpful, not
  intimidating, and a relatively low commitment."
- *Four Friends Ministry*. The name for this ministry is derived from
  a sermon preached on Mark 2:1–12, about the four men who low-
  ered their paralyzed friend through the roof so he could reach
  Jesus. Since public transport in Mexico City is "rough," someone
  arranged to purchase a bus, which is staffed with drivers and laypeople who minister to anyone who desires a ride to church. The
  bus is also equipped with dedicated space to transport a wheelchair. The initial outreach was so effective that a second vehicle
  was purchased. Family members, seeing their relatives trans-
  ported and treated kindly, often end up visiting the church at a
  later date. The idea came from a young lady whose grandmother

became disabled and was confined to a wheelchair. This ministry has expanded from only providing transportation to also including home visitation and prayer.

- *Adult literacy classes.* "We began teaching adults to read and write, because many members of our church never had the opportunity and longed to be able to read the Bible. Like most ministries, this one had humble beginnings. The goal was to teach illiterate older adults reading skills. As word got out [about] our free classes every Saturday, community members enrolled. The state government found out, accredited us, and offered grants. Now we not only provide basic literacy training but offer elementary and secondary school with full accreditation to adults over thirty. Over three hundred students have gone from functional illiteracy to achieving a GED high school diploma."

- *Eunice Project.* This is an outreach to the poorest of the poor in Mexico. The ministry is named after a young lady, tragically killed in an accident, who had a heart for the indigenous people. Every other month for the past five years, Tierra has organized teams that provide dental care and basic medical consultations and that bless families with school supplies, shoes, blankets, even haircuts— especially *hope*. The ministry involves about forty volunteers who serve wholeheartedly in different capacities.

Several church plants trace their beginnings to the impact of this ministry in their villages. The evangelistic fruit was "not in the original plan, but God always does more than we ask or imagine," says Stevenson.

How Tierra Prometida Does It

The mother and daughter churches take "doing works" seriously. As Stevenson explains, "We love Jesus, and we know that while we are saved by grace, we constantly teach that we are saved to do works" (Eph. 2:10). A tremendous advantage to the proliferation of this "doing" philosophy is how contagious it is.

You might think that it would be a challenge to keep people engaged in so many ministries, but we have found that the way to stay focused [is through] public testimonies from those who have served. Real-life testimonies keep the vision real and compel others to take a role.

Also, a constant voice from the pulpit and leadership in general, encouraging and exhorting every member to be a minister, fortifies efforts. Jesus's holistic ministry is often used as an example, and his teachings like Matthew 25:31–46 are crucial to maintaining the vision. We have a saying that members know by heart, "El que no sirve, no sirve," which literally translated is, "The one who doesn't serve, doesn't serve"; but the dynamic equivalent would be, "If you are not useful, you are useless." All our volunteers are not merely free laborers in the fields of our city; . . . they are workers of miracles.

Stevenson ministers in a context where nearly all his seekers and converts come from a Catholic background in which salvation is too often understood at the lay level as based on works.

Therefore, in our new believers' class we teach that we are indeed saved by grace through faith [Eph 2:8], but now that we are saved, works are an important expression of that saving faith [Eph. 2:10]. It is basically a question of getting the horse before the cart. To a people with a religious background, James 1:27 is meaningful: "Religion that is pure and undefiled before God the Father is this: to visit widows and orphans in their affliction and to keep oneself unstained from the world." By faith the blood of Jesus cleans our consciences from dead works so that we can actively do the works that adorn our salvation.

Stevenson maintains that vision and mission statements aren't nearly as powerful as pastoral example. "Not just preaching it," says Stevenson, "but doing it." While he participates in an occasional medical mission, he finds great personal blessing through regular ministry in the prison. When preaching for his local church body, he notes that both Old and New Testament passages are significant in promoting works of mercy and evangelism. Such texts include Matthew 25:31–46, James 1:27, the Prophets (especially Isaiah and Amos), and the story of the good Samaritan. Preaching is essential to keeping people focused and maintaining a culture of service: "I believe in the power of preaching to convince and persuade. If you preach inductively through the Bible, 'works' themes come out automatically. Frankly, call it preaching if you want, but we mostly just do Bible study." And these studies teach consistently that "every member is a minister." This theme is both heard in the preaching and displayed on the overhead screen before, during, or after the service.

Stevenson has a historical affinity with John Wesley and quotes him often. Because of the Catholic background of the church, Mother Teresa and St. Francis of Assisi are also helpful historical figures to reference. Another factor that keeps service at the forefront for the laity is having ex-prisoners living on the church grounds and working at Tierra's water business. People see these men performing their duties week after week, and they are reminded that transformation is possible—and actually happening before their very eyes.

Decades ago, Stevenson attended Fuller Seminary during the height of the church-growth movement, but he left before attaining his degree because the church-growth emphasis wasn't settling well in his spirit. He has since adopted a "works of mercy" approach, which, when accompanied by gospel presentation, provides a powerful model for becoming the church that Jesus desires. So has evangelistic growth come because of the interplay of works of piety and mercy?

> Indirectly, . . . although it is not the goal. I attended Fuller for church growth, but now I've died to all that. If this is the main goal, it is not good. You do what you do in ministry because it is the God thing—not primarily the growth thing—to do. In as huge a place as Mexico City, we teach people not to be discouraged but to be a drop of sweet water in an ocean of contamination—and just see what God can do. Trust.
>
> But growth spiritually—yes! The number one thing is to show Jesus's compassion to the world. Because we believe that everybody is created in the *imago Dei*, everybody needs to feel that touch, which begins to then proliferate in and through a church as amazing things happen.

Judging by the sheer growth in numbers among Tierra Prometida's network of churches, at least some of those "amazing things" involve church growth—both numerical and spiritual—in the best sense of the word.

Stevenson cautions, however, that as a pastor he is continually wooing people to persist in their works of piety lest their souls cease to grow and "we become merely professional":

You can too quickly become professional or political or prideful without a top-shelf devotional emphasis in your church. . . . An important part of compassionate ministry is a prevailing kingdom mentality and Christlikeness as the goal of every worker. The kingdom mentality helps us to realize that every act of service, no matter how small, is contributing to something much greater: the kingdom of God being proclaimed. The distinguishing feature of Christlikeness keeps us from pride and personal ambition when the Lord grants success to our endeavors.

The King found Stevenson in a prison cell many years ago, so he is adamant to make sure that the love offered there is carried from his ministry and his church to the places of need in Mexico City and beyond.

Immanuel Africa Gospel Church

Location: Kericho, Kenya
Denomination: Africa Gospel Church
Age: Birthed 1974
Pastor: Joyce Tonui
Size: 2,000

Immanuel Africa Gospel Church started through the evangelistic efforts of college students who desired to see a vibrant church in Kericho.[12] Beginning with two converts, the church met in various locations for almost a decade. In 1983 the congregation began holding two services. Eventually, they obtained land on a main highway. The current building was dedicated for use in 1993 by the second president of the Republic of Kenya, Daniel arap Moi, who himself attended an Africa Gospel Church.

The current pastor, the Rev. Joyce Tonui, is one of the few woman pastors in her denomination. Raised in Immanuel while her father was pastor, she was later appointed as pastor by the bishop. Tonui has commanded respect every step of the way, not only because of her lineage, but also due to her compassionate fervor for those both within and beyond her congregation.

12. Joyce Tonui, interview by Matt Friedeman, video call, January 11, 2022. Subsequent Tonui quotations are from that interview.

Vision and Mission

The Africa Gospel Church (AGC) has famously accentuated five "E's" that have enhanced the intentional discipleship of the Immanuel congregation:

E1—Evangelizing the unsaved
E2—Establishing churches
E3—Edifying believers
E4—Equipping leaders
E5—Exercising compassion[13]

The first two and the fifth of these emphases are definitely outward-bound and are taught from many AGC pulpits, including Immanuel's. Tonui notes that the denominational mission statement is "The whole church taking the whole gospel to the whole world," which, the pastor says, "we have adopted as our guiding principle and pillar as we do ministry."

Works of Piety

Pastor Tonui was adamant, as were all our interviewees, that the disciplines of Bible study, fasting, communion, small groups, and prayer—both corporate and private—are necessary underpinnings for works of mercy. Immanuel teaches about the means of grace from the pulpit and also offers multiple weekly opportunities for people to intercede for personal and corporate requests. There is a regular Wednesday night prayer meeting, a quarterly special emphasis on prayer, frequent all-night vigils, a regular emphasis on fasting, and a continual emphasis for people to pray privately and in their own homes.

Tonui's congregation leverages a discipleship-group model for small groups and distributes weekly Scripture passages for the congregation via social media platforms. Social media groups have been formed to enable people to pray and to share insights from their study of the Bible.

13. "AGC Vision and Five E's," Good Shepherd Africa Gospel Church, accessed October 21, 2022, http://www.goodshepherdagc.com/good-morning/.

At the beginning of every year, a twenty-one-day period of church-wide prayer and fasting sets the tone for the church's efforts.

> Quite a number of people get involved with that because we talk about it, we prepare for it, and we provide guides. And they actually come to the church over lunch hour. . . . Apart from just fasting from food, we try to help the children to fast from something that they like, so . . . we've done a TV fast, and that way we have the whole church fasting for twenty-one days. But we also then throughout the year have seven-day fasts, and generally that's when we want to pray for a specific thing. And we do that at least twice a year.

Immanuel divides the church into neighborhoods called "care groups." There are also "affinity groups" for people of similar gender, age level, and interests. Tonui emphasizes that engagement in these groups is perceived not merely as a church activity but as the means by which grace might flow to and through their works of evangelism and compassion.

Prayer is a critical component of effective outreach for those at Immanuel. People are encouraged to pray for their own participation in the harvest as well as to corporately intercede for those in the field. Empowering prayer is essential, says Tonui, to fruitful evangelism and compassionate ministry.

Works of Mercy

Key verses from Scripture inform Immanuel's involvement in compassionate ministry in and beyond Kericho. First, Proverbs 19:17: "Whoever is kind to the poor lends to the LORD, and he will reward them for what they have done." Tonui notes that people are inspired by the idea that "lending" to God brings significant blessing individually and corporately as a church. Concerning the New Testament, the pastor turns to John 13:35: "By this everyone will know that you are my disciples, if you love one another." This verse serves as a reminder that while a church can be immersed in doing exciting things and envisioning dynamic programs, the end goal is love. Underlying both verses is the Great Commission charge to go, baptize, and teach, with the goal of making disciples (Matt. 28:19–20). The latter passage also reminds the church that they do not exist simply for their own benefit, or even for that of

Kericho or Kenya. Their aim is to release workers for the harvest to the nations of Africa and beyond. These guiding Scriptures are regularly proclaimed from the pulpit and in church literature to keep the vision of an outward-bound church alive.

Hospital visitation looms large for Immanuel. Prior to the COVID-19 pandemic, staff and laity were organized into groups that went to the hospitals, hospices, and clinics to pray with and comfort the sick. Immanuel plans to expand the current prison ministry and discipleship initiative in response to a growing need. Through bereavement ministries, members of the church come to the aid of the poorest in their congregations with love and financial resources, supplying aid and counsel as family members navigate the future through grief and loss.

Immanuel maintains rural mission stations staffed by full-time missionaries who identify the most urgent needs. Teams from the congregation regularly mobilize to provide medical care, hold events for children and youth, and engage in evangelism. "We've also done veterinary medicine," Tonui says, "to reach especially those that are very dependent on the health of their animals to make their living. When economic disaster awaits because you lack veterinary medicine, it becomes more than just a luxury to provide help in this area."

Formidable funds are raised for these stations, but for Tonui, that is not enough. She insists that her people go and take part. Those who assist in these endeavors return with inspirational stories that serve to encourage and motivate others to participate in a missional movement. Tonui and other staff members use these stories when they are teaching. "One of the other things that we do is bring our missionaries we sponsor, that are in extreme places, to come and just talk about why they are there, how they are doing, what they are doing. Our people get inspired when they hear. Usually when we bring a missionary, that's when our giving goes up because people can see what their money is doing out in those places."

Immanuel holds an entire "missionary month" when members are encouraged to visit various ministry locations and also to give financially to evangelistic advance. Teams visit an orphanage with a baby center and a children's home to give gifts to the children; prison ministry is supported by offering discipleship classes and providing food during

special Christian holidays; discipleship classes and counseling are con-
ducted at a drug-rehabilitation center; and high school and university
settings are impacted by catechism and discipleship classes.

How Immanuel Does It

Tonui insists that strong and purposeful pastoral leadership is essential for a church that meaningfully engages works of both piety and
mercy. "If I can buy into something as a pastor, I will mobilize people
to do that which I am convinced is the way forward. If I am excited
about something, it's very easy for them to rally around; when there
is a lack of passion, I have found, people don't bother with it. If there
is something I want to see arise out of my congregation, I have to lead
from the front. And generally, when I provide that leadership, then the
church rallies much more easily behind that passion."

Tonui asserts that one aspect of this pastoral leadership is the powerful proclamation of the Christian's call to share God's love through word
and deed.

> The church will not be involved in the community if the pulpit is silent on
> the issue. As with all churches, it is so easy to get self-centered and focus
> on ourselves to the exclusion of those outside of our walls. So let's say we
> are going to have an evangelistic push with our church in the vicinity;
> in preparation we have a whole month where we teach on evangelism,
> where we teach on the importance of exiting to the mission, where we
> teach on the importance of being involved with the unchurched around
> us. We say, "Grow, then go."
>
> And you have to remind, remind, remind your people because it is
> very easy to forget to do evangelism and serve the poor and to dismiss
> missions. Preach about it! Often! The mobility and spiritual health of
> your congregation is at stake.

Missionaries from World Gospel Mission, based in the United States,
have enjoyed a long and fruitful relationship with the church in Kericho,
and Tonui cites them as a motivator in establishing their ministry with
local missionaries. She also points to transcontinental evangelist Billy
Graham as an inspiration and example for evangelism and compas-

sionate ministry. The Lausanne Movement,[14] for which Graham was largely responsible, attempts to promote the dual emphases of evangelism and compassionate ministry. Immanuel has sought to implement this strategy, particularly when the needs of a region are economically acute. Immanuel has also practiced Graham's approach of presenting an attractional event with significant follow-up.

> Our biggest challenge is consistency. People get excited during missions month, and by the time we get to actually going weeks or months later, many find that the "cares of the world" have moved in on them and day-to-day difficulties have made a motivated decision during our month less appealing later.
>
> Once people start going, not everyone hangs in there. Compassion sometimes, it's really a sweat-producing and rather heartbreaking job, getting people involved—especially consistent, ongoing, and day-to-day involvement. We find it easy for them to give, but then to give *and to go* is the hard part, because it is uncomfortable. Some get excited and want to continue doing, and others say, "Never again." We have many middle-class people who can't endure what the lower-class people might: . . . sleeping on the floor, bathing in the open area. And sometimes the people who have done it so consistently tend to block out others out of pride.

Evangelism and compassionate ministry can be demanding. But they are central to the message of Scripture and the call of the Christian. Churches must persist in finding ways to persevere, sometimes against all odds.

Involving people outside the walls of the church ought to be a lead pastoral initiative, maintains Tonui. She returns to the emphasis of the pulpit:

> Pastors should really preach about the church being involved with the community. If we don't speak to the issue, there is no question the church will not be involved in the community. As all churches are, we have a

14. The Lausanne Movement describes itself in this way: "For over 40 years, the Lausanne Movement has 'set the table' and convened leaders for a number of global gatherings and catalytic networks that, by God's grace, have impacted the scope of world missions." "The Legacy of the Lausanne Movement," Lausanne Movement, accessed October 21, 2022, https://lausanne.org/our-legacy.

tendency to become very self-centered. Like other churches, we send people out to needy places in the community but always try to extensively teach on evangelism before we go: where we teach on the importance of going out, where we teach on the importance of being involved with those around us. It is very easy to forget—to not just *want* to do evangelism, or *believe* in evangelism, but to actually *do* evangelism. It's very easy to forget missions if we don't preach regularly about it.

The emphasis to grow and then go is crucial to the mission of Immanuel. "Christian maturity needs to be a *going* maturity. In our instruction we teach how to go, what to do, and what it means to prepare yourself to go. We then teach people how to evangelize, how to get involved, how to pray for our missionaries, how to pray for unreached people, and finally, how to give financially to what God is leading us towards."

New initiatives for ministry typically start with the pastors. A current dream from church leadership is for an increased and enhanced prison ministry. This idea is taken to the church council; once a plan has been approved at that level, leaders are rallied, and leadership training is presented. "We involve as many people as we can. We bring it to the church after we have gone through it, have a budget for it, and have leaders for it; then we begin to recruit other people from within the congregation. And a lot of the way we do it is again from the pulpit, announcing it. There are times when we have announced and nothing else happened. Other times, we actually approach people one-on-one and ask them to volunteer and subsequently train them."

Recruiting people is usually not a problem.

We call it the Harambee spirit.[15] Africa is very communal; we seem to want to do everything in community. If it was planting, we came together to plant. If it was harvesting, people came together to harvest. For most Kenyans the Harambee spirit is an important part of who we are—certainly it is true of me—so I get satisfaction helping people accomplish things and knowing that you are helping others get what they desperately need. There is satisfaction in seeing success together. This is central to what it means to be Kenyan.

15. "Harambee" is Kenya's official motto. In Swahili it means "all pull together," and typically it is utilized verbally to suggest when community is necessary because mere individual effort could never get the task accomplished.

Even so, Immanuel's pastor recognizes the danger of developing a Messiah complex, where the desire to help ends up creating dependence, when independence was the goal. Further, less-than-humble missionaries may be perceived as "all-knowing rich people who have come to rescue us," potentially causing resentment. So Immanuel goes, but with a mindset that is humble and in a learning posture. According to pastor Tonui,

> The truth is, there is so much that the needy can teach us. We need to carve out mental, emotional, and practical ways that give us this learning opportunity. If we simply go in and do something for them, they abandon it, and we are disappointed that they did not benefit from the help we were giving them. But perhaps we have earned that disappointment because we didn't learn from them. They will, in the long term, probably disregard the help if we don't learn from them and subsequently teach them to be able to do things for themselves.
>
> And we have to guard ourselves from making mistakes. Our church is middle class. So when we go and hear all these sad stories, see all these needs, we get so emotionally involved and just want to do any- and everything we can to solve these people's problems. We make quick commitments on our own that are not sustainable.
>
> They pick up a kid and say, "I will take you and save you." Then when they find out what they have really done, the pocketbook cannot sustain their commitment. The spirit is willing but the flesh is unable to sustain some of the things that we will commit to, so a lot of times, before we become involved, we have to see: Is this a true need that we can legitimately help meet in the long term?
>
> God says he will give us the nations. But it is up to us to go and find out how we can really help this nation and eventually help them walk with God and not simply act like the Messiah we are not. As a pastor, I need to be very involved to make sure we are not hurting as we help.

Immanuel reminds other congregations desiring to emulate their outreach to start slow, then grow. "Too many churches want to immediately do what we are doing. But I have been in this church a long time—in fact, this is my home church—and we have grown slowly, slowly and learned first how to do what we have done with little in the way of financial resources. But still, we continued to grow." Immanuel has found that discipling smaller churches is a productive way to help them understand how to engage in evangelism and compassionate ministry. "We've brought other, smaller churches to go alongside with us so they can see what we do and how we do it, and we have sort of multiplied ourselves to other local churches around us. They eventually can go and minister creatively and effectively without us."

Genesis Project

Location: Fort Collins, Colorado
Denomination: Independent
Age: Birthed 2015
Lead Pastor: Rob Cowles
Size: 400

"Every church should have a bias for action. Our deeds must match our creed," says pastor Rob Cowles.[16] He means it.

The "genesis" of the Genesis Project in Fort Collins, Colorado, provides a clue to the distinctive emphases of this local church. Founder and lead pastor Rob Cowles recounts that there were several strip clubs in Fort Collins and Denver owned by three sons carrying on the family business. One of the brothers, who ran the club in Fort Collins, received a flyer in the mail advertising a Christian conference. He attended and, while there, was challenged to give his life to Jesus. Soundly converted, he soon recognized the incompatibility of attending a men's Bible study in the morning and opening a men's strip club at four o'clock in the afternoon. He concluded that he had to close the clubs and get out of the business. Unfortunately, that was easier said than done.

The brothers tried to sell the building, but at the last minute the deal inexplicably fell apart. God began to speak to the man's heart about how this whole situation could be redeemed for good. He approached several congregations in the area, and while all the pastors were encouraged about his recent conversion, none of them wanted a former strip club for church use. Two years into pitching the building, he approached a megachurch where Cowles was executive pastor. Before long, Cowles

---

16. Rob Cowles, interview by Matt Friedeman, video call, January 25, 2022. Subsequent Cowles quotations are from that interview.

and his senior pastor were checking out this old strip club to investigate the possibilities.

> So we toured the strip club. Obviously, it was in the early afternoon. It was closed, and man, God just hit me when I walked into the building. We went back into the locker room, and there were pictures of kids on lockers, and I just broke down and wept. And when we walked out of the club, I told my boss that we needed to plant a church here and that I wanted to put my name in the hat to do it. It just took me back to my roots of ministry for caring and loving really hurting broken people.
>
> There was a couple in Fort Collins that had a high capacity financially. I shared the vision with them, and they actually paid for the property, bought out the business, and put a half a million dollars toward the remodel, and we raised the rest. And so February of 2015 was our official launch in a debt-free, renovated strip club to be our church.

Vision and Mission

Part of the vision that was cast to the high-capacity donors was the proposed mission statement: "The Genesis Project exists to create space for people to discover new beginnings through transforming relationships with Jesus and others." That sounds like something you would read on the website of a typical evangelical church, but what Cowles had in mind were people he had recently ministered to in previous ministry locations—undocumented immigrants, members of gangs, alcoholics, drug addicts, strippers, pedophiles.

The Genesis Project wanted to ensure that everyone—all kinds of people and especially those who were significantly damaged—could come to a church and through real relationships be valued and learn that they're created in the image of God no matter how marred that image may be. People need a church, thought Cowles, that meets them where they are and is willing to journey with them.

> We often say we'll celebrate with your sobriety chip and we'll hold your hair during relapse. We're just going to be there. And so a lot more than what we do is just who we're trying to be in the community. We're very oriented to an incarnational style of ministry. The neighborhood that we're in is an industrial, high-crime area of Fort Collins, and again, we're not talking inner-city LA, but I think every community has an underbelly

of really broken and desperate people that are overlooked, especially in Fort Collins.

Now, Fort Collins is one of the top ten places in the country to live. It's the choice city. That's the city motto. But you would be surprised—or maybe not—that in a choice city people who are struggling are often overlooked. We wanted this church to focus on them, to love people that no one else wanted to love from the beginning, and so we've tried to do that.

Cowles describes their primary strategy: to "embed ourselves." Among other things, this suggests that the Genesis Project is not an "attractional" kind of a church. "If we're ever a stop on the church-hop train," says Cowles, "it's a brief stop. People don't stay with us. We try to do the best weekend service we can do, but we can't compete with 90 percent of the churches in our city." It's not that the staff and volunteers don't do a good job or aren't talented, according to the pastor. It's just that weekend services are not top priority. Building relationships with hurting people is.

Works of Piety

Key to the maintenance of a challenging mission is the indispensability of prayer. "You have to be a people of spiritual depth bathed in prayer and the Bible, and, well, I've never experienced spiritual warfare like we have in planting this church. It drives me to my knees constantly. I never took a class in school on what to do when a guy says, 'Can you throw my cocaine away, because I can't bring myself to do that?'"

A congregation that begins to live for transformation in the damaged people of their community experiences God differently than others do. A ministry in which you need to see God work miraculously will change the course of that people. "If a church has the greatest talent, powerful communicators, gifted musicians, you have a great experience at your worship service, and I don't know that God ever needs to show up," muses Cowles. "But put your ministry in the middle of *having to have him*, and watch the difference." Further,

I don't know if [anything has] ever forced me to pursue Jesus in my personal life more than pastoring this church, because I don't have all the answers. I don't know what to do most of the time. And I think it pushes me and all the rest of us to be more fervent in prayer, more fervent in what they believe and why they believe it, more dependent upon the work of the Holy Spirit. I just think we look a lot more like him when we desperately need him to live out our mission . . . to love the least of these.

The foregoing paragraphs reference Cowles's personal life, but he has also found it true congregationally. When a significant number of the laity are earnestly seeking to impact the hurting culture around them, they develop a hunger and a thirst for God—a prayer life and hearing from his Word. Cowles notes that in his church the demands of challenging ministry frequently lead people to take the works of piety much more seriously.

Works of Mercy

Cowles and his staff and volunteers have sought to create relationships using a strategy that they call ROCK: Random Outbreaks of Community Kindness. It is short-term ministry with no strings attached that sets up transformative longer-term relationships. These activities can take many forms:

- They show up at laundromats with rolls of quarters and pay for people's laundry.
- On Christmas Eve people bake dozens of cookies and deliver them to places where people have to work on the holiday and probably don't want to—especially locations like the seedy motels near the Genesis Project building, tattoo parlors, and liquor stores. Law-enforcement agencies are also recipients of the goodies.
- Every year the church holds a "Wanna Give Away" event, based on the Southwest Airlines slogan "Wanna Get Away?" This is a weekend of very intentional service projects, where 90 percent of the Genesis Project family engage in projects to benefit others in their city, especially low-income neighbors.
- They minister in a nearby trailer park. Americans with Disabilities Act–compliant ramps are built for wheelchair-bound residents. Someone donated a trailer to the church, which now enjoys a permanent presence from which to minister in that community.

The object of all this "random" ministry is building relationships that might lead to more meaningful community in the church. Activities and ministries are offered daily and weekly in the former strip club:

- *Zumba classes.* Dance fitness classes that get people together and help them to enjoy one another.
- *An open gym for tots and moms.* This provides a chance for mothers with young children to get together and enjoy fellowship.
- *Restore Ministry (a post-12-step ministry).* This group also does volunteer work in the local community, of their own initiative.
- *An in-house coffee shop that trains at-risk youth to become baristas.* A volunteer serves with each teenager for their entire shift. They personally invest in their lives to show them Jesus and to give them job skills.
- *Bible distribution.* Bibles in English and in Spanish are available to anyone who enters the building.
- *A playground and a community garden.* Instead of extending the parking lot between the church and the mobile-home park next door to the property border, the church left room for a playground and community garden area. The residents of the mobile-home park use the garden (which the church has fenced and irrigates) to grow their own food. The kids in the park now have a place to play. Genesis Project bought and installed all the playground equipment.
- *Prison ministry.* Genesis Project supports prison ministry by welcoming and accepting the formerly incarcerated who are sent to the church.
- *Rent assistance*
- *Parents' Night Out.* The church provides pizza, and its youth plan activities and staff the event, while parents enjoy free time. This serves married couples and single parents.
- *A two-day event that allows families to come into the church to pick out age-appropriate toys for their kids for Christmas.* The church even wraps the gifts for them.
- *Food distribution.* During the COVID-19 pandemic, food distribution became a huge concern. A local billionaire gave Genesis

Project money to ensure that any food-insecure residents nearby might be fed. Local restaurants also donated to this cause.

Five years ago, two young, recent Colorado State University graduates heard that the church needed interns to live in the aforementioned trailer park, serving the church and building relationships with the neighbors. Cowles says,

> I just figured these are going to be two guys, because it's a dangerous place to live. Well, it was these two girls, and man, God had called them. It was clear. So we met, they moved into that trailer park, and the whole agenda was just to teach us how to love our neighbors. Our goal was to get them to come to our church and love our neighbors and work with the people who live there to make our community better.

Since a number of the residents in the park were undocumented, fear and distrust were widespread. Additionally, most of the parents and grandparents raising their kids there didn't speak English. The two young women lived there for about three years before one of them had to move to Denver to finish her master's degree. The other one got married, and she felt so attached to that community that she and her husband bought their own trailer in the park and have continued to serve on church staff part time in a community-development position. Says Cowles, "That opened so many doors for us to engage with our neighbors." A few of the current ministries include soccer for the kids from the trailer park, English as a second language for its residents, and food distribution on a regular basis to its residents as well.

Cowles coaches his congregation to keep the "why" of this method of ministry in mind. "A holistic transformation in the lives of people is inherent to the good news of Jesus. New beginnings and people becoming a new creation in him is fundamental to the gospel. It is crazy to debate the social gospel. It's 'both/and' and 'all of the above.' Further, it's what we see with Jesus. It's care and compassion for the poor that cannot be a forgotten segment of our communities."

How Genesis Does It

Cowles notes how Fort Collins is a great place to live and thus attracts new residents ripe for involvement in churches, particularly new churches. But, says Cowles, many of them seem to be aiming for the same kinds of people. "There are tons of church plants since we planted this church that come into Fort Collins . . . that all target the same audience, and it's a pretty affluent audience that can pay the bills. And I get it." But the Genesis Project has felt called in another direction—one that, frankly, looks a bit insane to anyone with a penchant for a more traditional model.

> None of what we do makes any sense financially. It's the worst business plan. But this is God's economy that blesses when you love and care for the least of these. We just finished an expansion that cost five million dollars, and one group of donors, because they believed in what we were doing, wrote a check for 4.4 million of that. It's impossible for us to even consider being in the building we're in now. It just doesn't make sense apart from God just moving the hearts of people. And so I think that's probably it. I just fundamentally believe that the gospel includes a holistic approach to people's lives and that God so loves to see a group of people do that that he blesses it.

Cowles ministered in Colorado Springs before moving to Fort Collins. While there, he was in a restaurant and heard a group of movers in the booth behind him discussing how horrible the city was and how they hated living there. As a relatively new pastor in town, Cowles wondered what caused this city that he had been born in to become a place that these men so passionately wanted to leave. The men finally collectively settled on the culprit: it was the influx of evangelical ministries that had relocated to Colorado Springs. In fact, one of them remarked, "My dream is to build a strip club right next door to Focus on the Family and call it Focus on the Fanny." That comment elicited laughter, but Cowles's heart sank, and he felt God speak to him in that moment: *Establish a ministry that will demonstrate love in tangible ways with no strings attached.*

Cowles has become skeptical that churches that aren't already doing that can easily adopt a compassionate ministry approach.

> I don't know if it can happen, honestly. I think pastors and leaders have to be prepared to take some lumps, because everyone wants that as part of their creed. . . . But they don't want someone tweaking on meth next to them at a Sunday morning service.

If it could happen, maybe there's just a group of people that have that heart and passion within the church and can get approval to begin to just meet needs in really simple ways. And really, once it starts, it becomes contagious when you really begin to see people's lives changed. But that kind of turn is typically a massive congregational headache.

And many of the headaches come from the reality of the addicted and impoverished world entering the four walls of the church. "We've had a couple of instances of violence at the church with people tweaking on meth," says Cowles. "I've had to flush cocaine down the toilet. I mean, it's not safe. It's *not* safe. Ministry like this is messy." He continues:

> We lose a lot of people, or at least we did when we first started, because they just said, "I don't feel safe there," and my response was always, "Yeah, it's not." But I don't think we've ever been called to be safe. I don't think that's what Scripture teaches. I don't think that's what the history of the church teaches. This isn't safe. We're not called to be safe. Now, we don't take foolish risks. Obviously, our kids are our priority when it comes to safety, but we don't want to be a hopelessly consumer-oriented church in America that leaves the hurting behind.

Cowles appreciates Gary Haugen, founder and CEO of International Justice Mission, who describes the "Christian cul-de-sac."[17] Haugen says that cul-de-sacs were devised by suburban planners to create safety. Since there would be no through traffic, kids could run free without fear of harm. But after decades of study, researchers discovered that more children are hit by cars backing out of driveways than by those moving forward on streets. It is so obvious now that some cities are prohibiting cul-de-sacs because of the danger.[18]

In other words, what was created for safety turned out to be dangerous. And churches can do the same thing by making their experiences totally safe and shielded from all manner of harm but then find that another kind of harm makes itself known. Specifically, Cowles wonders if our Christian cul-de-sac creates a spiritual danger for congregants,

17. Gary A. Haugen, *Just Courage: God's Great Expedition for the Restless Christian* (Downers Grove, IL: IVP Books, 2008), 31–32.
18. See the NPR story "Cul-de-Sacs: Suburban Dream or Dead End?," June 7, 2006, https://www.npr.org/templates/story/story.php?storyID=5455743.

who were never created for "safety first." Ministry the Genesis Project way is dangerous. But so is ministry in the Christian cul-de-sac.[19]

o————◇————o

We have looked at four churches, three different nations, substantially different contexts. And yet the pastor of each of these congregations knew what the loving grace of God had meant to their own salvation and fully intended that it wouldn't end there with their lives or the lives of their congregations. And years after the emphasis of shared love had taken root, many come to each of these churches and ask, "How do you do all that you do?" Answer: One step out of the door of the church at a time. Find a ministry of compassion. Celebrate it. Share the story. And then watch others who want to take those same steps with you and begin adding feet to kingdom dreams. And soon, at least with these churches, you have a movement. But for every one of these churches, it started with a first inspired step out of the door.

19. See Rob Cowles and Matt Roberts, with Dean Merrill, *The God of New Beginnings: How the Power of Relationship Brings Hope and Redeems Lives* (Nashville: W Publishing, 2018).

CHAPTER 6

Strategic Pastoral Leadership

Toward Valuing Works in the Local Church

I f one peruses church websites, queries pastors, calls district and national denominational headquarters, and observes what happens in
most communities, it becomes clear that works of mercy are rarely
a week-by-week, consistent commitment. To be sure, many churches
frequently have sporadic efforts in play for their church year—a Thanks-
giving or Christmas emphasis, an annual or biannual workday of sorts,
or short-term forays to mission fields whether foreign or domestic.
But far fewer efforts are made to engage congregants in weekly, even
monthly, compassionate outreach to the unevangelized and the dis-
advantaged. In our calls to churches, we found many megachurches,
for instance, that could testify that they had substantial efforts toward
helping hurting people in their communities and around the world. But
when queried further, proportionately few could attest to more than
low single digits in percentage of their congregation who were engaged
weekly or monthly toward that need.

But such churches do exist and tend to have reputations that are
enviable among congregational leaders who know them. So after inter-
viewing the pastors of the four churches featured in the previous chapter, we identified additional congregations whose pastors were willing
to affirm that at least 20 percent of those attending were engaged weekly
in works of mercy or evangelism:

Sean Kelly, Greenford Christian Church (Greenford, OH)

Leland Lantz, Lutheran Church of the Cross (Laguna Woods, CA)

Elbert McGowan, Redeemer Church (Jackson, MS)

Cindy Molnar, Table of Grace Church (Apache Junction, AZ)

Kristen Raine, Sharpstown United Methodist Church (Sharpstown, NJ)

Brian Rice, Living Word Community Church (Red Lion, PA)

Jeff Stachmus, First Baptist Church (Fairfield, TX)

Rob Strickland, Highland Community Church (Columbus, GA)

We integrated their comments with those of the preceding four pastors to formulate workable strategies for local churches seeking to involve more laity in outreach. As in the last chapter, we place a special emphasis on works of mercy, knowing that nearly every congregation gives significant attention to works of piety—worship, small groups, Bible study, prayer, and communion. Far, far fewer place a similar accent on works of mercy. Here are a number of leadership principles that we gleaned from the pastors of churches that are active in works of mercy.

- Lead by example (personally adopt the means of grace).
- Be intentionally biblical.
- Learn from your community.
- Start something.
- Let laity lead.
- Be compassionate *and* evangelistic.
- Build a culture of participation.
- Open wide the doors.
- Plant.

Lead by Example

Rob Strickland of Highland Community in Columbus, Georgia, is as bold as Jesus and Paul at the point of the admonition, "Follow me" and "Come be like me." "I seek to articulate to everyone that my life is my sermon," Strickland says. "I do what I can to conduct my life in a way that aligns with Scripture and the mission the Lord has brought to life here by being consistent in my walk and talk."[1] In Highland Community's work with the poor, such an exemplary emphasis is necessary.

"So," Strickland says, "they see me humbly trying to work out my own sanctification with fear and trembling . . . , and they're having the chance to see what that looks like—in me. . . . For the most part, the people who come to our church have not seen that—previously—but have seen the opposite. They've seen what it looks like to work out impurity and wickedness, so it is exciting for them to be able to hold onto and see someone value God's Word enough to be willing to work out their own sanctification." He adds, "Our church is located smack-dab in the middle of an extremely impoverished neighborhood. . . . We have been intentional about being in proximity to the people that are who the Lord has called us to serve, and they are within this neighborhood. Additionally, we impart to them the good news of the gospel, walking alongside them with counsel and discipleship." Strickland recognizes that for a people to change their direction, they have to see churches and their leaders live faith with integrity and live it close to the people they serve.

This "gospel by example" is neither brash nor antithetical to the New Testament. Throughout the Gospels, Jesus challenges people, "Follow me." Paul issues similar directives. Note the following verses where Paul admonishes believers to emulate *his* life:

> I became your father in Christ Jesus through the gospel. I urge you, then, *be imitators of me.* That is why I sent you Timothy, my beloved and faithful child in the Lord, to remind you of my ways in Christ. (1 Cor. 4:15–17 ESV)

> Give no offense . . . , just as I try to please everyone in everything I do. . . . *Be imitators of me, as I am of Christ.* (1 Cor. 10:32–11:1 ESV)

> Brothers, *join in imitating me,* and keep your eyes on those who walk according to the example you have in us. (Phil. 3:17 ESV)

---

1. Rob Strickland, interview by Matt Friedeman, video call, February 2, 2022. Subsequent Strickland quotations are from that interview.

What you have learned and received and heard and seen in me—*practice these things*. (Phil. 4:9 ESV)

You yourselves know how *you ought to imitate us,* because we were not idle . . . to give you *in ourselves an example to imitate*. (2 Thess. 3:7–9 ESV)

You . . . have followed my teaching, my conduct, my aim in life, my faith, my patience, my love, my steadfastness, my persecutions and sufferings. (2 Tim. 3:10–11 ESV)

The Greek word *mimētēs,* translated as "imitator," appears only six times in the New Testament. Five of those instances are from Paul's writings, and only he uses the term this audaciously: be imitators or followers of *me* (1 Cor. 4:16; 11:1)! It is a bold but probably necessary leadership style that seems to be reflected in Strickland's understanding.

Leading by example is essential to ensuring an active church. Sean Kelly's congregation, Greenford Christian Church in Greenford, Ohio, was planted in 1831 in a community that today numbers about 350 people. The church itself, though, consists of about 2,000 each Sunday, with people traveling from all over the region to attend. He recalls a recent staff meeting whose main topic was "How do we [the staff] get out of the building more? How can we get out of the daily grind of internal ministry and *go and do* ministry?"[2] There is much that needs to be done by a staff within the building, but Kelly knows that it is all too easy to get caught up in this work and forget why your ministry was established: primarily, to touch those *outside* the building.

Roberto Stevenson (Tierra Prometida) maintains that one of the keys to motivating his laity to action is to "get a ministry yourself." After decades in Mexico City, he has noticed that people tend to follow the pastor's lead, both theologically and practically. If the pastor is active, the people will be too. If the pastor is stagnant and inert, the people will likely reflect a similar habit. Stevenson oversees a church of 8,000 as well as sixty church plants. But ministries like street evangelism, through which Tierra's founding pastor initially discovered Stevenson, still captivate his heart. As a result, all of Tierra knows that their pastor is deeply committed to ministry among the downtrodden, especially

2. Sean Kelly, interview by Matt Friedeman, video call, January 26, 2022. Subsequent Kelly quotations are from that interview.

the prison community where he ministers regularly and, because of his own prison background, finds personal refreshment. When he announces a new ministry or the expansion of an existing one, his congregation knows that it issues from one whose heart resonates with the poor and who is himself personally involved with them on a weekly basis. Laity could (and often do) follow the example of a pastor who talks about but doesn't participate in works of mercy.[3]

Many of the pastors interviewed for this chapter contend that the same principle of pastoral example holds regarding the disciplines of personal prayer and Bible study, fasting, and small groups. Rob Strickland explains that the "'works of piety' serve as the nutritious part of our church." They are important for far more than the pastor and staff; they are also important for individual members and the wider body. The sanctification that begins with personal and corporate devotional life "flows into missional work, the outworking of what we sow and encounter in our relationship with the Lord personally. Works of piety are how health is built and maintained and how it becomes the sustainer of works of mercy. Without them, everything would topple over."

Be Intentionally Biblical

The pastors in our sampling have outward-bound churches to the needy because they *earnestly desire* such churches. And basically, they want this because they find prominent evidence for such an emphasis in Scripture. Naturally, this spills over into all aspects of the church, not least the pulpit.

Joyce Tonui (Immanuel Africa Gospel Church) constantly reinforces from the pulpit the necessity of outward-bound ministry. Without frequent emphasis on such ministry, she says, "churches can get very self-centered."[4] Every pastor we interviewed agreed. Much of what happens outside the church begins with a robust pulpit presentation of pertinent pericopes from both the Old and the New Testaments,[5] with particular emphasis on the words of Jesus.

3. Roberto Stevenson, interview by Matt Friedeman, video call, December 13, 2021.

4. Joyce Tonui, interview by Matt Friedeman, video call, January 11, 2022.

5. It may be interesting to readers to note which pericopes were cited by these pastors as they instructed their people in compassionate ministry. We didn't ask for an exhaustive list, but these were

Rob Strickland asserts that, without a doubt, congregational effort toward the serious needs of the community starts with "healthy preaching."

> By that I mean that it is important that we look at the Bible and allow it to interpret us as opposed to looking at the Bible in a way that we're looking to get something for ourselves. I think that has been the most important ingredient. . . . If we didn't have a good grip on Scripture at church and handle Scripture with integrity, then all of this wouldn't have a healthy foundation for the church to stand on. With all of these programs and ministries going on, you're going to have storms and sunny days. When people saw that a healthy view of Scripture was a priority here, they began to buy in to what God was calling us to do.

Even so, Sean Kelly proposes that the best pulpit is one that is not "overvalued": "I don't want to devalue Sunday morning; I want to *rightly value* Sunday morning. I think there are a lot of churches that overvalue the gathering and forget that we have to live out our faith the other six days of the week. If we claim that this is a place of not only spiritual nourishment but training . . . , there is a *going and doing* to it. We teach it, but we must also live it." Passionately communicating "works" from Scripture and being persistent in the message across time is a powerful means to lay the groundwork for moving people from inside the building outward to a hurting world. Churches that are doing so have pastors who use the pulpit mightily to this end.

Learn from Your Community

Darrell Whiteman, anthropologist and former missionary, cautions that too often pastors who leave comfortable confines to minister go "with too high an opinion of ourselves."

> How often do we go consciously expecting to learn? We don't. We go as the teachers and as the authorities. If we go as theologians, we've been trained with all the right doctrine; if we go as doctors, we've been trained

---

the ones mentioned: Gen. 12:1–3; Prov. 19:17; 29:7; Isa. 58:6–12; Mic. 6:8; Matt. 22:36–38; 25:31–46; 28:18–20; Luke 4:18–19; 10:25–37; John 13:35; James 1:27; 1 John 3:16–17.

with all the right surgical techniques. If agriculturalists, we go with all the right grains of river rice to grow. . . . It creates an endless mentality of the expert. I find that people learn and will be more open to what you had to say if you take the posture of a learner and fellow pilgrim.[6]

In this spirit, it is important to resist the temptation to present ourselves as some sort of savior who has all the answers to rectify the circumstances of those whom we seek to help. As agents of God's grace, we should go as learners, grow in relationship with them, and absorb insights about them and their culture in order to discern how the church might be able to lend aid.

Sean Kelly explains,

> A question we always ask as a gospel-centered community is, "What is good news to your community?" Every community has a different set of good news. We have a community not far from us that is just riddled with drug abuse. So good news for them is not painting their fire hydrants. You have to find what is good news to them. Is there a felt need that we can meet? If you meet felt needs with no strings attached, then people get curious and ask, "Why would you do this?"

Jeff Stachmus pastors First Baptist Church in Fairfield, Texas, a congregation of 175–200 in a town of about 4,000. The best way to know and be known there is to encourage the church to get involved in the civic community and consider that involvement a part of intentional ministry. Stachmus says, "Being part of the community is huge. We go to the football games, work concessions during the season, feed the football team breakfast on game day, for instance. We are there for all of the school events—band concerts, athletics, other special things. Whatever is going on, the church is there because the church is made up of the community."[7]

Laity are encouraged to attend these events, but staff is also expected to get involved at the community level. As senior pastor, Stachmus leads the way by participating in advisory councils at the high school. When

---

6. Matt Friedeman, *The Master Plan of Teaching: Understanding and Applying the Teaching Styles of Jesus* (Wheaton: Victor Books, 1990), 43. The quotation is from an original interview with Whiteman.

7. Jeff Stachmus, interview by Matt Friedeman, video call, January 26, 2022. Subsequent Stachmus quotations are from that interview.

he arrived at First Baptist in 2019, the church's motto was prominently displayed on the walls of the church and on a billboard in town: "It's all about relationships!"

> Whether it's doing the community events through the chamber of commerce . . . , we are trying to interact with the community, trying to get to know them. And this leads you into all kinds of specific mission partnerships by networking in the community. You put yourself in the position to discover a variety of needs by getting to know a variety of people—say, the sheriff or even other church leaders. From this has come jail ministry on Thursday nights for both men and women, working with a local nondenominational church that operates the local food pantry, intercommunity prayer groups at the courthouse.

Staff and laity at First Baptist have also partnered with Casas por Cristo,[8] building houses at the border between El Paso and Juarez. Stachmus affirms, "It inspires you. It fans the flame that is inside you. It reignites the passion for faith, and as James said, 'Faith without works is dead.'"

Elbert McGowan of Redeemer Church in Jackson, Mississippi, continually evaluates needs in the surrounding community with his interracial congregation. McGowan describes this process as holding themselves up to the "light of Jesus" and "our commitment to this parish." He notes, "That ebbs and flows. It changes. It's dynamic. Communities change. As residents change and people move as people do, we're always assessing what we're doing. Who is in our parish? What are the needs there? How can we intersect with them with the gospel?"[9]

Steve Moore, who helped revitalize the Wesley Foundation at Texas Tech, utilized six questions to formulate a direction for ministry.[10]

1. What are the needs of the people of this campus?
2. Where are these people spiritually, intellectually, and emotionally?
3. What is the message we really desire to communicate to this campus?

---

8. To learn more about Casas por Cristo, go to their website: https://casasporcristo.org.

9. Elbert McGowan, in-person interview by Matt Friedeman, January 25, 2022. Subsequent McGowan quotations are from that interview.

10. See Friedeman, *Master Plan of Teaching*, 43–44.

4. What is the most effective way to communicate our message as good news and not as bad or irrelevant news?

5. What will this good news mean in terms of behavior, values, and worldview to the people of this setting?

6. How can we appeal to the university mindset with our message?

Moore sent out a handful of college students with these questions to poll and observe the campus community. After gathering and analyzing the data, the group took bold steps to structure its basic program to meet the many needs of the Texas Tech community. The Wesley Foundation grew from under a dozen students involved to a ministry of eight hundred people weekly. McGowan deems this kind of work—in the terminology of a former professor—*theography* (combining two words, "theology" and "geography"). The process involves discerning the needs of a particular geographical context and finding applicable theological answers.

Leland Lantz, pastor at Lutheran Church of the Cross in Laguna Woods, California, advises canvassing the neighborhood.[11] He recalls Rick Warren's initial survey of the Saddleback Valley area, in the early days of Saddleback Church. Warren and his team went door to door in their community and asked the following:

• What do you think is the greatest need in this area? (This question simply got people talking to me.)

• Are you actively attending any church? (If they said yes, I thanked them and moved on to the next home.)

• Why do you think most people don't attend church?

• If you were to look for a church to attend, what kind of things would you look for?

• What could I do for you? What advice can you give to a minister who really wants to be helpful to people?[12]

A couple who now attends Church of the Cross remembers one of Warren's team coming to their door. That inspired Lantz to think, "Why

11. Leland Lantz, interview by Matt Friedeman, video call, January 27, 2022. Subsequent Lantz quotations are from that interview.

12. Rick Warren, "Understanding Unbelievers," *Christian Post*, April 13, 2007, https://www.christianpost.com/news/understanding-unbelievers.html.

not canvass?" And further, why not pose some questions to the next larger-than-usual crowd at Church of the Cross—Christmas Eve services? Lantz and his staff and laity distributed surveys to both visitors and members, asking what might interest them—from Bible studies, to movie nights, to children and youth activities, to volunteering to help the community. From that questionnaire, dozens of community members who hardly ever came to services volunteered to engage in compassionate ministry with Church of the Cross. Key to this style of theography is not simply going door to door with questions but making significant inquiries when the community comes to the church. And canvassing the community need not be complicated. DaySpring Community Church's oft-stated hope is to "run to the sound of the pain." This commitment prompts relatively simple questions: Where is the pain? Who needs us? Where can we help? The answer has been an activated response toward abortion clinics, prisons, nursing homes, schools, a strip club.

Rob Strickland of Highland Community Church is an admirer and literary protégé of John Perkins.[13] Perkins is well known for advocating "relocation": to best reach a people, it is necessary to live in the same community with them. Strickland explains, "The work of the church is based on the reality that I not only pastor here, but I live here. I am a neighbor here, first. We do life together, not just on Sundays, but on Tuesdays on the sidewalks; we eat dinner together, have coffee, and exchange life together. We have become not just neighbors, but family." This approach brings credibility, positioning those who minister not as outsiders but as residents with the same challenges of crime, poor infrastructure, and broken families, while building relationships to open avenues of communication and hope.

John Perkins puts it this way:

> Without relocation, without living among the people, without actually becoming one of the people, it is impossible to accurately identify the needs as the people perceive them. And once outsiders misdiagnose the problem, their proposed solutions cannot help but miss the mark. They will almost always treat symptoms without touching the disease. In fact, the relief of the uncomfortable symptoms may remove the incentive to

---

13. Perkins was mentioned as significant by four pastors featured in these latter chapters: Rob Strickland, Elbert McGowan, Brian Rice, and Matt Friedeman.

cure the disease. The person in need becomes addicted to the program that provides temporary relief while the disease eats away at his humanity. The very program designed to save the victim destroys him.[14]

There are various ways to relocate, but one thing is certain among those who practice compassionate ministry in earnest: staying in the building and waiting for people to come to the church is generally not effective. The church needs to go.

Start Something

Churches working in their communities tend to initially engage members in less challenging or short-term outreach activities. As passion is ignited and confidence and skills increase, they often progress to deeper involvement in ministry. In the discipleship ecosystem of Sharpstown United Methodist Church of Sharpstown, New Jersey, pastors Doug Smith and Kristen Raine promote smaller, short-term ministries as a gateway to more substantial and regular outreach. To this end, Sharpstown United Methodist focuses each month on a different ministry effort, to propel members to get involved:

January	Code Blue Angel Tree gift ministry, Cookies for Jail
February	Cornerstone Pregnancy Center fundraiser and collection
March	Homeless help on streets in Philadelphia
April	Stop Hunger Now food-packing event
May	iServe
June	"Church has left the building to serve the community"
July	Delanco Camp
August	VBS
September	Yard-sale fundraiser
October	See You at the Pole, Water Walk
November	Operation Christmas Child collection and preparation
December	Operation Christmas Child packing party and collection center

14. John Perkins, *With Justice for All: A Strategy for Community Development* (Ventura, CA: Regal, 2007), 65.

From this beginning, members who serve are often inspired and motivated to more regularly engage serious need. Sharpstown has developed ministry foci to meet those aspirations: an intensive weekly prayer hour, jail ministry, outreach to widows, crisis pregnancy center involvement, visitation to shut-ins and hospitals, MOPS (mothers of preschoolers) mentors, involvement in multiple recovery groups, and mission trips.[15]

Sean Kelly's church, Greenford Christian, ministers to twenty-two different high schools. Their strategy is simple: they contact superintendents, schools, and city hall and simply ask, "What are your needs? How can we help you?" The genius of the approach is persistence and longevity. The church keeps making those calls to the leaders, schools, and city halls year after year after year. The church regularly cleans up five parks in the community. They paint fire hydrants. They repaint walls that have been defaced by graffiti. They send people into towns to sanitize the public bathrooms. They donate coffee shop gift cards to nursing-home staff and to fire departments to express appreciation for these essential services. And they repeat these acts of service over many years. Kelly elaborates,

> Now, we have done so much of this for so long that we actually have communities calling us when there is a need because we have built this rapport with our community leaders. The hard part is that the impact is not instantaneous. This is where a lot of churches miss it. They want an instant impact after an event. . . . For us, we decided to attack it from a completely different standpoint. We just want to be in our community and impact it as much as we can. We want to be a presence in our community so that when people have spiritual questions, issues, they remember us because they have seen us in action.

Not all the emphases are short-term, albeit annual, approaches. For instance, the church operates the Big Reach Center of Hope with weekly food and clothing distribution. Other community pantries have come to rely on Big Reach for food items. The important thing, stresses Kelly, is that "we are not an inward-focused church." In other words, the desire is to be not a "come and see" ministry but a "go and do and

15. Kristen Raine, interview by Matt Friedeman, video call, February 16, 2022.

be" ministry. Maintaining this consistent witness across years may eventuate in a teacher visiting the church and remarking, "I've been getting these welcome-to-school gifts, and we just decided that we wanted to check you out." Very often those visitors become members and then themselves begin serving. Kelly explains, "Again, it is not gimmicky. . . . I think it is what Jesus did. He just showed the love of God to people, and it makes them curious. . . . We don't pass out tracts or whatever; people just get curious and want to know what it is about."

Let Laity Lead

"Staff" is a necessary, if potentially problematic, reality in many local churches. They can be immensely helpful to a growing church. The problem arises when the staff assumes the majority of organizing and running a ministry and risks undermining lay involvement. At Day-Spring Community Church, the congregation is frequently admonished, "If you have an idea for a new ministry, let's talk!" That conversation might result in the idea being promoted, tweaked, or shelved. But typically, the nascent ministry idea is presented to the congregation in order to gauge interest; those who sense a call to the potential ministry then gather and begin to pray and plan. When things are in order, they return to the congregation to launch the new ministry and recruit volunteers.

Redeemer Church's similar policy is more firmly codified in a document, "How to Begin a New Outreach/Mercy Ministry at Redeemer." That statement explains,

> We encourage the development of grassroots efforts of ministry within the body of Christ at Redeemer. This means that primarily our ministries will derive from the hearts and the passion of the members of Redeemer as God moves among His people.
>
> Ministries should be managed, operated and serviced primarily by members of church versus the paid staff or the officers of the church. (This core value does not preclude the involvement and leadership of officers and staff but is meant to encourage the development of new leadership and the involvement of all the members of Redeemer.)

And then the particulars:

Process for Starting a Ministry at Redeemer:

Research the Field: When a member of Redeemer senses a desire
to create a new ministry effort to reach the lost or to minister to
the hurting and those in need, that person is encouraged to call
the church office and seek counsel from a pastor (or team leader,
committee head). . . . Together they can look to see if there is a
ministry that we already have in place that is either doing that
same ministry or something similar. Second, they can check
to see if Redeemer is already in partnership with a ministry in
the city that is accomplishing the same or a similar goal. If so,
it might be more advantageous for the body of Christ and that
member to work alongside an already established ministry.

Launching Discovery Prayer: If there is no similar ministry effort,
or the local ministries cannot accommodate to include this ministry's vision and goals, then the member will be encouraged to
begin a 30-day season of prayer and can invite people with similar interests or calling and passion to join in a time of discovery
prayer. That member and interested parties can seek God for his
guidance, his resources and his people to be led in regard to a
workable vision and sustainable mission for our church in the
new ministry effort. This is a great time to pray for the target audience who will benefit from this ministry. (Col. 4:1–6 is a good
guide to follow in prayer.)

Report Back to Move Forward: After the 30 days of prayer, the person will report back to the committee to let them know where
the Lord is leading in this area. If everyone is in agreement that
we are to proceed to the next level, the person will be asked to
submit a written proposal, a working model of what the ministry
would accomplish, its mission and goals, identifying the key leadership of the ministry effort, the number of team members that
will be required, a beginning budget, location of the ministry,
needed supplies and how this ministry will be sustained. Once
a workable, sustainable vision and mission has been created, a
written proposal will be presented to the Mercy Ministry Committee or the Home Missions Committee. . . .

Recognition of a New, Established Mercy or Outreach Ministry: Upon
approval of the session, the ministry will be recognized as an

official ministry of the church . . . with its own planning, programming, budgeting, communications, reporting and recruiting functions and responsibilities. Regular reports will be made to the committee of the church or the diaconate in writing.[16]

Pastor McGowan adds, "I tell our people in our New Members class that if there is something that Redeemer ought to be doing that we aren't doing, this is where you come in." Redeemer embraces the concept of the priesthood of all believers and anticipates that many new initiatives will begin with both established members and those who are newer to the body. New ministry at Redeemer is thus encouraged, guidelines provided, prayerful discernment advised, clear expectations given for its development, and resources made available (if necessary) for continuance.

At Living Word Community Church in Red Lion, Pennsylvania, missional movement toward the community is promoted from the pulpit and in small groups. But pastor Brian Rice recognizes that good intentions don't always translate into action. "You've got to create practical avenues to actually get involved. Most people will not do it on their own, so we just have to make it as easy as possible for them."[17] "We have four core words: connect, grow, serve, reach. The word 'serve' is an internal component where we want everybody to be serving someplace. But then 'reach'—we're just constantly telling the congregation, 'You gotta reach! Get out into your neighborhood, you've got to get into places and people that you don't know.'"

Living Word clearly publicizes where people can sign up and show up to participate in various ministries with which the congregation partners—a community rescue mission, a food bank, a ministry to unwed mothers, a local school outreach, a moving ministry that assists low-income people, and a car-care ministry that changes oil and performs minor repairs for those who can't afford to pay for these services. These activities provide a missional platform that facilitates not only the meeting of needs but also building relationships that the church hopes to leverage for sustained community.

16. Redeemer Church, "How to Begin a New Outreach/Mercy Ministry at Redeemer."
17. Brian Rice, interview by Matt Friedeman, video call, February 3, 2022. Subsequent Rice quotations are from that interview.

Be Compassionate *and* Evangelistic

An unfortunate dichotomy exists in the minds of too many evangelicals who perceive a bifurcation between evangelism and compassionate ministry. George G. Hunter III, in his volume *To Spread the Power*, recounts the experience of Father Vincent J. Donovan among the Masai tribes of eastern Africa. When he arrived, he observed schools, hospitals, and other services, established for the benefit of the Masai. Interestingly, however, no Masai had committed their life to Christ. Missionaries who had served before him were so absorbed in the ministry of compassion that they had lost the initial vision of evangelization. Donovan explained to one of the Masai chiefs that he intended to take the spiritual side of the matter much more seriously. The chief asked, "If that is why you came here, why did you wait so long to tell us about this?"[18]

While the churches and pastors we surveyed apply a variety of approaches to engaging their communities, all seek to evangelize and make Christ known through various endeavors. Roberto Stevenson is the hands-on leader of a megachurch, overseeing a large staff, a school, sixty church plants, and a handful of businesses. But I (Matt) have seen him hustle into the front seat of a cab after ordering his companion into the back seat for prayer support, so that he could lead the cab driver to the Lord (which, he did). Stevenson is a busy man with an enormous load of ecclesiastical responsibilities; nonetheless, he clearly understands that his first business is the saving of souls for the kingdom. I have also had opportunity to minister with him in Mexico City's maximum-security prison. Because he himself found salvation while incarcerated, preaching to prisoners is high on his list of passions. Meeting people at the point of their need often creates receptivity, especially to someone offering hope. And from compassionate ministry typically arise excellent opportunities for evangelism and discipleship.

Often an evangelism mindset needs to be cultivated, not because people are resistant to sharing the gospel but because they're unprepared. Brian Rice notes, "Most people don't do evangelism because they're not good at it."

---

18. George G. Hunter III, *To Spread the Power: Church Growth in the Wesleyan Spirit* (Nashville: Abingdon, 1987), 16–17.

> We're trying to get people out there with ministries of compassion and care, building relationships, getting to know the stories of other people, telling our stories. You just have to get them out of their comfort zones. In these ministries there is the greater likelihood of real, meaningful sharing of our faith. . . . We don't expect most Christians to be able to do that . . . , but if you can get those you are ministering to connected with our church in some way, we can wind up helping them. We like to use the language "Cross the lines of faith." So our biggest thing is getting people mobilized to take care, to serve, to connect outside of their Christian sphere.

Do that, says Rice, and new connections to the church are the natural by-products.

Build a Culture of Participation

Mission statements and their actual impact can be vastly overestimated; if they are generic in nature or simply not incorporated into church life, they have little effect. Rob Strickland's church, Highland Community, avoids those pitfalls. Boldly embedded on their website and in the heart of the pastor is this objective: "To give the Gospel to the poor through our lives laid down and the name of Jesus Christ being lifted up as Savior." According to Strickland, it's more than a mission statement. "It's my life. It has become the very fiber of who I am as a person, in the role of shepherd or pastor, and the life of our church as a whole." Springing from Highland are three ministries intended to change the community in which it resides:

- a private Christian school for neighborhood kids
- a trade school where adults can learn culinary arts, urban farming, janitorial and construction skills, how to study Scripture, how to budget, how to parent, how to handle job interviews, and a plethora of other proficiencies designed to establish them as productive citizens
- a housing initiative in which dilapidated structures are acquired and are subsequently renovated by the trade school construction team, thus rebuilding the community through neighborhood hands

These initiatives are rooted in a corporate commitment that has become enfleshed in the life of its members.

The approach of Redeemer Church under Elbert McGowan's leadership is similar. He clearly presents the church's fivefold philosophy of ministry. Redeemer wants every member to have an opportunity

- to worship,
- to give,
- to learn,
- to connect, and
- to serve.

"That," says McGowan, "describes health."

Recall Joyce Tonui's church in Kenya and their emphasis, as an extension of their denominational commitments, on the five "E's":

E1—Evangelizing the unsaved

E2—Establishing churches

E3—Edifying believers

E4—Equipping leaders

E5—Exercising compassion[19]

These are not just fodder for websites or bulletins. Rather, they are talked about much, preached on, brought up in board meetings, and leveraged in efforts practically expressed through medical camps, veterinary medicine outreach, ministry to the bereaved, visitation to the sick, prison ministry, and disaster relief.

All the pastors we interviewed agreed that individual and corporate prayer are essential to the ongoing outreach and impact of their congregations. But a few were adamant that prayer is not enough. Prayer that gets stuck in prayer alone is probably not healthy for churches. And the same seems to be the case for financial giving. For international missions in particular, financial support is critical, especially so

19. "AGC Vision and Five E's," Good Shepherd Africa Gospel Church, accessed October 21, 2022, http://www.goodshepherdagc.com/good-morning/.

for the relatively wealthy American church. But while some congregations allow their charitable giving to stop at the support of ministry, the churches in this study never let it end there. DaySpring actually has a policy with this in mind: when considering financial support of ministries in the community, we are open to giving if we have the laity of our church actively involved with that ministry.

Working against an "involvement culture," asserts Jeff Stachmus, is the modern tendency toward being "consumer driven, turning inward and becoming about programs"—an "If you build it, they will come" mindset. "It's easy to get caught up in that," says Stachmus. "It's the way the world thinks. What makes my life easier? What will help me have the better, more comfortable life?" As an extension of this concern, he says, the general understanding of "the building as geography" is not helpful.

> I think sometimes we think of church as "the location"—that, geographically, the church is the goal. We need to be intentional that we think of ourselves not going to church, not coming to church, but that we need to be the church. Now, those things have become cliché over the years, but we are very intentional about that. The destination is not here. . . . The destination is to get people into the kingdom of God and to see him glorified.

"Get people involved outside of the building," says Brian Rice of Living Word Community Church, "and in a way that obviously engages congregational gifts with serious human need, and you will find that it changes them." Whether through a global mission trip or local outreach, they typically describe the experience as one of the most impactful things they have ever done, and they start operating with a kingdom mindset that had hardly, before their involvement, been tapped.

Open Wide the Doors

Loving people on the margins of culture, as do many of the churches described in these pages, often draws the marginalized into the center of church life. Both Elbert McGowan and Rob Cowles have described that process as "messy." Cowles advises that this "messiness" can be very uncomfortable for people used to a more traditional church setting.

I remember one homeless guy in his late 20s who used to come hang out in our coffee shop for hours on end. We would talk with him and try to advance our relationship.

Then one Sunday morning he arrived strung out on some drug; I don't even know which one. Suddenly he was reaching into the tip jar at the coffee bar and grabbing all the cash. Mark Orphan, our associate pastor, saw him and said, "Hey, man—you're going to have to put that back. I mean, if you need help with something, tell me about it, and we'll see what we can do. But that money in your hand needs to go back into the jar."

He got belligerent. I ended up nudging him outside the building, quietly repeating what Mark had said. He tightened up his muscles, got within 2 feet of my face, and I honestly thought he was about to take a swing at me with his fist.

"Hold on, man," I said. "You know we love you and care about you here. We always have. We've helped you however we could. But right now, you need to leave. Come back when you're sober, and we can have a conversation."

He walked away. I went back inside to start the morning service. I was into my sermon that day when I glanced out toward the coffee shop—and there he was again, more agitated than ever. Mark was trying once again to handle the situation, when all of a sudden, I saw Mark's body go flying backward. The guy had pushed him, almost knocking him to the ground.

We ended up having to call the sheriff's department, which came out and told him in no uncertain terms he'd better move along, or he'd be charged with trespassing. Fortunately, he at last got the message. Unfortunately, he never did take up my offer to come back in a sober state and continue talking.

So it goes in ministering to troubled souls. It's never going to be a cakewalk.[20]

Often observing these interactions are families, and parents have to make a decision when such chaos ensues: "Is this the kind of church we want to attend?" But if churches are going to reach hurting people, expect these moments.

Cindy Molnar planted Table of Grace Church in Apache Junction, Arizona. From the outset, they opened up their facility for any community groups that needed a meeting place. The United Way and the

---

20. Rob Cowles and Matt Roberts, with Dean Merrill, *The God of New Beginnings: How the Power of Relationship Brings Hope and Redeems Lives* (Nashville: W Publishing, 2018), 203–4.

Homeless Coalition took the church up on that offer, met with Cindy, and explained the possibilities for involvement in the city. Molnar resonated with the homeless problem of Apache Junction and decided to serve them any way she could. While other churches were doing everything they could to put distance between themselves and the homeless population, "homeless people just started flocking into our church." Table of Grace, as a small church of thirty to fifty members, didn't have a huge program; they simply opened the church doors for coffee, and the homeless (whom they call "the overcomers") would come and hang out. "We don't give them money or solutions or clothes, but we do give them Jesus," not infrequently through "healing and deliverance."

At one point, a gentleman was invited to live in the church building. That was a step too far for some in the relatively new congregation, and "we had some leave the church." But subsequently,

> Our congregation has built up. God has led those with a heart for this to our church. We are so deep and strong in this ministry now. He pruned us out, and now he is bringing back the people with the heart for this. They see the vision and back me on it. We do not have any criticism, blame, guilt, or shame. If we have an issue, we go into the prayer room and we pray, empty ourselves, and the Holy Spirit always unites us in our decisions. It is miraculous.[21]

The day after David Wilkerson, of Times Square Church and Teen Challenge fame, died, author Nancy French wrote a remembrance that recalled the first time she attended the church that Wilkerson pastored. Wilkerson said during the service, "Ladies, when we stand to sing, please don't leave your pocketbooks on the ground. Some thieves are here in the sanctuary, so keep an eye out on your belongings. And for those of you who came here expressly to steal, we welcome you. You came here thinking you'd leave with a few bucks, but you'll leave knowing the life-changing love of God. Stay as long as you'd like."[22]

We should be mindful that reaching and receiving people with challenging backgrounds is woven into the earliest church traditions. Paul

---

21. Cindy Molnar, interview by Matt Friedeman, video call, February 2, 2022.
22. Nancy French, "Remembering David Wilkerson," *The Corner* (blog), *National Review*, April 28, 2011, https://www.nationalreview.com/corner/remembering-david-wilkerson-nancy-french/.

challenged the church at Corinth with these words: "Do not be deceived: Neither the sexually immoral nor idolaters nor adulterers nor men who have sex with men nor thieves nor the greedy nor drunkards nor slanderers nor swindlers will inherit the kingdom of God" (1 Cor. 6:9–10). Many evangelicals would give that passage a resounding "Amen!" But in the next sentence, Paul goes on to say, "That is what some of you were. But you were washed, you were sanctified, you were justified in the name of the Lord Jesus Christ and by the Spirit of our God" (6:11). That is a beautiful Pauline expression. But those "washing," "sanctification," and "justification" steps aren't likely to happen if the church isn't, first, ministering on the margins and, second, willing to allow hurting people from those margins into the life of the church.

Plant

In the conventional wisdom of church planting, it is frequently easier to plant a new church than to turn an inward-focused church into an outward-bound one. Rob Cowles's congregation, the Genesis Project, is located on the northeast side of Fort Collins near Interstate 25, which he describes as a "seedy industrial area."[23] But he is thrilled to be there, because a church a couple of hours away, near the same highway, didn't want to have anything to do with his passion toward the disenfranchised.

> I tried it in my church in Colorado Springs and got crucified for it. So I don't have a ton of confidence that [the shift from inward to outward] can happen. That's pretty pessimistic, but it's one of the reasons I really believe in church planting, especially churches that will be planted to reach this segment of society and will be based around demonstrating concern for the same people Jesus seemed concerned with.[24]

McGowan's efforts in Jackson, Mississippi, reflect the same concern. He describes how compassionate ministry was "in our DNA" from the very beginning of Redeemer Church. This church plant had a somewhat unusual start. The original church had decided to leave the area,

23. Cowles and Roberts, with Merrill, *God of New Beginnings*, 3.
24. Rob Cowles, interview by Matt Friedeman, video call, January 25, 2022.

but nearly ninety members decided that they didn't want to leave and were concerned about the void they might leave in a needy area. Their hearts were "tethered" to the people of the area, and they wanted to continue to minister there. The eighty-nine people who stayed in the original location and planted Redeemer Church not only maintained their witness in the community but also ended up growing substantially in attendance and influence and have become a multiethnic example of community ministry. God seems to have blessed them in numerous ways for their commitment.

Robert Dale, in *To Dream Again*, notes the typical organizational health cycle.

> A healthy church is born out of a dream. A group of persons dream of a redemptive ministry in a community. They sense and share what they feel God wants from them in their setting at that moment. Then they take ownership of their vision, band together, and organizational life begins. They clarify their beliefs by Bible study, doctrinal statements, and the hymns they sing repeatedly. They set goals and priorities. They develop programs, policies and procedures, budgets, and institutional habits called norms. Finally, they minister out of the focused dream and the trust that has developed within the congregation.
>
> Then, if the congregation doesn't take steps to open itself to revitalization, a plateau occurs. Decline begins. First, people doubt the structures. . . . Next, they doubt the goals. . . . Then, they doubt the organization's basic beliefs. . . . Finally, they become completely alienated and drop out in total disillusionment. This is absolute doubt and marks the death of the kingdom dream in these persons.[25]

This is all part of the natural life cycle: churches are born, churches grow, churches finally die. But this "open to revitalization" phase matters, and it can happen not only in the way that Dale suggests but also by planting new churches to proliferate the redemptive dream. In fact, given that churches eventually die, planting is one of the best strategies available to a healthy church.

DaySpring was planted, in part, out of a bias toward outreach that had not been evident in the local church that its core group came from.

25. Robert D. Dale, *To Dream Again: How to Help Your Church Come Alive* (1981; repr., Eugene, OR: Wipf & Stock, 2004), 14.

As the fledgling congregation put feet to faith, a new church culture in the plant was created. In recent years, another congregation has been planted out of DaySpring; Foundry Church is thriving and reaching many previously unevangelized, primarily young, people. Foundry's core group was largely composed of young adults whose ministry habits were formed in the context of DaySpring. From the outset, Foundry leaders have successfully incorporated an outward-bound ethic into their church identity. Together, DaySpring and Foundry hope to continue planting additional congregations for whom works of piety and works of mercy are foundational realities.

Tierra Prometida's church planting efforts have been much more extensive, with more than sixty daughter churches throughout Mexico and beyond. Recall that Tierra began as a plant from an inward-focused Catholicism. What is heartening about Tierra's plants is that many are a direct result of compassionate outreach by Tierra; all of them are shaped by the vision and mission of the mother church. Church planting represents a powerful avenue for outward-bound churches to multiply their impact.

Conclusion

Brian Rice says, "A missional God sent a missional Messiah to build a missional church." In other words, Scripture is missional from beginning to end. "You can't be a church without being a missional church. And you have to do it globally and locally, and that is just the core of everything we do." But beware, he says, of an evangelicalism that almost wholly touts receiving Christ as Savior so one can get to heaven but, because of such a bold accent, creates a privatized, nominal, conservative Christianity.

The churches surveyed here span a range of theological and ecclesial traditions, but all have effectively mobilized a significant portion of their congregations for evangelistic and compassionate ministry. They hold in common a commitment to faithfully heed the Great Commandments (Matt. 22:37–39): "'Love the Lord your God with all your heart and with all your soul and with all your mind.' This is the first and greatest commandment. And the second is like it: 'Love your neighbor as yourself.'" Through works of piety, they cultivate a strong spiritual life, and through works of mercy, they express their devotion to God in service to others. Whether a congregation of dozens or of thousands, these churches and their pastors bear witness that faithfulness to God means a life wholly given to his purposes. Salvation is not merely a gift received; it is a reality that by its very nature transforms the recipient into an active conduit of God's grace and mercy to others.

Conclusion

United with Christ, Filled with the Spirit,
Zealous for Good Works

Good News and Good Works

In this book, we have worked to recover a classical Protestant doctrine of good works. We first surveyed important (if sometimes largely forgotten) contributions to Anglican, Lutheran, and Reformed theology with respect to good works. Here we saw that good works are anything but ancillary to salvation and the Christian life; in no sense whatsoever can works of piety and works of mercy be considered optional or "add-on" accessories. No, to the contrary, such works are nothing less than necessary for the Christian. We followed the historical survey with a closer look at the biblical basis for a doctrine of good works. Here we saw that an active and vibrant concern for love of God and love of neighbor pervades not only the Law but also the Prophets, not only the exhortations of James but also the theology of Paul and the teachings of Jesus. Putting the historical and biblical elements together, we then offered a systematic summary of the theology of good works. Then, moving from historical, biblical, and systematic theology to pastoral praxis, we explored some case studies. Here we saw, in real time and real life, not only the doctrine but also the practice of good works in the twenty-first century. Here are examples of Christian ecclesial communities in very diverse settings and in challenging contexts that are, however imperfectly and humbly, intentionally focused on concrete and meaningful expressions of their love for God and their neighbors.

This is a thoroughly Protestant doctrine of good works. We are not engaged in polemics against Roman Catholic accounts; instead, we are, as Protestants, focused on pursuing not only "peace" but also "holiness, without which no one will see the Lord" (Heb. 12:14). We are aware of residual and deep-seated Protestant concerns about the "dangers" of good works. With the confessional Protestant traditions, we deny that good works are meritorious; we do not earn salvation by our good deeds. But we are, following classical Protestant theology, also concerned about the dangers of neglecting good works. More than that, however, we are energized and motivated by the grace of God, which comes to us again and again. This grace prepares the way for salvation, justifies sinners freely through faith alone, brings new life, and produces genuine holiness of heart and life—and calls us to join in the work that God is doing in the world.

Good works are not antithetical to the good news. To the contrary, good works are part of that good news; God works on us and in us so that God can work through us. God justifies us freely by grace alone through faith alone, and good works necessarily follow justification as the "fruit" or evidence of it. God regenerates and sanctifies his people as he prepares them for the glorification of the beatific vision, and God uses good works to do so. And God's grace is even so amazing that it can transform broken and perverted sinners into agents of his redemptive work in the world.

The Call to Discipleship

We learn from Scripture that to belong to God is to belong *wholly* to God. To know Christ as Savior is to know Christ as Lord. To be saved is to be joined in union with Christ, and there is no salvation apart from union with Christ. And to be joined in union with Christ is to come to share not only in Christ's benefits but also in Christ's sufferings; it is *both* to be "crucified with Christ" (Gal. 2:19–20) and participate in the "fellowship of his sufferings" *and* to know "the power of his resurrection" (Phil. 3:10). It is to come to share Christ's affections; it is to love what—*and who*—he loves and to abhor what he abhors.

To be joined in union with Christ is to labor with him in love of God and neighbor.

Make no mistake: when Jesus calls us to himself, he is calling us to a life of radical discipleship, and when he unites us to himself, he unites us with the one who is rejected and crucified. "Whoever wants to be my disciple must deny themselves and take up their cross and follow me. For whoever wants to save their life will lose it, but whoever loses their life for me will find it" (Matt. 16:24–25).

We must be realistic. To be joined in union with Christ, to know him as Savior and confess him as Lord, is to renounce all competing ideologies. To love God supremely—with all one's heart, mind, and strength—is to live in opposition to all regnant ideologies. To love one's neighbor as oneself—to share and extend Christ's love not only to those like us but also to those who are radically unlike us—is to live in open and pronounced defiance of political totalitarianisms and indeed in tension with common political allegiances and alliances.

Commitment to works of piety and works of mercy will call Christians to live in such a way that their most basic commitments and even their very identity stand as a challenge to the ideologies that polarize and divide twenty-first-century culture. Christians make a profound political statement every time they confess Jesus as Lord and express their love for God above all: they belong to God and cannot be "bought." And when Christians actively seek to love their neighbors, they will be called to pursue good deeds that cross tribal allegiances and trespass common "party lines." They will, for instance, be concerned to protect not only the most vulnerable humans in the womb but also their mothers and their siblings who struggle against injustice. They will be exercised not only to oppose legally codified systems of oppression and injustice that haunt modern societies but also to promote methods of personal accountability that foster human flourishing. They will be committed not only to rescue individuals from systems of oppression but also to stand against those systems that oppress. They not only will run into the burning building to rescue people trapped within it but also will seek to diminish and extinguish the fires. They will work not only for the reform of penal institutions but also for the discipleship of prisoners.

But if we must be realistic about grace, we should also be hopeful. Indeed, we should be filled with joy. Think about it: the same God who has worked graciously for us promises to continue his good work within us even as he calls us to join in his work in the world. The same God who draws us into union and communion with Christ also indwells and empowers his people in the person of the Holy Spirit. God has not called Christians to frenetic activity *for God*—as if we are commanded to do our best to try to impress God with how good or holy we are. No, instead God has summoned us to live and work *with God*. We—finite and feeble, broken and weak creatures that we are—are invited and commanded to join God's work in the world. We are not told to do what is impossible and then thrown back upon ourselves to somehow find the resources and the strength to do it. No, the God who calls us into his own life and labor is the same God who fills us with his Holy Spirit. God's salvation—and the good works that are part of it—is all of grace.

This is the good life. The full means of grace is the life of abundance. There is, as we noted, a cost. But the real cost—the unbearably high cost—is for those who turn away from God's commissioning call. The life of the full-orbed utilization of the means of grace—the life of wholehearted love of God and like-minded love of neighbor—is the life of abundance promised in Scripture. The good life—the life promised and provided by God—is the life that promotes human flourishing, the life that seeks the welfare of the city, the life that gives itself away.

Saved by Grace . . . to Do Good Works

Those who are joined in union with Christ by faith are justified. They are in a right relationship with God, and now they are truly free to love God and neighbor. Now what? We recognize that our best efforts to love God and neighbor will sometimes fall short. Our good works are not perfect. But that should not stop us from the pursuit of them. How do we love God more fully? How do we grow in love of God? By committing ourselves to the means of grace. By serious and joy-filled engagement in public worship as expressed in preaching, teaching, public prayer, confession, the celebration of the sacraments, and hymns and other music that bring praise to God. By equally serious devotion to personal discipleship as expressed in prayer, fasting, and accountability.

And how do we love our neighbors more fully? How can we grow in love of neighbors near and far? By serving them (and, of course, by allowing them to serve us). By showing hospitality to strangers and immigrants. By caring for those we may deem to be deficient or inferior or undeserving and those who seem different or threatening. By being advocates for the most defenseless in our communities. By the hard and sometimes frustrating work in prison ministries and homeless shelters and immigration centers. Sometimes simply by showing up again and again and again.

Sometimes it may seem like our efforts are in vain. Sometimes we may be humbled by recognition of our own laziness or complicity in settling for what is comfortable. Sometimes we may realize that we vacillate between periods of energized activism and times of apathy and exhaustion. Sometimes we are convicted by our sloth, and sometimes, when we are industrious, we are guilty of a "holier than thou" mentality that is not edifying for anyone. But we should not be discouraged by our ineffectiveness or our shortcomings or even any remaining sinfulness in our best efforts. Instead, we should "fix our eyes on Jesus, the author and perfecter of our faith" (Heb. 12:2). We should rest secure in the knowledge that to be joined in union with Christ is to be saved and thus to be safe. We should "keep on loving" and helping strangers (13:1–2) as we rejoice in the affirmation that "God has said, 'Never will I leave you; never will I forsake you'" (13:5). We should understand that we are commanded, "Continue to work out your salvation with fear and trembling, for it is God who works in you to will and to act in order to fulfill his good purpose" (Phil. 2:12–13).

Perhaps nowhere is the radically gracious nature of salvation more evident than in the crucifixion of Jesus. In Luke's account of the passion narrative, we see this part of the story: "One of the criminals who hung there hurled insults at him: 'Aren't you the Messiah? Save yourself and us!' But the other criminal rebuked him. 'Don't you fear God,' he said, 'since you are under the same sentence? We are punished justly, for we are getting what our deeds deserve. But this man has done nothing wrong.' Then he said, 'Jesus, remember me when you come into your kingdom.' Jesus answered him, 'Truly I tell you, today you will be with me in paradise'" (Luke 23:39–43).

Two important observations stand out as particularly relevant for us. First, we can see that as soon as this criminal begins to respond to God's grace, he engages in "works of piety" and "works of mercy." For he both admits his position before God and looks to Christ for rescue as well as entreats the other criminal to reconsider and repent. And second, this criminal is saved by grace. He has done nothing to merit salvation; by his own admission, he is a criminal and a sinner who has not earned salvation. Nor can he do anything to build up enough spiritual or moral credit with God, for he has only hours or perhaps minutes of restricted and excruciatingly painful life left. He cannot save himself; without grace there is no hope for him. But there is grace—and thus there is hope. Jesus says to him, "Truly I tell you, today you will be with me in paradise." We are saved by grace from first to last. And we are saved so that we can do good works (Eph. 2:8–10).

Scripture Index

Old Testament

Genesis

1 26n1
1–2 26, 30, 58
1–3 25–26, 31
1:1–25 27
1:1–2:3 26, 27
1:4 26
1:10 26
1:12 26
1:18 26
1:21 26, 27
1:24–25 27
1:25 26
1:26 27, 103
1:26–27 26, 27n4, 28, 29
1:27 103
1:28 27, 31, 32, 33, 58, 103
1:31 27, 101
2:2–3 26, 43
2:4 28
2:4–25 27, 28, 29
2:5 29n9
2:5–6 28
2:7 62
2:7–8 28
2:7–17 28
2:9 29n9, 94

2:10–14 94
2:15 28, 29
2:16–17 30
2:18–20 28
2:21–25 28
3 26, 30
3:4–5 30
3:16 31
3:17–19 31
3:19 31
3:23 28
5:15 43
6:9 32
9:6 27n4
11:4 32
12:1 34
12:1–3 32, 104, 166n5
12:2–3 33, 34, 132n7
12:4 34
15 34, 36, 37n29, 92
15:1 35
15:1–20 104
15:2 35
15:4–5 35
15:5 83
15:6 35, 38, 85, 91, 92
15:7 35
15:8 35
15:9 35

15:10 35
15:13–14 39
15:17 35
15:18 35, 36
17 37, 37n29
17:1 37
17:2 33
17:5 34
17:6 33
17:8 33
17:10 37
17:12 37
17:14 37
21:1–3 37
21:5 37
22 37, 92
22:2 37
22:9–10 92
22:12 38
22:16–18 33
26:3–4 33
28:3 33
35:11–12 33
47:27 33
48:3–4 33

Exodus

1:7 33
2:24 39

3:2 35n20
13:21 35n20
19:1–6 104
19:3–6 39, 41
19:4 39
19:5 39
19:6 105
19:8 40
19:18 35n20
20:3–17 41
20:8–11 42–43
20:14 65
20:18 35n20
22:22–24 54n47
23:30 33
31:14–15 43
32:13 33
35:2 43

Leviticus

19:18 41, 55, 67, 72
26:9 33

Numbers

15:32–36 43

Deuteronomy

1:10–11 33
5:7–21 41
5:14 43
6:5 41, 67
7:13–14 33
8:1 33
10:18 54n47
14:28–29 54n47
15:4 77n37
16:11 54n47
16:14 54n47
24:17 54n47
24:19–21 54n47
26:12–13 54n47
27:19 54n47
28:63 33
30:5 33
30:16 33

31:16–17 44
31:19 44
32 44

Joshua

24:19 110

1 Samuel

9:2 45
10:8 45
11:1–11 45
13 46
13:8–9 45
13:13–14 45
13:14 46, 59
15 46
15:3 45
15:13 45
15:14–15 45
15:21 45
15:22 46
15:22–23 45–46
15:25 46
15:30 46

2 Samuel

7:1–17 105
7:9–11 47n39
7:11b–16 47
7:14 47
7:15 47
11 46
12:13 46

1 Kings

2:3–4 48
3:6 46n38
3:14 46n38
6:12 48
8:25 48
9:4 46n38
9:4–9 48n40
11:4 46n38
11:6 46n38

11:31–33 48n40
11:33 46n38
11:34 48n41
11:38 46n38
11:39 48n41
14:8 46n38
15:3 46n38
15:4 48n41
15:5 46n38, 47
15:11 46n38

2 Kings

8:19 48n41
14:3 46n38
16:2 46n38
18:3 46n38
19:34 48n41
22:2 46n38

1 Chronicles

29:3 39

2 Chronicles

6:16 48n40
7:17 46n38
7:17–18 48n40
17:3–4 46n38
21:7 48n41
28:1 46n38
29:2 46n38
34:2 46n38

Psalms

1:6 49
2 49n42
5:3–7 50n44
5:4 9
7:8 50, 51
7:10–17 50n44
8 27n4
11:5–7 50n44
14:3 51
15 51
15:1–2 51
15:1–5 50n44

17:1 50
17:3–5 50
18:20 51
18:20–24 50–51
18:24 51
24:3–5 49
25:7 51n46
25:11 51n46
26:1–12 51n45
28:3–5 50n44
28:4 50
32 51n46
34:8 100
34:12–16 49–50
36:10–12 50n44
37:37–38 50
41:1 50n44
41:4 51n46
41:12 51n45
50:1–23 50n44
51 46, 51, 51n46
51:16–17 46
51:17 59
58:10–11 50n44
62:12 50, 87
85:1–3 51n46
89:30–32 47
94:21–23 50n44
95 49n42
100:5 99
103:8–12 51n46
106:1 99
107:1 99
125:4–5 50n44
132:11–12 48n40
140:13 50n44

Proverbs

19:17 146, 166n5
24:12 87
29:7 166n5

Ecclesiastes

2:8 39

Isaiah

1–5 54
1:2–4a 52
1:11–15 52–53
1:16–17 53
6 54
6:3 100
6:5 54
6:6–7 54
6:8–10 75n27
6:8–13 54
8:16–9:2 75n27
29:13 54
40–66 54
42:6–7 75n27
43:8 75
43:8–14 54
43:10 75
43:12 75
49:5 54
49:6 54
53:12 54
58:6–12 166n5
60 95n74, 97
60:3 95
60:6–7 95–96
60:9 96
60:11 96
60:13 96
60:19 95
61 63
61:1–2 62, 62n2, 63, 77
61:3 54
65–66 97
65:17 94
65:21–22 94–95
66:22 94

Jeremiah

31:31–34 105
34:18–22 36n23

Ezekiel

17:15 9
36:22–28 54

Amos

2:6–8 55
4:1–2 55–56
4:1–3 55n49
5:7 55n49
5:11–13 55n49
5:14–15a 56
5:21–23 56
5:24 56
5:27 56
6:1 56
6:1–7 55n49
6:4–6 56
6:7 56
7:11 56
7:17 56
8:4–6 55n49

Micah

1:1 57
1:7 57
2:2 57
2:6 57
2:8–9 57
3:1–4 58
3:4 58
3:5–7 57
3:8 57
3:9–10 57–58
3:11 58
3:12 57–58
4:1–8 58
5:2–4 58
6:8 58, 166n5
6:11–12 57
6:12 58
7:2 58

Zechariah

8:17 9

Malachi

3:17 40

New Testament

Matthew

1:1 105
1:21 105
1:23 105
3:10 66n10
3:16 76n32
4:1–11 62
5–7 64–67
5:17–20 64–65
5:20 65
5:21–48 65
5:43–48 72
5:46–47 72
6:1 65
6:7 76n32
6:9–13 76n32
7:12 72
7:13–14 66
7:13–27 65, 71n18
7:15–20 66
7:16–20 69
7:17–20 66
7:21–23 66
7:24 67
7:26 67
7:27 67
8:12 69, 122
10:40–42 71
11:25–26 76n32
12:48–50 72
13:24–30 71n18
13:36–43 71n18
13:42 69, 122
13:47–50 71n18
14:23 76n32
16:13 76n32
16:24–25 189
16:27 71, 71n19
17:1 76n32
18:6 72
18:10 72
18:14 72
19:13 76n32

19:18–19 68
22:13 69, 122
22:36–38 138, 166n5
22:37–38 106
22:37–39 184
22:37–40 41, 67
22:39 106
22:40 106
24:4–25:46 70
24:9 71
24:14 71
24:36–25:30 71
24:51 69, 122
25 68, 72
25:14–46 68–73
25:16 69
25:21 69
25:23 69
25:25 69
25:30 69, 122
25:31 71n19
25:31–33 70, 122
25:31–46 73, 142, 166n5
25:32 70
25:35–36 70, 122
25:37 70
25:40 70, 72, 122
25:41 70, 122
25:42–43 73
25:45 70, 72, 122
25:46 70, 122
26:39 76n32
26:42–43 76n32
28:10 72
28:18–20 73n24, 138, 166n5
28:19 71, 132n7
28:19–20 146

Mark

1:10 76n32
1:35 76n32
2:1–12 140
6:46 76n32
8:27 76n32
9:2 76n32

10:17–19 42
10:19 68
10:45 106
12:29–31 41, 67
14:32 76n32
14:35–36 76n32
14:39 76n32

Luke

1–4 62–64
1:3 74
1:35 62, 75
3:21 76n32
3:23–38 75
3:38 62, 75
4:1–13 62
4:3 62
4:9 62
4:14 62
4:16–21 77
4:18–19 62, 62n2, 166n5
4:21 63
4:31–35 63
4:38–41 63
4:43 63
5:1–11 63
5:16 76n32
5:27–28 63
6:12 76n32
6:12–16 63
6:20 63n3
6:20–21 77n40
7:22 63, 77n40
8:1 63
9 63
9:6 64
9:18 76n32
9:28–29 76n32
10:9 64
10:21 76n32
10:25 68
10:25–28 42, 67
10:25–37 166n5
10:27–28 41
10:29 67

10:33–34 107
10:36 107
10:37 67, 107
11:1 76n32
11:1–4 76n32
12:33 77n40
14:12–14 77n40
14:13 63n3
14:21 63n3
16:16 63
16:19–31 77n40
18:18–20 68
18:21 68
18:22 63n3, 68, 77n40
18:23 68
18:27 68
19:1–10 68
20:1 63
22:14–23 77
22:32 76n32
22:41–42 76n32
22:44–45 76n32
23:34 76n32
23:39–43 191
23:46 76n32

John

3:16 100
11:41–42 76n32
12:27–28 76n32
13:35 146, 166n5
14:6 73n24
16:5–15 108
16:8–14 108
17:1–26 76n32
17:24 101
20:30–31 73n24

Acts

1:1–8 74–76
1:8 74, 75, 76
1:9 74
1:14 76n28
2 108
2:1–8:1a 74

2:21 73n24
2:22 77
2:33 74
2:33–34 77n37
2:38 73n24
2:42 76nn28–30
2:43 77n34
2:46 76n30
3:1 76n28
3:6–8 77n35
4:12 73n24
4:16 77n34, 77n39
4:22 77n34, 77n39
4:24–31 76n28
4:25 49n42
4:30 77n34
4:32–37 77n37
4:34 77n37
5:12 77n34
5:15–16 77n35
5:16 77n36
5:42 76n29, 77n33
6:1–7 77n38
6:4 75n28
6:6 76n28
6:8 77n34
7:59 76n28
8:1b–11:18 74
8:4 77n33
8:6 77n34, 77n39
8:6–7 77n36
8:7 77n39
8:12 77n33
8:13 77n34
8:15 76n28
8:24 76n28
8:25 77n33
8:35 77n33
8:40 77n33
9:4–5 74
9:10–12 74
9:11 76n28
9:15–16 74
9:34 74
9:40 76n28

10:9 76n28
10:36 77n33
10:43 73n24
10:48 73n24
11:5 76n28
11:19–28:31 74
11:20 77n33
11:29–30 77n37
12:5 76n28
12:12 76n28
13:3 76n28
13:22 46
13:32 77n33
14:3 77n34
14:7 77n33
14:15 77n33
14:21 77n33
14:23 76n28
15:7 77n33
15:12 77n34
15:17 71n20
15:35 76n29, 77n33
16:10 77n33
16:18 77n36
16:25 76n28, 76n31
17:18 77n33
18:11 76n29
19:4–5 73n24
19:11 77n34
19:11–12 77nn35–36
20:7 76nn29–30
20:11 76n30
20:20 76n29
20:24 77n33
20:36 76n28
21:5 76n28
21:28 76n29
22:7–8 74
22:16 73n24
22:17 76n28
26:14–18 74
27:35 76n30
28:8 76n28
28:8–9 77n35
28:31 76n29

Romans

1:1–2 85
1:16–17 85
1:18–3:20 85
1:18–4:25 85
1:21 110
1:32 9
2:5 110
2:6 78n42, 87, 89
2:13 87
2:16 87
3:9 51
3:10 85
3:10–12 51
3:20 82n51
3:21–24 85
3:21–26 73n24
3:21–4:25 85
3:22 81
3:25–26 84
3:28 82n51
4 81
4:1–5 82, 83, 91
4:1–25 32, 35
4:2 82n51
4:3 82, 83, 85
4:4 82
4:6 82n51
4:9–12 83
4:9–13 92
4:19 91
4:20 91
4:21 91
5–6 81n48
5:1 86
5:1–8:39 85
5:9 86
7:7–11 38
7:16 38
8:12–13 88
8:13 88
14:10 87
15:11 71n20
16:25 85
16:26 71n20

1 Corinthians

3:10–15 88
3:12–15 88n61
3:14 88n61
3:15 88n61
4:3–5 86
4:5 87
4:15–17 163
4:16 164
6:9 21
6:9–10 182
6:10 21
6:11 86, 182
10:5–10 88
10:32–11:1 163
11:1 164
11:7 27n4

2 Corinthians

5:10 87, 88
5:21 106
11:15 78n42, 87

Galatians

2:16 87, 107
2:19–20 107, 188
3:1–9 32
3:9 34, 38
5:4 86n58
5:4–5 86
5:5 86n58
5:19–21 21
6:7–9 88
6:8 88

Ephesians

2:1 110
2:8 142
2:8–9 79, 89
2:8–10 78–79, 81, 84, 192
2:9 87
2:10 79, 108, 141, 142

Philippians

2:12 23, 88
2:12–13 191

3:10 188
3:17 163
4:9 164

1 Thessalonians

4:6 9

2 Thessalonians

3:7–9 164

1 Timothy

1:8 38

2 Timothy

3:10–11 164
4:14 78n42, 87

Titus

2:14 xv, 99, 120, 125
3:5 86
3:7 86

Hebrews

2:14–15 106
4:7 49n42
10:38 9
11:8 34
12:2 191
12:14 125, 188
13:1–2 191
13:5 191

James

1:27 xii, 142, 166n5
2:14–17 90, 91
2:14–26 90, 90n66, 91
2:18a 90n67
2:18–20 90
2:18–24 32
2:20–23 38
2:21 90
2:21–23 92

2:21–24 91
2:24 91
2:26 90
3:9 27n4

1 Peter

2:9–10 120
2:21 105
3:18 106

1 John

1:5 100
2:6 105
3:8 106
3:16–17 166n5
4:8 100
4:16 100

Revelation

1:20 93
2–3 93
2:5 93
2:23 93, 123
3:1b 93
3:4–5 93
12:5 71n20
13:8 93
17:8 93
20:12 93
20:12–13 93, 123
20:15 93
21–22 94
21:1 94
21:16 97
21:22 97

21:23–26 95
21:24–26 95
21:26 96
22:1 94
22:2 94
22:3 97, 123
22:5 97, 123

Other Ancient Sources

Genesis Rabbah

14.6 34
16.5 29n8

Subject Index

Abraham
  blessing to all peoples of the earth, 34
  call and response, 32–34
  as example of faith, 82–83
  faith that works, 38
  justified by faith, 84–85
  justified by works, 90
  sacrifice of Isaac, 37–38
Abrahamic covenant, 34–37, 104
abundant life, 190
Acts, book of, 74–78
Adam, as son of God, 75
Adam and Eve, rebellion of, 30–32
adult literacy classes, 141
Albert Magnus, 8
Allison, Dale C., 71nn20–21
Alsted, Johann Heinrich, 16–17
Amos, 55
analogia fidei, 8
ancient Near East, covenants in, 35–36
Anglican theology, 15
  on justification, 112
  on sanctification, 115
antinomians, 8
apathy, 104
apologetics, xi
apostasy, warnings against, 9
Aristotle, 8
Arminians, 9

assurance, and good works, 12
Augsburg Confession, 3, 6, 10
Augustine, 8

Babel, 32
Barclay, John, 80–81, 89, 110
Barlow, Thomas, 16
Beatitudes, 64
Belgic Confession, 11, 12–13
believers, created to do good works, 79, 81, 83–84
Beza, Theodore, 14
Bible distribution, 156
Biel, Gabriel, 8
blind, 63
Blomberg, Craig, 88n61
broken and contrite heart, 59
Bull, George, 16

Calvin, John, 112, 115
Campos, Heber Carlos de, 18n81
Canons of Dordt, 12
car-care ministry, 175
Carpe Diem (discipleship ministry), 136
Casas por Cristo, 168
Cassuto, Umberto, 28–29
casting out unclean spirits, 77
charis, 79–80

"Christian cul-de-sac," 159–60
Christian life, and good works, 2, 12, 23, 187
Christian school, 177
Chrysostom, John, 1–2
church, as community of good works, 120–21, 125
church-growth movement, 143
Church of the Cross (Laguna Hills, California), 169–70
church planting, 182
circumcision, 37
Clark, R. Scott, xv n. 7
community canvassing, 169–70
community garden, 156
community rescue mission, 175
compassionate ministry, 139, 144, 158, 160, 170, 171, 182–83. See also evangelism and compassionate ministry
Compton, Henry, 15
concurrence, 102
covenant faithfulness, 38–44, 51
covenants, 34–36, 58, 104–5
Cowles, Rob, 152–60, 179, 182
"cows of Bashan," 55–56
Cranmer, Thomas, 115
creation, goodness of, 101, 102
Crouch, Andy, 96–97
culture of participation, 177–79

Dale, Robert, 183
damnation, 121–22
dance fitness classes, 156
Davenant, John, 18–21, 111
David
    as man after God's own heart, 45–47
    sin and repentance, 45
Davidic covenant, 36, 47–48, 105
Davies, John A., 37
Davies, W. D., 71nn20–21
DaySpring Community Church (Clinton, Mississippi), 130–37, 170, 173, 179, 183–84
Decalogue. See Ten Commandments
deSilva, David, 79–80
devotion to apostles' teaching, 76

DeYoung, Rebecca Konyndyk, 104
discipleship, 145, 188–90
divine command, for good works, 7
divine life, as actus purus, 124
domestic-violence counseling, 140
Donovan, Vincent J., 176
drug rehabilitation, 148

early church, 74–78
Eden, 123
Edwards, John, 15, 16
efficacy, of gift/grace, 80
efficient cause, 13, 17, 18
embedded ministry, 154
Erickson, Millard, xiii–xiv, 111
eschatology, and good works, 121–23, 125
eternal life, 67–68, 88
eternal punishments, 9
Eucharist. See Lord's Supper
Eunice Project (outreach to poor), 141
evangelical theology, downplays good works, 24
evangelism and compassionate ministry, 129, 146, 149, 152, 176–77, 184
exile, 48, 54, 56

faith, 78, 81–84
faithfulness, 83
false disciples, 66
false prophets, 57, 66
fasting, 139
fatherless and widow, justice toward, 54
final cause, 14, 17
final justification, 92
First Baptist Church (Fairfield, Texas), 167–68
five E's (discipleship program), 145, 178
Fleming, Daniel, 31
food distribution, 156–57, 172, 175
Forde, Gerhard, 117
formal cause, 14, 17
Formula of Concord, 6
France, R. T., 66
Francis of Assisi, 143
freedom, 6

French, Nancy, 181
fruit of good works, 14
Fuller Theological Seminary, 143
future justification, 86–87

Gallic Confession, 11
gathered church, 120
Genesis Project (Fort Collins, Colorado),
152–60, 182
Gentry, Peter, 36, 40
Gerhard, Johann, 4, 5, 8–11
gift, response to, 89
glorification, 22, 114, 119–20, 125
glory of God, and good works, 12, 14
God
concurs with creaturely action, 102
goodness, 99–101, 121
holiness, 100
love, 100–101
opera ad extra, 101, 124
opera ad intra, 124
primary efficient cause of good works, 13
as a worker, 26
good life, 190
good works
and assurance, 12
bring glory to God, 12
in the Christian life, 2, 12, 23, 187
commanded by God, 7, 8, 10, 15
as condition of salvation, 16
as covenant faithfulness, 38–44
declare the goodness of God, 121
as detrimental to salvation, 6–7
in the early church, 76–78
edify others, 12
and eschatology, 121–23, 125
essential to true worship, 51–52
as evidence of saving faith, 12
in final judgment, 65–67
as fruit of justifying faith, 10
in the garden of Eden, 27–30
and glorification, 22, 114, 119–20, 125
and God's final intent, 94–97
and judgment, 65–67, 112–14
necessity, 5–11

not antithetical to the good news, 188
not efficient cause of justification, 113
not *locus* in theology textbooks, xi n. 1
not meritorious, 19–20, 113, 119, 188
related to justification consequently and
declaratively, 7, 113–14, 124
and salvation, xv, 2, 15, 16–17
and sanctification, 22, 114–19, 124–25
"gospel by example," 163
grace, 78–81, 83
Graham, Billy, 148–49
gratitude, and good works, 7, 10
Great Commandments, 184
Great Commission, 146
greater righteousness, 64–65
greatest commandment, 41–42, 106, 108
Greenford Christian Church (Greenford,
Ohio), 164, 172
Gundry, Robert, 66
Gupta, Nijay K., 81n49, 82n52

Hafemann, Scott, 27n6, 28–29, 43
Hamilton, Victor P., 26n1, 29–30
Hampton, Stephen, 16
Harambee spirit, 150
Haugen, Gary, 159
healing the sick, 77
Heidegger, Johannes, 116
Highland Community (Columbus, Georgia),
162–63, 170, 177
historical prologue (Mosaic covenant), 41
historic Protestantism, on good works, xiv,
23
holiness, 100, 120
Hollaz, David, 4–5
Holy Spirit
empowers for witness and service, 108–9
indwelling, 190
principal efficient cause of good works, 5
Hooker, Richard, 115
hospitality to strangers, 191
hospital visitation, 147
housing initiative, 177
human agency and responsibility, 5
human flourishing, 189, 190

humanity, created and commissioned for
  good works, 124
Hunter, George G., III, 176
hypocrisy, xii

image of God, 26–27, 29, 58, 102–3
Imes, Carmen Joy, 42n36
Immanuel, 105
Immanuel Africa Gospel Church (Kericho,
  Kenya), 144–52, 165, 178
incongruity, of gift/grace, 80
inheritance, 15–16
initial justification, 92
injustice, struggle against, 189
inner-city school ministry, 134
instrumental cause, 14, 17
intentionally biblical, 165–66
intentional outreach, 130, 132
"involvement culture," 179
Isaac, 37
Isaiah, 52–53
Israel
  disobedience, 59
  as holy nation, 40, 105
  as kingdom of priests, 40, 104

James, on faith and works, 90–92
Jesus
  active obedience, 124
  came to do good works, 106
  as climax of the covenant, 105
  crucifixion, 191
  on good works, 61–73
  intensifies and internalizes the law, 65
  as new Adam, 62–64, 75
  passive obedience, 124
John of Damascus, 8, 101, 102
John Paul II (pope), 64
joint attention, 107
joy, 189
judgment, and good works, 58, 92–94,
  112–14, 121–22
justice and mercy, xi
justification, 124
  distinct but not separate from sanctifica-
    tion, 85

as forensic, 85, 89, 112
and good works, 78, 84–89
not the whole of salvation, 110–11
present and future dimensions, 86, 92

Keener, Craig, 122
Kelly, J. N. D., 110n14
Kelly, Sean, 164, 166, 167, 172
Kidner, Derek, 49

laity, leading ministries, 173–75
Lantz, Leland, 169–70
Lausanne Movement, 149
Law and the Prophets, 106
leaders, injustice of, 57–58
leading by example, 162–65
learning from your community, 166–71
"least of these," 72
Levenson, John, 41
Libertines, 21
"little ones," 72
Living Word Community Church (Red Lion,
  Pennsylvania), 175
Lord's Supper, 76, 139
love
  for enemies, 72
  for God, xi, 41–42, 53, 106, 108, 113, 184,
    189
  for neighbor, xvi, 41–42, 53, 55, 68, 72,
    105, 106, 108, 113, 184, 189, 190–91
Luther, Martin, 23, 73, 117–18
Lutheran theology
  on good works, 2–11
  on sanctification, 117–18

Mastricht, Petrus van, 16, 116
material cause, 14, 17
Mayes, Benjamin T. G., 2–3
McGowan, Elbert, 168, 169, 175, 178, 179,
  182
means of grace, 190
medical mission, 140
Melanchthon, Philip, 117
Methodist Articles of Religion, 112
Micah, 57–58

ministering on the margins, 182
missional church, 184
Moi, Daniel arap, 144
Molnar, Cindy, 180–81
Moo, Douglas J., 82nn51–52, 83, 86, 87, 88, 90n67
Moore, Steve, 168–69
Mosaic covenant, 36, 41, 104
Mosaic law, 38–41, 43–44
Mother Teresa, 143
Mouw, Richard, 96
moving ministry, 175
Muller, Richard, 17n78
mysterium tremendum et fascinans, 100

narrow gate, 66
necessary by precept, 15
necessity, 6
  of the consequent, 8
  of hypothesis, 8, 11
neighbor, 72, 106–7
new birth, 114
new covenant, 105
new creation, 94–98, 123
new life, 118
Nicene Creed, 120n51
Noah, 32
non-circularity, of gift/grace, 80
nursing home ministry, 134

obedience, 59, 83
obedience of faith, xiv, 37–38
oppression, 55, 189
ordo salutis, 22
organizational health cycle, 183
Orphan, Mark, 180
Oswalt, John, 54
Otto, Rudolph, 100
outreach ministries, 134–37

parable of the good Samaritan, 72, 107, 142
parable of the talents, 121–22
Paraclete, 108
parents' night out, 156
pastoral leadership, 161–85

patronage system, 79–80
Paul, on faith and works, 78–89
Pelagianism, 109–10
Pelagius, 109, 115
Pennington, Jonathan, 64
Perkins, John, 170–71
Piper, John, xiv–xv
Polanus, Amandus, 14
poor, 56, 63, 68, 77
prayer, 76, 146, 174, 178
preaching, 166
presence, of good works, 7
priestly kingdom, Israel as, 105
primary efficient cause, 13, 17, 102
priority, of gift/grace, 80
prison ministry, 134, 140, 150, 156
prison reform, 189
proclaiming good news, 77
pro-life ministry, 131, 134, 189
prophets, on good works, 52–58
prosperity gospel, xii
protology, 121
Psalms, works and worship in, 48–52

Quenstedt, Johannes, 4, 7, 10

Raine, Kristen, 171
recovery ministry, 134
Redeemer Church (Jackson, Mississippi), 168, 173–75, 178, 182–83
redemption, frees us for work, 58
Reformed theology
  good works in, 11–22
  on sanctification, 115–16
religion that is pure and undefiled, xii
Remonstrants, 9
rent assistance, 156
repentance, 54, 58, 59
Revelation, and good works, 92–97
revitalization, 183
Rice, Brian, 175, 176–77, 179, 184
righteousness, 84
  and act of justifying, 84
  greater than that of the Pharisees, 64–65

imputation of, 112
in the Psalms, 51
ROCK (Random Outbreaks of Community
    Kindness), 155
Roman Catholics, on good works, 23
royal grant, 36, 40, 47
ruling sins, 9
rural missions, 147
Rutherford, Samuel, 18

Sabbath, 42–43
sacrifice, as mere performance, 52–53
Sailhamer, John, 28–29
salvation
    equated with justification in contempo-
        rary evangelical theology, xiii–xiv
    for good works, 192
    more than justification, 13
Samuel, 45–46
sanctification, 22, 114–19, 124–25
Saul (king), 45–46
scattered church, 120
Schreiner, Tom, xiv–xv
Scots Confession, 12
Scripture, as missional, 184
secondary efficient cause, 13–14, 17, 102
selfishness, 103
semi-Pelagianism, 110
Sermon on the Mount, 64, 68
servant of the Lord, 63
service, 190–91
sharing of possessions, 77
Sharpstown United Methodist Church
    (Sharpstown, New Jersey), 171–72
sheep and goats, 70–71, 122
short-term missions, 171
sick, visiting, 129–30
signs and wonders, 77
simil justus et peccator, 117
sin, 103–4
singing, 76
singularity, of gift/grace, 80
sloth, 103–4
Smith, Doug, 171
sola fide, 11

Solomon, 47–48
Song of Moses, 44
"son of David," 105
spiritual growth, 132
Stachmus, Jeff, 167–68, 179
Stevenson, Roberto, 137–44, 164–65, 176
stipulations (Mosaic covenant), 41
Strickland, Rob, 162–63, 165, 170, 177
strip club ministry, 134
superabundance, of gift/grace, 80
suzerain-vassal treaty, 36, 40–41, 47
sweat, as anxious fear, 31

Table of Grace Church (Apache Junction,
    Arizona), 180–81
temporal punishments, 9
Ten Commandments, 41–42, 68, 106
Teresa, Mother, 143
theography, 169
theological anthropology, 124
theology proper, 124
Thielman, Frank, 91
Thirty-Nine Articles of Religion, 112
Thomas Aquinas, 8
Thyatira, church at, 123
Tierra Prometida (Mexico City), 137–44,
    164–65, 184
Tonui, Joyce, 144–52, 166, 178
trade school, 177
transportation ministry, 140
Trelcatius, Lucas, Jr., 13–14, 116
Trinity, and love, 100–101, 124
Turretin, Francis, 13, 21–22, 113, 118, 119–20
tutoring ministry, 135

union with Christ, 107–9, 115–16, 188–90
unwed mothers ministry, 175
Ursinus, Zacharias, 116

Velázquez, Aurelio Gómez, 137
via salutis, 110–11
vice-regents over creation, 27
vocation, and image of God, 26–27
Voetius, Gisbertus, 18

Warren, Rick, 169
wealthy, 56
Weinfeld, Moshe, 36
Wellum, Stephen, 36, 44
Wesley, Charles, 109n12
Wesley, John, 21, 92n71, 112, 128–30, 139,
    143
Wesley Foundation (Texas Tech), 168–69
Westminster Confession of Faith, 12, 13
Westminster Shorter Catechism, 112
Whiteman, Darrell, 166–67
widows, providing for, 77
Wilkerson, David, 181
witnesses, 75–76
Wollebius, Johannes, 15–16, 18, 116
work
    as burdensome, 25–26
    corrupted by the fall, 30–32
    part of humanity's rightful calling, 30, 43
working faith, 127
works, and final judgment, 50
"works-haters," 8
works of mercy, xvi, 1, 103, 128–30, 189
    at DaySpring Community Church, 133–35
    in the early church, 76, 77–78

    at Gospel Project, 155–60
    at Immanuel Africa Gospel Church, 145–48
    as love of neighbor, 113
    necessity, 125
    as second table of the law, 106
    of thief on the cross, 191–92
    at Tierra Prometida, 139–44
    transformation from, 119
works of piety, xvi, 1, 103, 189
    at DaySpring Community Church, 132–33
    in the early church, 76–77
    as first table of the law, 106
    at Gospel Project, 154–55
    at Immanuel Africa Gospel Church, 145–46
    as love of God, 113
    necessity, 125
    of thief on the cross, 191–92
    at Tierra Prometida, 138–39
    transformation from, 118–19
works of the law, 82n51
World Gospel Mission, 148

Zacchaeus, 68
Zanchi, Jerome, 18
"zealous for good works," xv, 120, 219